T0295854

Fronsperger and Laffemas

ECONOMIC IDEAS THAT BUILT EUROPE

Economic Ideas That Built Europe reconstructs the development of European political economy as seen through the eyes of its principal architects and interpreters, working to overcome the ideological nature of recent historiography. The volumes in the series – contextualized through analytical introductions and enriched with explanatory footnotes, bibliographies and indices – offer a wide selection of texts inspired by very different economic visions, and stress their complex consequences and interactions in the rich but often simplified history of European economic thought.

Fronsperger and Laffemas

Sixteenth-Century Precursors of Modern Economic Ideas

Leonhard Fronsperger and Barthélemy de Laffemas

Edited by Erik S. Reinert and Philipp Robinson Rössner

ANTHEM PRESS

Anthem Press
An imprint of Wimbledon Publishing Company
www.anthempress.com

This edition first published in UK and USA 2023
by ANTHEM PRESS
75–76 Blackfriars Road, London SE1 8HA, UK
or PO Box 9779, London SW19 7ZG, UK
and
244 Madison Ave #116, New York, NY 10016, USA

Part of The Anthem Other Canon Economics Series
Series Editor Erik S. Reinert

British Library Cataloguing-in-Publication Data
A catalogue record for this book is available from the British Library.

Library of Congress Control Number: 2022940884
A catalog record for this book has been requested.

ISBN-13: 978-1-83998-708-3 (Hbk)
ISBN-10: 1-83998-708-1 (Hbk)

Cover Credit: Reinert family library

This title is also available as an e-book.

CONTENTS

INTRODUCTION

The series *Economic Ideas That Built Europe* aims at making classical economic texts – first published on the European Continent – available in English. We aim at finding and making available important works that provide insights that are lost in today's mainstream and neoclassical traditions. This tone was set already in the first text published, in 2011: Antonio Serra's *A Short Treatise on the Wealth and Poverty of Nations* (1613). Serra introduced the dichotomy of increasing and diminishing returns to explain the wealth-creating capacity of manufacturing (operating under increasing returns to scale) and the lack of generalised wealth in countries specialising in activities where one factor of production is limited by nature (agriculture, fisheries, mining) and therefore, after a certain point, are subject to diminishing returns.[1] This counterpoint – a key to understanding the wealth and poverty of nations – is not compatible with *equilibrium,* and therefore disappeared from mainstream economics in the early 1900s.[2]

We have published first ever English translations of key works on economic policy from Italian, both published in Naples – Antonio Serra (1613) and Carlo Tapia's *Treatise on Abundance* (1638) – in a period (1503–1707) when the Kingdom of Naples was ruled by the kings of Spain. From German, we published Wilhelm von Hörnigk's highly influential *Austria Supreme (if it so wishes)* (1684), and from Spanish, Gaspar Melchor Jovellanos' *Report of the Agrarian Law* (1795). In addition, we have republished Martin Luther's work *On Trade and Usury* (1524). The first English translation of Albert Aftalion's *Periodic Crises of Overproduction* (1913) is forthcoming in this series.

In this volume we combine two small works representing the economics of the 1500s. With a work authored by Barthélemy de Laffemas (1545–1612) we add an important French text, and with Leonhard Fronsperger (ca. 1520–1575) a pioneering German text. Despite their age, these two pragmatic texts still provide important insights.

We are pleased to present the first-ever translation of Barthélemy de Laffemas *Reiglement (sic) général pour dresser les manufactures en ce royaume,* originally a 40-page booklet, and also a 15-page addition – with questions and answers – entitled *Response aux difficultez proposées à l'encontre du règlement géné-ral touchant les manufactures.* The first work is dated 1597, and Bibliothèque Nationale de France also considers the second work as published in that year. The two are sometimes, as here, bound together. At the end of this second part, in a note to the reader Laffemas indicates he has been working on these matters since 1585.

Laffemas' booklet was published both in Paris and in Rouen, but today this theoretically important and politically very influential work is extremely rare. WorldCat – a website where the major libraries of the world participate – only finds three printed copies of the original Paris edition and one copy of the Rouen edition, all in Paris libraries.

Leonhard Fronsperger is best known as a theorist of warfare. In the 1564 work presented here – *Von dem Lob des Eigen Nutzen/On the Praise of Self-Interest* – Fronsperger enters a completely different field, anticipating a paradox that much later, in 1714, was introduced by Bernard Mandeville in his *Fable of The Bees: or, Private Vices, Publick Benefits.* Comparing Fronsperger and Mandeville, Fronsperger's approach to the role of Self-Interest in economic development comes across as pragmatic rather than ideological. Mandeville being often seen as a predecessor of neoliberalism, Fronsperger's approach avoids this ideological bias.

As editor of the series, we wish to thank the Institute of New Economic Thinking (INET) for their grant to Sophus Reinert and Francesca Viano that made the translation of Laffemas and some of the other works in this series possible.

In these volumes that historically were extremely influential, it is possible to trace changes of national economic fortunes over time. Laffemas' work – published in 1597 – attempts to free France from its economic dependence on Italy.[3] Less than hundred years later – in 1684 – Hörnigk's work built national strength to Austria, geographically situated between the diminishing military power of the Turks and the rising economic power of the French. During the seventeenth century the economic strength of France had increased, particularly so under the economic regime of Colbert (1665–1683). Laffemas may have been the main French inspiration for Colbert's economic policy.

In his *History of Economic Analysis* (1954) Joseph Schumpeter mentions Antonio Serra's 1613 book – the first published in our series – and Laffemas' text together on three different pages[4]. Schumpeter credits Serra with being 'the first to compose a scientific treatise, though an unsystematic one, on Economic Principles and Policy'. In a footnote to this paragraph Schumpeter finds only one person to compare Serra with: Laffemas. But Laffemas recommended a certain policy, while Serra gave the explanation *why this policy would work*. This explains the apparently negative footnote by Schumpeter:

'Almost immeasurably inferior to Serra in grasp of economic principle and analytic power, but not dissimilar from him in views on the issues of practical policy, was B. de Laffemas, who wrote around 1600' (footnote p. 195). Yet, twice in the same volume, Schumpeter puts Laffemas, just the two of them, in the same positive light as Serra: '(Serra) refuted the bullionist doctrine of exchanges (as had Laffemas before him)' (p. 354) and when discussing the work of Thomas Mun (1571–1641) – the first English economist of fame – Schumpeter remarks, 'We also know the analytical progress involved was anticipated by Laffemas and Serra' (p. 357)

Schumpeter, however, surprisingly does not mention Giovanni Botero (ca. 1544–1617) in his work. Botero's 1589 work *Della Ragion di Stato*[5] was clearly an important forerunner both of Laffemas and Serra, except that it did not contain Serra's path-breaking dichotomy between increasing and diminishing returns to scale.[6] Botero was the true best-seller of these three authors, with a total of 80 editions in six languages before 1800. Seeing that, in 1597, Laffemas finds it necessary to inform his readers that he has worked on these problems since 1585, the thought comes to mind that this just might have been written to establish precedence over Botero.

It is our hope that the richness of theoretical thinking and practical policies found in early Europe may bring back insights and nuances that to a large extent were lost in Cold War economics, but to some extent are finding their way back in modern industrial policy.

Erik S. Reinert, Series editor
Hvasser, Norway, February 2023

Notes

1 Our publication led to new interest in Serra's works leading to two conferences – in Oslo and Naples – resulting in an edited volume: Rosario Patalano and Sophus A. Reinert (eds), *Antonio Serra and the Economics of Good Government* (London: Palgrave, 2016).

2 It should be noted that in two articles, from 1979 and 1980, US economist Paul Krugman reintroduces the simultaneous existence of increasing and diminishing returns to scale and produces models that agree with Serra – without mentioning him – as well as traditional development economics and even, specifically, with Lenin's theory of imperialism: the countries exporting articles subject to diminishing returns (raw materials) will stay poor! See Erik S. Reinert and Vemund Riiser, https://www.networkideas.org/featured-articles/2020/11/recent-trends-economic-theory/, pp. 17–18.

3 See Henry Heller, *Anti-Italianism in Sixteenth Century France* (Toronto: University of Toronto Press, 2003).

4 Joseph Schumpeter, *History of Economic Analysis*, edited from manuscript by Elizabeth Boody Schumpeter (New York: Oxford University Press, 1954), pp. 195, 354, 357.
5 Venice: I Gioliti.
6 For a discussion of Botero and Serra, see Erik S. Reinert, 'Giovanni Botero (1588) and Antonio Serra (1613): Italy and the Birth of Development Economics', in *Handbook of Alternative Theories of Economic Development*, ed. Erik S. Reinert, Jayati Ghosh, and Rainer Kattel (Cheltenham: Elgar, 2016), pp. 3–41.

Chapter 1

BARTHÉLEMY DE LAFFEMAS (1545–CA. 1611) AS AN EARLY ECONOMIST: CONTEXT AND SCHOLARLY VOICES IN THE ENGLISH-LANGUAGE LITERATURE

Erik S. Reinert and Philipp Robinson Rössner

Context

Laffemas' work takes us back to the early beginnings of political economy, and – as part of that *Zeitgeist* – an emphasis on manufacturing as an indispensable ingredient. Laffemas came to the fore when the fiscal-military state was still in the making but took more and more visible shape;[1] during that time an economic ideology grew ground which established, in economic reasoning as well as practice, a connection between state consolidation and the raising of the wealth of the nation: in order to generate a better, stronger state apparatus, the economy needed some attention as well.[2] Economic policy often took the shape of merchants and other economic actors asking for privileges and monopolies, but Laffemas' text presents an understanding that policy ought to be more than rent seeking serving the interest of the few. Policy was to feed on a mutual relationship or symbiosis: a strong manufacturing economy was the foundation of a strong state, and vice versa. The best way to curb domestic factionalism, monopoly and rent seeking, and to defend France's political and economic interest internationally was to promote domestic economic growth. During the process industry was identified as a key candidate to achieve this simultaneous strengthening of the nation's power and its wealth, and the main source of the wealth of nations – the birth of modern political economy.[3]

This is borne out in the further works in Laffemas' oeuvre and career as a writer and 'consultant administrator' (using Schumpeter's famous classification), in which he often returned to themes including the dichotomy of

agriculture and manufacturing as two very different forms of economic activity, with radically different chances for the growth potential of the nation's
wealth. Laffemas also sported an anti-bullionist perspective, never confusing –
as a very common allegation against 'mercantilism' goes[4] – money with real
wealth, advocating for free money flows in and out of the country instead.[5]
With his emphasis on import substitution, the prohibition of vital raw material exports (which better be worked into manufactures domestically), promoting manufacturing and national productivity, stimulating domestic
employment, increasing 'industry' (at that time still meaning *industriousness* or,
in German, *Fleiss*) across the French lands, encouraging the immigration of
skilled foreigners (technology transfer) Laffemas' work classifies as 'mercantilist' in the traditional sense, but also matches *Cameralist* economic thought.
Kameralwissenschaften – cameral sciences was a doctrine flourishing from the
later seventeenth century across Europe (especially the German-speaking
lands, but also in Sweden and Italy).[6] Like mercantilism, Cameralism or
Kameralwissenschaften – cameral sciences – sported an edge towards manufacturing empowered through conscious industrial policy. Aimed at increasing the availability of economic resources, national productivity and infinite
growth, from a Cameralist (and slightly later) perspective Laffemas' ideas
strike a familiar chord. Laffemas thus was, in doctrinal or intellectual-history
terms, part of an emerging and increasingly transnational field of economic
discourse, contributing to a broader European tradition of thinking about
manufacturing as the origin of the wealth of nations, something for which
'mercantilism' in particular is a label less than helpful and which ought only
to be retained for convenience and want of a better alternative term.

As former World Bank chief economist Justin Yifu Lin put it very suc-
cinctly, 'Except for a few oil-exporting countries, no countries have ever got-
ten rich without industrialization first.'[7] Laffemas encapsulated this principle
in his 1597 text thus: 'And following the example of the queen of England and
other princes neighboring France who allow no manufactured merchandise
to enter their country, it shall also be forbidden to any person to bring into
said kingdom any sort of foreign manufactured merchandise unless it be of
new invention and unknown to the French.' His urge to survey the country
for possibilities of growth and to substitute imports, trying to produce or imi-
tate any goods that any other trading nation of his time produced, became
better known, and treated more systematically, through Philipp Wilhelm von
Hörnigk's (1684) best-seller on Austrian economic development, also published for the first time in English in this series.[8] The 'Hörnigk Strategy' was
based above all on rigorous analysis of the economic status quo, through systematic lists and thorough statistical surveys of the nation's productive capacities, from which suggestions were derived on how to improve the situation (or

raise the future wealth of the country), especially where such capacities were found to be lacking, in relation to other competitors.

The practice of often heavy-handed industrial policy may in fact be traced to England during the 1400s. Arguments about the importance of adding value to raw materials were sometime presented, like this incisive one by Luis Ortiz, the Spanish minister of finance to King Philip II in 1558:

> From the raw materials from Spain and the West Indies – particularly silk, iron and cochinilla (a red dye) – which cost them only 1 florin, the foreigners produce finished goods which they sell back to Spain for between 10 and 100 florins. Spain is in this way subject to greater humiliations from the rest of Europe than those they themselves impose on the Indians. In exchange for gold and silver the Spaniards offer trinkets of greater or lesser value; but by buying back their own raw materials at an exorbitant price, the Spaniards are made the laughing-stock of all Europe.[9]

However, the theoretical arguments as to why manufacturing was important were only coherently formulated by Giovanni Botero in his 1589 best-seller *On the Greatnesse of Cities*.[10] When the first French translation of Botero's work appeared two years after Laffemas' work – in 1599 – it was given prominence.[11]

Notwithstanding his obviously exposed political position and enduring relevance for France's long-run economic development, in the historical literature early French economists have – in modern economic literature – been completely overshadowed by the later Physiocrats, whose preference was for agriculture rather than manufacturing. The main author here being François Quesnay (1694–1774). There is not much French literature on Laffemas.[12] Like many other thinkers of his ilk he has never made it squarely into either a history, economics or history of economics book, beyond casual references or brief discussions, often in footnotes. What is often emphasised is Laffemas' humble background as tailor and manservant to King Henry IV of France.

At his time Laffemas was at the forefront in French politics; after the decennial religious wars that had hampered France, he was charged with reforming the existing tariff and revenue system, and in the course of events came to publish more than 25 treatises on economic matters, with the present one relating in as succinct and concise style as possible at the time what could be done to improve France's position on the international market and stimulate domestic economic development.

In the modern literature this has earned him a reputation as an economic nationalist[13] and 'protectionist',[14] but what scholars often tend to forget is that in early modern Europe protectionism was never meant to be absolute or across the board, and no policy makers and consultant administrators advocated generally high tariff walls across the spectrum of the world of goods. Protectionism was selective, targeting specific branches of economy identified as particularly important for the nation's wealth while leaving others less regulated and less protected (and in many cases completely unregulated), and it is exactly this style of 'listing' or enumerating that we find in works like Laffemas (1597) or Hörnigk (1684), singling out specific economic activities as they contribute to, or decrease (or simply are irrelevant for) the wealth of the nation which makes for a very distinct style and technique of economic reasoning in early modern Europe. It should prevent us from quick and haphazard assumptions and careless allegations of early modern Europeans using economic nationalism as tools or acts of (economic) warfare, or rulers trying to close off their economies from international markets. Even in the depths of Anglo-French warfare in the eighteenth century, trade routes remained open (as in the case of tobacco[15]); and when Colbert occasionally alluded to trade as being a means of continuing war with different means, this was intended to talk Louis XIV out of, not into, real-life wars.[16]

Laffemas came to see manufacturing in a way analogous to the slightly later and more popular saying of seeing manufacturing as the 'real gold (or silver) mines' of a nation. This referred to the gold and silver that flowed into Spain, deindustrialising that country, whereas the gold and silver accumulated in cities like Venice and Amsterdam which had no mines, but abundant manufacturing plants.[17] This metaphor became somewhat ubiquitous, especially in seventeenth-century German, Swedish and English economic writings after Giovanni Botero had popularised it in his 1589 book on cities and the reason of state.

In lieu of a still outstanding monographic study of Laffemas and his contribution to economic thought, the following provides a collection of snapshots on Laffemas from the Anglophone scholarly literature on the author.

A Summary

French economic and social reformer, Laffemas was born in Dauphiné of a family of impoverished Calvinist nobility. Having adopted the vocation of *tailleur* he was engaged sometime around 1566 by Henry of Navarre, whose continued favour after his coronation as Henry IV of France[18], gave Laffemas an opportunity to become a prosperous merchant. The commercial experience thus gained inspired him to write a number of tracts, twenty-three in all, sketching a program for the economic and social reform of the nation. Although these reveal their author's lack of scientific training, their basis in direct observation gives them a decidedly practical quality and often results in striking ingenuity in matters of detail. In opposition to the agrarian doctrines of his friend Sully[19], Laffemas upheld an industrial policy. He assumed that the quantity of gold and silver, provided it was in active circulation, was an infallible index of a nation's wealth. But the drain of money into other countries was to be prevented, according to his view, not by prohibiting its exportation but by stimulating the manufacture of more and better goods to the point where foreign nations would be forced to buy in France. In his program for the reorganization of national industry were included the development of the cultivation of the mulberry tree with a view to increasing silk production, the creation of new factories, bans upon the export of raw material and the extension of government protection to industry. On its social side Laffemas' plan envisaged the creation of an autonomous industrial class which should have high powers to control the labouring energy of the nation in the interests of industrial aggrandizement. He proposed toward this end the straight enforcement of the edict of 1581, which had expanded the system of *jurandes*; the establishment of bureaus of manufactures in each diocese endowed with police jurisdiction and the right to settle industrial conflicts; and the creation of workhouses for habitual idlers. Henry IV manifested respect for Laffemas' ideas by appointing him controller general of commerce in 1602 and so far followed his advice as to reissue the edict of 1581 in 1597 and to found a council of commerce and manufactures in 1601. In spite of these measures Laffemas' social program was doomed to oblivion because it conflicted with the royal conception of centralization. The economic and mercantilistic aspects of his system also failed to produce a significant effect at the time. But in their essentials they were later revived by Montchrétien and eventually translated into legal fact by Colbert[20].

Paul Harsin, Encyclopaedia of the Social Sciences, *vol. 9 (New York: Macmillan, 1953), p. 12.*

On Laffemas and Industrial Policy

Finally, in 1614, the Third Estate demanded that no foreigner should be permitted to levy farm taxes. Undoubtedly, under the influence of Laffemas, the Trade Council, of which he was president between 1602 and 1604, proposed that foreigners producing manufactured goods should be allowed to become French naturalized citizens and that it should be made compulsory for all foreign manufacturers to employ French apprentices so that the latter could learn their manufacturing

secrets. (...) These measures bring to mind a macro-economic view of
international trade according to which the import of manufactured
goods gives rise to competition that can prove fatal for domestic manufacturers. This was a sensible opinion given the prevailing circum-
stances because, even though nineteenth-century liberalism advocated
the opening of borders to revive sectors that had become stagnant due
to systematic protectionism in the form of high import duties, no such
theory had been developed in the sixteenth century which would have
permitted the analysis of protectionism in these terms.

Yves Charbit, The Classical Foundations of
Population Thought: From Plato to Quesnay
(New York: Springer, 2011), p. 79.

But real thinking on industrialization began with Barthélémy de
Laffemas. He was convinced, on the one hand, that France owed her
wealth to her diversity and, on the other, that strict bullionism was not
effective since it was too rigid. He believed that the restoration of industries ruined by the wars of religion would reduce poverty and enrich the
King and his subjects. Taking into account the influx of English goods
in the fairs, he recommended a ban on the entry of foreign goods into
France. But more than anything else, he was responsible for the first
steps to develop sericulture (cultivation of silkworms to produce silk).

Charbit (2011), p. 86.

Laffemas and the Spirit of Capitalism

As things stood, more treasure was going out of than coming into the
kingdom, and the chief reason for that, thought Laffemas, was the
decline and poor quality of French manufactures (for which he blamed
'the laziness and carelessness of the French') and the willingness of
French merchants, moved by Self-Interest rather than considerations
of the Common Good, to bring goods from abroad. To correct this
lamentable state of affairs, he proposed the establishment and regulation of native manufactures, especially silk, and the prohibition of all
imports of manufactured goods, 'whether it be cloth of gold; of silver;
textiles; serges; leathers gilt and tooled, or in the form of gloves, or
otherwise; iron; steel; copper; bronze; watches; clocks; and in general
all products whatsoever used as furniture, ornaments, and clothing, of
whatever quality they may be and for whatever purpose they may be
employed'. (Interestingly, he excepted from this prohibition *bons livres*

and works of art made during or before the reign of Francis I.) The emphasis of these measures, both positive and negative, was on luxury goods. Love of luxury among the French nobility and the better-off bourgeoisie was also among the factors Laffemas considered responsible for the drain of money out of France. This was a sin that the overwhelming majority of the French population could not afford, but the majority of the French population clearly little interested this early secretary of commerce. Laffemas also wished to involve the impoverished nobility in manufacture and trade, proposing that nobles be forced to grow mulberry trees and advocating special concessions to the glass industry, in which a nobleman could participate without losing status (*sans déroger*).

> *Liah Greenfeld,* Spirit of Capitalism: Nationalism
> and Economic Growth *(Cambridge, MA: Harvard
> University Press, 2009), p. 117.*

On the Man

In summing up the work of Barthélemy de Laffemas it is hard not to be prejudiced in favour of this sturdy Huguenot who gave himself to the unaccustomed pursuit of the literary muse, not from inclination, but because he felt that France must be stirred from her lethargy. His ideas were in large part practicable and derived not only from the theories made current in the sixteenth century but also from his own experience and observation. Only when he visioned immediate results flowing from the application of his ideas, wholesale reforms put into effect without a hitch, or changes in the habits of a people following close upon a royal edict, did he assume the role of a dreamer.

> *Charles Woolsey Cole,* French Mercantilist
> Doctrines before Colbert *(New York: Richard
> R. Smith, 1931), p. 110.*

On the Relationship between Manufacturing and Agriculture

Laffemas did not ignore the value of agriculture. It was to him an important resource of his native land. But commerce was more important. Through it gold and silver entered or left a country. It must, therefore, be regulated so as to prevent foreign exploitation of France. … But of all things it was most necessary to establish manufactures.

> *Cole (1931), p. 110.*

Laffemas and French Nationalism

In contradiction to the cosmopolitanism of Bodin[21] and Sully of which even Laffemas had a trace, Montchrétien[22] hated all foreigners, with a bitter, biting scorn and deep-seated antipathy that is hard to rival. It was the foreigners who were encroaching on French manufactures, stealing her commerce, creating her unemployment, maltreating her merchants.

Cole (1931), p. 159.

At the same time an assertive economic protectionism implemented by Barthélemy de Laffemas led to a gradual decline of Italian control over the French economy.

Henry Heller, Anti-Italianism in Sixteenth-Century France *(Toronto: University of Toronto Press, 2003), p. 18.*

Attacks on the dominance of Italian imported silk in France were at the heart of the mercantilist program of Laffemas. Laffemas called for the banning of Italian silk and the building up of a national silk industry by the encouragement of widespread cultivation of the mulberry and by state support of silk manufacturing.

Heller (2003), p. 220.

The King's Controller General of Commerce Barthélémy de Laffemas, seconded by the somewhat reluctant Sully, attempted to revive agriculture, strengthen manufacturing and provide employment. In order to do so lower interest rates were imposed. A major programme of public works including the construction of new roads and bridges was made a priority. An industrial policy entailing economic protectionism and strict control of manufactures including financial aid to inventors and new industrial enterprises was set in place. The purpose of these measures was in the first place to help France recover from the material devastation and economic decline suffered during the religious wars that marked the second half of the sixteenth century. But they were also meant to endow France with a manufacturing base which would enable it to compete with the economically more powerful neighbouring states of England and Holland. Such initiatives apparently helped to sustain a period of renewed economic growth which lasted into the late 1620s.

Henry Heller, 'Primitive Accumulation and Technical Innovation in the French Wars of Religion', History and Technology, an International Journal *16, no. 3 (2000): pp. 243–262, p. 245.*

It is from the deliberations of Laffemas' Commision du commerce as well as the published and unpublished decisions of the royal Conseil d'état, Paris Parliament and Court of the Châtelet that we learn most about economic and technical innovations in the reign of Henri IV. (...) Scores of new mechanical devices were patented during this period. Among these were new agricultural implements, irrigation works, mills, pumps, furnaces, clocks, anti-rust agents, treadmills, carriages, barges, presses, cranes, brush clearing and earth moving machines and tile making devices. As to new enterprises created with the support of the crown, the number of so-called royal manufactures established under Henri IV between 1600–10 has been estimated at more than 250.

Heller (2000), p. 245.

Foreign craftsmen and entrepreneurs were clearly an important source of new techniques and manufacturing processes during the religious wars and into the reign of Henri IV. Recruitment of foreign craftsmen, not only from Italy and the Low Countries, but as far afield as Africa and Asia, was one of the objectives of Laffemas' Conseil du Commerce.

Heller (2000), p. 254.

Laffemas' Plan Revived after Almost a Century

A quite different means of aiding agriculture was employed by Louvois,[23] when he revived a project that had originated with Barthélemy de Laffemas at the end of the sixteenth century. In 1688 Louvois entered into an agreement with a certain sieur Silvestre de Sainte-Catherine, whereby the latter undertook to establish in the south of France nurseries of mulberry trees to encourage the production of silk. Silvestre planned to bring in workers from Italy who were expert in both the preparation and the manufacture of silk.

Charles Woolsey Cole, French Mercantilism 1683–
1700 *(New York: Octagon Books, 1971), pp. 220–221.*

Laffemas the Moderniser: On Infrastructure, Inventions and Standardisation

Not only was Sully not opposed to Laffemas over royal regulation of trade and industry; many of their schemes and interests in fact coincided. One of the chief preoccupations of the *conseil de commerce*, over which Laffemas presided, was precisely that canalization of the rivers and development of the sea-ports which Sully directed as *grand voyer* and *surintendant des fortifications*. Like Laffemas, Sully tried to encourage inventors(…).

> David Buisseret, Sully and the Growth of
> Centralized Government in France 1598–1610
> *(London: Eyre and Spottiswoode, 1968), p. 173.*

[Here] may be mentioned the *Sources des abus et monopoles glissés sur le peuple de France,* and *Trésors et richesses pour mettre l'état en splendeur* (1598), in which [Laffemas] advocates, among other regulations, the establishment of a uniform system of weights and measures for the whole kingdom ….

> *R. H. Inglis* Palgrave, Dictionary of Political
> Economy, *vol. 2 (London: Macmillan, 1900), p. 533.*

Though Laffemas and not Sully was the chief instigator of all this policy, it does not mean that the latter was of no account in the development of town life and the growing wealth of the industrial classes, for as *grand voyer* he did more than anyone else to improve transport both by land and water, and nothing was more necessary for the establishment of markets and the spread of prosperity than an improvement in the means of communication.

> *Eleanor C. Lodge,* Sully, Colbert and Turgot;
> a Chapter in French Economic History
> *(London: Methuen, 1931), pp. 106–107.*

Botero's and Bodin's ideas were echoed by the counselor to Henry IV of France, Barthélemy de Laffemas. In 1600, he wrote *Le sixiesme traicté du commerce,* one of many pamphlets about commerce and industry that modern historians equate with the idea of mercantilism. Laffemas believed that the way France could return to wealth after the long, bloody Wars of Religion (1562–98) was to favor urban industry over agriculture. Working to support the French monarchy after the wars' destruction, he followed Bodin and Botero when he said that princes became rich by levying fair taxes on rich merchants and artisans. Kings had to make strict regulations to stop both foreign goods and internal monopolies from undermining national industries. (…) Doing so, however, would help merchants create more competitive businesses and industries and spark unfettered, unmonopolized national trade. Thus, Laffemas called for protectionism, state support of industry, and versions of internal laissez-faire to catalyze economic development in France. This mixture of protectionism and liberalism would characterize the most important French works of political economy of the seventeenth century's initial decades. Most notably, Laffemas's formula appears in Antoine de Montchrestien's 1615 *Traicté de l'oeconomie politique*. Montchrestien coined the term political economy. He declared that 'mechanical arts' would flourish only through royal regulations and that wealth for the king would, in turn, come from manufacturing rather than from agriculture. Regulations would act to stop fraud, monopoly, and wasteful lawsuits and thereby open up the internal market.

> Jacob Soll, *'For a New Economic History of Early Modern Empire: Anglo-French Imperial Codevelopment beyond Mercantilism and Laissez-Faire'*, The William and Mary Quarterly *77, no. 4 (October 2020): 525–550.*

On the Impact of His Work

It is difficult to evaluate the success of Laffemas' efforts. But some facts are clear. He paved the way for the titanic efforts of Colbert. He disseminated his own ideas in a fairly large and important circle. He accomplished something at least toward the early industrialization of France. It is almost impossible to deny him the rank of the first mercantilist minister of France, and not see in him the Colbert of the reign of Henry IV.

> *Cole (1931), p. 112.*

There may even be some connection between the fact that Laffemas and others in the late sixteenth and early seventeenth centuries sought so ardently to make France a producer of luxuries, and the fact that since the seventeenth century France has supplied a large part of the world with its luxury goods.

> *Cole (1931), p. 216.*

The origin of this French singularity is associated with France's history and more specifically with two of its outstanding figures. The first is that of Sully, Superintendent of Finance of Henri IV, who sought, with the advice of Barthélemy de Laffemas, to develop national production through a whole series of actions ranging from the improvement of infrastructures (backfilled, paved and passable roads) to the abolition of small financial and judicial offices, including the abolition of tolls and the development of plantations and industry (for example, the Gobelins Manufactory). The second historical figure is that of Colbert (...)

> *Joël-Thomas Ravix and Marc Deschamps,* Innovation and Industrial Policies *(London: Wiley, 2019), p. 8.*

Laffemas and Laissez-faire

Indeed, in both France and England, experienced merchants and financiers such as Thomas Mun, Edward Misselden, Roger Coke, John Cary, Barthélemy de Laffemas, Jean-Baptiste Colbert, Jacques Savary, François Véron Duverger de Forbonnais, the Pâris brothers (Antoine Paris, Claude Pâris La Montagne, Joseph Paris Duverney, and Jean Paris de Monmartel), and the Swiss transplant Jacques Necker all questioned the totalizing laissez-faire policies of the physiocrats and advocated much more mixed approaches.

Soll (2020), p. 526, n. 6.

Lessons from History?

'In his role of Controller General of Commerce and President of the Conseil de Commerce, Barthélemy de Laffemas devised a public institution dedicated at encouraging entrepreneurship and regulating industries. Despite being judged by historians as a cumbersome machine generating endless meetings of doubtful utility, Laffemas's *Commission de Commerce* did everything conceivable to encourage industrial investments in France. In an estimated 150 separate sessions over the 1601–1602 period only, the Commission investigated matters relating to trade in goods and services, including textile manufacturing, horse breeding, leather works, glass, tiles, tapestry, rival and canal works, shipbuilding and much more.'

Simone Raudino, Development Aid and
Sustainable Economic Growth in Africa. The
Limits of Western and Chinese Engagements
(Cham: Palgrave Macmillan, 2016), p. 96, ch. 3.

Work Continued by His Son

LAFFEMAS, ISAAC DE, sieur de, son of Barthélemy de Laffemas, civil lieutenant of Paris and subsequently member of the council of state, wrote a *Histoire du Commerce de France* (1606), in which he follows his father's footsteps and insists on the usefulness of acclimatising the breeding of silkworms and of prohibiting the introduction of foreign silks.

Palgrave (1900), p. 532.

Works by Laffemas[24]

1. *Source de plusieurs abus et monopoles qui se sont glissez et coulez sur le peuple de France, depuis trente ans ou environ, à la ruyne de l'Estat, dont il se trouve moyen par un réglement général d'empescher à l'advenir tel abus, présenté au Roy et à nosseigneurs de l'assemblée* (1596)

2. *Reiglement général pour dresser les manufactures en ce royaume et couper le cours des draps de soye et autres marchandises qui perdent et ruynent l'État. Avec l'extraict de l'advis que MM. de l'Assemblée tenue à Rouen ont baillé à S. M., que l'entrée de toutes sortes de marchandises de soye et laines manufacturées hors ce royaume, soient deffendues en iceluy. Ensemble le moyen de faire les soyes par toute la France* (1597)

3. *Responce à messieurs de Lyon, lesquels veulent empescher, rompre le cours des marchandises d'Italie, avec le préjudice de leurs foires, et l'abus aux changes* (1598)

4. *Les Trésors et richesses pour mettre l'Estat en splendeur et monstrer au vray la ruine des François par le trafic et négoce des estrangers* (1598)

5. *Advertissement et responce aux marchands et autres, où il est touché des changes, banquiers et banqueroutiers* (1600)

6. *Advis et remonstrance à MM. les commissaires députez du Roy au faict du commerce, avec les moyens de soulager le peuple des tailles, et autre bien nécessaire pour la police de ce royaume* (1600)

7. *L'Incrédulité ou l'ignorance de ceux qui ne veulent cognoistre le bien et repos de l'Estat et veoir renaistre la vie heureuse des François. Ce discours contient cinq petits traictez* (1600). Contient: *Le Cinquiesme traité du commerce parlant des procez et chiquaneries et voir l'honneur que l'on doit porter aux juges de la justice, avec la faute et la création de celle des consuls, et autres telles préjudiciables au public. Second traité : Advertissement et responce aux marchands et autres, où il est touché des changes, banquiers et banqueroutiers. Troisiesme traité: Les moyens de chasser la gueuserye, contraindre les fainéants, faire et employer les pauvres*

8. *La Commission, édit et partie des mémoires de l'ordre et établissement du commerce général des manufactures en ce royaume, proposés par Barthélemy de Laffemas* (1601)

9. *Les Discours d'une liberté générale et vie heureuse pour le bien du peuple* (1601)

10. *VIIe traicté du commerce, de la vie du loyal marchand, avec la commission du Roy, et bien qu'il faict aux peuples et royaumes* (1601)

11. *Neuf advertissements pour servir à l'utilité publicque, advenus sur le bonheur de la naissance de Mgr le Daulphin, assavoir est, d'un bon et rare ouvrier françois : faire fil d'or au tiltre de Milan ; faire croistre le ris en France ; bluter les farines par des enfants ; faire fromage à la vraye mode de Milan ; faire croistre esperges grosses de deux poulces, et longues d'un pied ; comme les estrangers possèdent la navigation de la mer et les richesses des foires; certain advis de fabriquer toutes étoffes en France; le désordre des monnoyes* (1601)

12. *Remonstrance au peuple suivant les édicts et ordonnances des roys, à cause du luxe et superfluité des soyes, clinquants en habits, ruine générale* (1601)

13. *Remonstrances politiques sur l'abus des charlatans, pipeurs et enchanteurs* (1601)

14. *Comme l'on doibt permettre la liberté du transport de l'or et de l'argent hors du royaume et par tel moyen conserver le nostre, et attirer celuy des estrangers. Avec le moyen infaillible de faire continuellement travailler les monnoyes de ce royaume, qui demeurent inutilles* (1602)

15. *Le Tesmoignage certain du profict et revenu des soyes de France, par preuves certifiées du païs de Languedoc* (1602)

16. *Lettres et exemples de feu la Royne mère, comme elle faisoit travailler aux manufactures, et fournissoit aux ouvriers de ses propres deniers. Avec la preuve certaine de faire les soyes en ce royaume pour la provision d'iceluy et, en peu d'années, en fournir aux estrangers* (1602)

17. *Le Mérite du travail et labeur, dédié aux chefs de la police* (1602)

18. *Le Plaisir de la noblesse et autres qui ont des éritages aux champs, sur la preuve certaine et profict des estauffes et soyes qui se font à Paris* (1603)

19. *La Façon de faire et semer la graine de meuriers, les eslever en pépinières et les replanter aux champs, gouverner et nourrir les vers à soye au climat de la France, plus facilement que par les mémoires de tous ceux qui en ont escript* (1604)

20. *Le Naturel et profit admirable du meurier* (1604)

21. *Recueil présenté au Roy, de ce qui se passe en l'Assemblée du commerce, au Palais à Paris* (1604)

22. *La Ruine et disette d'argent, qu'ont apporté les draps de soyes en France, avec des raisons que n'ont jamais cogneu les François, pour y remédier* (1608)

23. *Advertissement sur les divers crimes des banqueroutiers. Suivant les édits et ordonnances des rois de France* (1609)

24. *Advis sur l'usage des passements d'or et d'argent* (1610)

25. *Le Terme de Pasques sans trébuchet, en vers burlesque* (1649)

Notes

1 See, for example, Jan Glete, *War and the State in Early Modern Europe: Spain, the Dutch Republic and Sweden as Fiscal-Military States, 1500–1660* (London: Routledge, 2006); Bartolomé Yun-Casalilla and Patrick K. O'Brien (eds), *The Rise of Fiscal States: A Global History, 1500–1914* (Cambridge: Cambridge University Press, 2012); Richard Bonney, *The Rise of the Fiscal State in Europe c.1200–1815* (Oxford: Oxford University Press, 1999).

2 The political-discursive history of this line of reasoning is covered in Istvàn Hont, *Jealousy of Trade. International Competition and the Nation State in Historical Perspective* (Cambridge, MA: Belknap Press at Harvard University Press, 2005); the economic part in Sophus A. Reinert, *Translating Empire: Emulation and the Origins of Political Economy* (Cambridge, MA: Harvard University Press, 2011), ch. 1.

3 Rosario Patalano and Sophus Reinert (eds), *Antonio Serra and the Economics of Good Government* (London: Palgrave, 2016); Philipp Robinson Rössner (ed.), *Economic Growth and the Origins of Modern Political Economy: Economic Reasons of State, 1500–2000* (London and New York: Routledge, 2016).

4 See Cosimo Perrotta, *Consumption as an Investment: The Fear of Goods from Hesiod to Adam Smith* (New York and London: Routledge, 2004); and also his 'Antonio Serra's Development Economics: Mercantilism, Backwardness, Dependence', *History of Economic Thought and Policy* 2 (2013): pp. 5–19.

5 See list of Laffemas' work, according to Wikipedia, at the end of the chapter.

6 Ere Nokkala and Nicholas B. Miller (eds), *Cameralism and the Enlightenment: Happiness, Governance, and Reform in Transnational Perspective* (London and New York: Routledge, 2020); Marten Seppel and Keith Tribe (eds), *Cameralism in Practice: State Administration and Economy in Early Modern Europe* (Woodbridge: Boydell & Brewer, 2017); Philipp Robinson Rössner, 'Marx, Mercantilism and the Cameralist Path to Wealth', *Vierteljahrschrift für Sozial- und Wirtschaftsgeschichte* 108, no. 2 (2021): pp. 224–254.

7 Justin Yifu Lin, *New Structural Economics: A Framework for Rethinking Development and Policy* (Washington, DC: World Bank Publications, 2012), p. 350.

8 Philipp Robinson Rössner (ed.), *Philipp Wilhelm von Hörnigk's Austria Supreme (if It So Wishes): 'A Strategy for European Economic Supremacy' (1684)*, translated by K. Tribe (London and New York: Anthem, 2018).

9 *Memorial del Contador Luis Ortiz a Felipe II. Valladolid, 1 de marzo, 1558* (Madrid: Instituto de España, 1970).

10 Giovanni Botero, *Della Ragion di Stato, con Tre Libri delle Cause della Grandezza, e Magnificenza delle Città* (Venice: I Gioliti, 1589).

11 *Raison et gouvernement d'Estat, en dix livres. Du seigneur Giovani Botero Benese. Traduicts sur la quatriesme impression italienne, plus ample que les autres premieres, la version respondant à son original, colomne, pour colomne, par Gabriel Chappuys secretaire, interprete du roy: & dediez a monsieur d'Incarville* (Paris, 1599).

12 Exceptions include Fernand Hayem, *Un Tailleur d'Henri IV. Barthélemy de Laffemas* (Paris: Guillaumin, 1905); Enea Balmas, *Le idee di Barthélemy de Laffemas* (Milan: Editrice Viscontea, 1957), or Pierangelo Bulgari, 'Pour une approche à l'enseignement des langues spécialisées en diachronie: la langue de l'économie et du commerce dans l'œuvre de Barthélemy de Laffemas', *Plaisance* 26 (2012): pp. 231–258. On Laffemas and his contribution to economic thought, see Henri Hauser, *Les débuts du capitalism* (Paris: F. Alcan, 1927), pp. 161–180.

13 Liah Greenfeld, *Spirit of Capitalism: Nationalism and Economic Growth* (Cambridge, MA: Harvard University Press, 2009), p. 117.

14 See Jean-Baptiste Vérot, 'Barthélemy de Laffemas: protectionnisme, innovation et émergence de l'économie politique sous Henri IV', in *Libéralisme et protectionnisme. Économie politique des relations internationals*, ed. André Tiran and Dimitri Uzunidis (Bruxelles: Peter Lang, 2019), pp. 101–121.

15 Jacob M. Price, *France and the Chesapeake: A History of the French tobacco monopoly, 1674–1791, and of its Relationship to the British and American tobacco trades*, 2 vols (Ann Arbor: University of Michigan Press, 1973).

16 See an unpublished *Habilitationsschrift* by Moritz Isenmann, *Der 'Colbertismus' und die Ursprünge des wirtschaftlichen Liberalismus. Französische Außenhandelspolitik im Zeitalter Ludwigs XIV* (University of Cologne, 2015), pp. 126–161. We are indebted to Moritz Isenmann for granting us access to this thesis. It is the most intelligent and up-to-date

reassessment of Colbert's economic policies in their historical and international setting.

17 The econometrics of this have been sketched in Adam Brzezinski, Yao Chen, Nuno Palma and Felix Ward, eds., 'DP14089 The Vagaries of the Sea: Evidence on the Real Effects of Money from Maritime Disasters in the Spanish Empire', CEPR Press Discussion Paper No. 14089. https://cepr.org/publications/dp14089.

18 Henry IV (1553–1610), also known as Good King Henry, was king of France from 1589 to 1610. Baptised as a Catholic but having been raised in the Protestant faith by his mother, Henry shared a non-Catholic background with Laffemas. He survived several assassination attempts, but was in the end killed by a Catholic fanatic.

19 Maximilien de Béthune, 1st Duke of Sully (1560–1641) was a nobleman, soldier, statesman and faithful right-hand man who assisted King Henry IV of France in the rule of the country. Although he counselled King Henry to convert to the Roman Catholic faith, he steadfastly remained a Protestant himself.

20 Jean-Baptiste Colbert (1619–1683) – often referred to as *The Great Colbert* – was a French politician who served as the minister of finances of France from 1665 to 1683 under the rule of King Louis XIV. Through relentless hard work and thrift he improved the state of French manufacturing and brought the economy back from the brink of bankruptcy.

21 Jean Bodin (1530–1596) was a French jurist and political philosopher, member of the Parlement of Paris and professor of law in Toulouse. He is best known for his theory of sovereignty. His most famous work *Les Six livres de la République* (The Six Books of the Republic) (1577) had lasting influence. Bodin became one of the founders of an inter-confessional group that ultimately succeeded in ending the Wars of Religion, with the Edict of Nantes, in 1598, the year after Laffemas' main work was published.

22 Antoine de Montchrétien (c. 1575–1621) was a French soldier, dramatist, adventurer and economist. His *Traicté de l'économie politique* (1615) was to a large extent based on the works of Jean Bodin. In this work he employs the term 'political economy' which had first been used by Louis de Mayerne in his *La monarchie aristodémocratique* (Paris: Jean Berjon & Jean Le Bouc, 1611).

23 François-Michel Le Tellier, marquis de Louvois (1639–1691) was secretary of state for war under Louis XIV of France and his most influential minister in the period 1677–91.

24 https://fr.wikisource.org/wiki/Auteur:Barthélemy_de_Laffemas.

Chapter 2

GENERAL REGULATION FOR THE ESTABLISHMENT OF MANUFACTURES (1597)

Barthélemy de Laffemas

Translated from the original French by Philip Stewart

Full title:

General regulation for the establishment of manufactures in this kingdom to contain the cost of silk fabric and other merchandise that harms and ruins the state, which is the true way of restoring France to her splendor, provide work for the poor, and keep them from begging for a living.

With an extract of the opinion which the Lords of the Assembly held in Rouen have sent to his Majesty, that the entrance of all sorts of gold thread and woolens manufactured outside the kingdom be prohibited here, and that levies on woolens and raw silk be suppressed.

Along with the means of producing silks throughout France.

[By Barthélemy de Laffemas.]
Paris: C. de Monstr'oeil et Jean Richer, 1597.
By privilege of the king.

A note by the translator and the general editor.

The introduction will show that Mr. Laffemas was not raised as a man of letters. If anything, the author of this treatise was certainly more accustomed to legal documents than anything else. His language is often rigid and haphazardly punctuated, so I have had to take some risks in modernising it. Its pre-economic and pre-industrial vocabulary is fraught with difficulties, of which the most general are these:

1. **Police** is used to designate a system: an economic policy but also the structure that is adopted to support it. Thus, it should be understood that *policy* in this document does not mean only policy but also this frame. Accordingly, a dictionary of 1606 gives this complex definition: *Police* 'is a regulation of a state and community, whether monarchical, aristocratic, or democratic, in supplies, clothing, trade, and other things that concern the welfare of all. It comes from the Greek *politéia*, derived from *polis*, city, because the city was first subject to such regulation [...].'[1]

2. **Manufacture** as a noun has no obvious equivalent in modern English. It means a place or structure where things are made by man, as opposed to the production of raw materials, or the process itself. The same dictionary just quoted calls it 'the making of some piece of work by hand'.[2] Here we use the term in the same sense as Alexander Hamilton's famous 1791 *Report on Manufactures* to the US House of Representatives.

3. **Marchandise** can be either singular or plural; in the latter case, it is pretty close to *merchandise*, but in the singular is closer to *product*.

4. The state or government is sometimes designated as **république** or **chose publique**. It needs to be understood that these terms are etymologically identical – *res publica* (in Latin) = *chose publique* (in French), but 'public thing' has no such resonance in English and thus is not an acceptable substitute. The Dictionary of the Academy in 1694 notes that *republic* 'often stands for any kind of state or government'.[3] Thus does not mean what we do by *republic*, which would be anachronistic, but the government as public institution or the public weal. I have used an asterisk to mark terms that stand for *chose publique* in the original.

5. **Chambre** in the proposal means a sort of guild cell; the only survival of this word in today's English is the expression 'chamber of commerce', which will convey the sense of *chamber* in this context. It has a physical office, but the term designates the structure rather than the physical location. These *chambers* are run by unpaid senior guild members called *jurés* (in other words, those sworn to office),[4] which I have translated as *officers*.

6. There are many terms used to designate various types of fabric and stages in producing them. I have done the best I can to make distinctions among them, but in order to sort them out with any precision, it would be necessary to work directly from the original document.

Reiglement general pour dresser les manufactures en ce royavme, et couper le cours des draps de soye, & autres marchandises qui perdent et ruynent l'Estat. Avec l'extraict de l'advis que Meßieurs de l'Assemblee tenue à Rouen ont baillé à Sa Maiesté, Que l'entrée de toutes sortes de fil d'or & d'argent, & marchandises de soye & laines manufacturees hors ce Royaume, soient def-fendues en iceluy: & d'oster les imposts sur les laines et soyes escrues. Ensemble le moyen de faire les soyes par toute la France.
A Paris. Par Claude de Monstr'oeil, & Jean Richer, 1597. *Avec Priuilege du Roy.*

The French text of this document duplicates the typography of the source edi-tion for the first part (Bibliothèque Nationale de France microfiche R-40327) and for the second part *Response aux difficultez proposees à l'encontre du Reglement* from the Reinert family library, with the following exceptions:

—Long *s* (*ſ*) is transcribed like any other *s*, but the character ß for double *ss* is retained in the few places where it occurs in the original.

—The letters *u* and *v* and *i* and *j*, conflated in the original and often used interchangeably, are separated in this transcription; thus the reader will see *j'ai* and *peuvent* instead of *i'ay* and *peuuent.*

Mistakes are not corrected but obvious anomalies are noted by a bracketed [*sic*].

[3]

AU ROY.

SIRE,

Ayant eu c'est honneur que d'estre vostre domestique depuis trente ans passez, & vous ayant fait service en mon estat de tailleur & varlet de chambre, & depuis marchant en vostre argenterie, la longueur du temps & le trafic que j'ay fait avec plusieurs marchans estrangers, m'a fait avoir l'experience pour cognoistre le mal secret & caché qu'aporte en vostre Estat les draps de soye, toilles d'or & d'argent, & autres marchandises venant des pays d'Italie, de Flandres, Angleterre, & autres lieux; & pour cest effet en ayant communiqué à plusieurs personnes, c'est chose tres veritable que si le cours de ces abus estoient retranchez, ce seroit une espece d'actions de graces envers Dieu, des benedictions qu'il a tant departies en vostredit Royaume, qu'il semble qu'il l'aye designé pour avoir auctorité & commandement sur tous les autres, l'ayant si bien constitué & pourveu de tout ce qui est necessaire pour la vie de l'homme, & en telle abondance, qu'il se peut passer de tous ses voisins, & nul ne se peut passer de luy: Pour exemple il est de besoin considerer les richesses & moyens qui peuvent venir des loingtains pays, la pollice & manufacture establie, sça- [4] voir est des bleds, vins, sel, pastel, tailles, & grand nombre de draps, qui souloyent fournir tout le pays de levant, ce qui se peut faire encore les atteliers desdites manufactures estant dressez, & außi de plusieurs autres sortes de marchandises, dequoy les pays estranges ont affaire, & ne s'en peuvent passer, qui seront les vrais thresors des Indes, pour remplir la France de deniers & richesses, empeschant d'aller chercher aux estranges pays, ce qui se peut faire & travailler en France, pour le bien de vos subjets: cela m'a occasionné, & ay pris la hardiesse vous faire entendre les moyens qui semblent estre propres pour empescher tels abus. Et d'autant, SIRE, que je n'ay n'y l'eloquence n'y la hardiesse de proposer à vostre Majesté de bouche le remede qu'il y faut apporter, cela m'a fait vous importuner de ce petit livret, avec la forme d'un reiglement general, où j'ay mis par escrit ce peu que je vous presente, qu'il vous plaira faire voir à vostre Assemblee, & je prieray le Createur,

SIRE,

Que de santé & felicité vous ne puissiez jamais manquer, par celui qui est nay pour mourir.

Vostre tres-humble, tres-obeyssant, & tres fidelle serviteur,

LAFFEMAS dit
Beau-Semblant.

[5]

Pour bien reigler, maintenir & faire fleurir la chose publique, il est de besoin que le chef d'icelle cognoisse les membres, ainsi les Republiques doyvent estre tenues en tel estat, que le Prince en puisse estre secouru, le pauvre aidé & survenu, & un chacun selon son grade, attendu que les communautez ne peuvent subsister n'y s'entretenir, sans la puissance du souverain, la vertu du Prince, & auctorité du Magistrat.

Il est donc expediẽt oster & retrancher les malversations qui s'y commettent, sçavoir est, les abus, tromperies, monopoles, assemblees, & autres telles mangeries & yvrogneries, qui par ce moyen seront abolies, ainsi qu'il sera declaré, & facile par un reiglement generale, pour le bien & utilité du public, & conservation de l'Estat.

Avant que parler du bien qui se trouvera audit reiglement, il est besoin parler des monopoles & malheurs que nous ont apporté les draps de soye, d'or & d'argent, & autres telles marchandises venant des pays estrãges, qui est en partie la ruyne de l'Estat, ainsi que l'on verra, & se pourra cognoitre par les plus ignorans du monde.

Lesdites soyes, toilles d'or & d'argent qu'apportent les estrangers, ont enlevé les cens [6] & cinq cens mil escus à la fois, qui leur ont servy à faire le fonds des affermes & grands partis, lesquels ont ruiné & ravagé toutes les Provinces du Royaume, & si les Françoys estoyent aussi braves à la manufacture, comme ils sont à plaider, ils empescheroyent lesdits estrangers à faire lesdites affermes, & partis changes & rechanges qui achevent d'epuiser l'or & l'argent de la France.

Il semble que lesdits fermiers, & ceux qui ont inventé les doüanes à Lyon, ont predit ou desiré le malheur de la France, il donnoyent à entendre au Roy, qu'il en viendroit deux ou trois cens mil escus à son domaine; mais ils ne disoyent pas qu'il[s] les prenoyent dans sa bourse, ou en celle de ses pauvres subjets, & par le moyen de ses ruses & inventions de chaque cent mil escus qu'il donnoyent au Roy, ils en tiroyent dix milliõs hors de la Frãce.

Jugez s'il vous plaist, si la doüane qu'a estably le duc de Savoye à la Suze, aux frontieres de son pays, qui luy vaut tous les ans grand nombre de deniers, à cause des draps de soye, toille d'or & d'argent, & autres telles marchandises qui viennent à Lyon, je vous laisse à penser s'ils apportent les deniers d'Italie pour payer ladite doüane, & si ce ne sont pas des deniers clairs de la France.

Et par l'industrie de ceux qui ont envoyé si grãd nombre de draps de soye manufacturez en France, ils ont fait un grand service aux ennemis du Roy & de l'Estat: car ils ont tiré les thresors hors de France, que l'on dit estre le nerf de la guerre, voila pourquoy le Roy & son peuple sont desnuez de moyẽs, l'on à veu le temps que l'on eust plus trou- [7] vé d'or & d'argent par les simples villages ruinez, qu'aujourd'hui on ne sçauroit trouver en tout le Royaume, à cause des grands thresors que lesdits draps de soye & autres ont tiré de France, & montent plus de sommes de deniers trois fois que n'ôt cousté toutes les armees.

Exemple de ce que dessus, à sçavoir que tous les marchans qui trafiquent en draps de soye, par toute la France, qui sont en grand nombre, tesmoin en la ville de Paris, l'on à veu qu'il n'y avoit que cinq ou six marchans de soye trafiquant à Lyon, & à present ils son un nombre infiny, & toutes les villes de France ainsi munies desdits marchans de soye, ils sont comme facteurs ou commis de ceux qui nous envoyent lesdits draps de soye d'Italie, & d'ailleurs, pour raison que tous les jours & à toute heure ils sont apres à trouver de l'or & de l'argent de tous costez, & cherchêt toutes les bonnes bourses, pour avoir argent, & y employent tous leurs amis & credit pour faire grands amas de deniers pour porter à Lyon, ou en Italie, & ailleurs, qui est un vray moyen d'achever de ruyner l'Estat: Si Dieu par sa misericorde ne coupe le cours de ceste mechante invention, qui ne porte que la ruine des François.

Autre abus grandement prejudiciable, touchât la permission qui se fait de laisser faire dans la ville de Paris & ailleurs, un si grand nombre de passemêt d'or & d'argent, qu'autant vaudroit-il permettre de mener les finances de France à charretees dedans la mer, attendu que ce sont besongnes perdues au monde, dont il ne revient aucun profit, & pareille- [8] ment que se sont estoffes qui ne se doyvent porter qu'aux Rois & aux Princes, le tout à faute d'une bonne reigle & police, qui se peut faire avec celle des draps de soye, par le moyen dudit reiglement.

Qu'on prenne exemple aux bas de soye qui viennent tous les ans en France, il se trouvera plus de cinquante mil personnes qui en portent, plustost moitié d'avâtage que moins, quand ils ne cousteroyent que quatre escus l'un portât l'autre, & chacun en peut user quatre paires par an, c'est article seul monteroit à huit cens mil escus, & qui le pourroit sçavoir au vray, il s'y en trouveroit davantage.

Or est-il que si les bas de soye reviennent à une si grand[e] somme de deniers tirez hors de la France, les draps d'or & d'argent, & de soye, reviendront à vingt fois d'avantage, ayant esgard au grand nombre qui s'en porte par toute la France, tant grands que petits, jusques aux bourgeois, bourgeoises, & autres qui en sont ordinairement vestus, au grand prejudice du public, d'autant que l'on peut avoir moyen de faire marchandise en France, pour en estre vestus, & par ce moyen l'on feroit travailler les pauvres; car à faute de leur donner moyen ils demeurent à rien faire, & se perdent de tout, soit de pauvreté ou autrement.

Que si les Princes ou Princesses ont affaire de toille de drap d'or & d'argent, & autres estoffes rares, elles se peuvent manufacturer & travailler en France, belles & bonnes sans nulle difficulté, & peut-on aisémêt faire venir du pays de

Perse & de levant, les soyes toutes escruës, & mesmes en chan- [9] ge d'autres marchandises, sans tirer l'or & l'argent de la France.

Outre ce qu'avec le temps il se plantera parmy la France des meuriers pour nourrir des vers à faire la soye, à l'exēple du Languedoc, qu'ils en ont grand nombre, mêmes le Sieur de saint Privat, gentilhomme du pays, qui à fait des pepinieres desdits meuriers, que depuis deux ou trois ans ils en ont planté dans le pays, mêmes en Provence, Orange, & Conté d'Avignon, plus de dix millions, outre ceux qu'ils avoyent auparavant, sont arbres faciles à venir, & qui aportēt grand profit, soit du bois que l'on coupe de cinq à cinq ans, ou de la feuille pour nourrir lesdits vers, qui font grand nombre de soye, il y a tel meurier qui a porté du profit à son maistre plus d'un escu, & s'aferme les communs à vingt ou trente sols tous les ans, il y a pareillement des meuriers en Touraine, qui font des soyes belles & bonnes, voire des meilleures qui se puisse trouver, ce memoire servira d'instruction à plusieurs, qui pourront planter desdits meuriers, la terre est propre en plusieurs endroits de la France, desquels meuriers se nourriront les vers, qui embesongneront plusieurs mesnages lesquels en tireront du profit, & est chose certaine & veritable.

Autre instruction pour les cuirs en la ville de Nerac en Gascongne, il y a un maistre conroyeur [sic] nommé Bernardin, fait qu'il acoutre des cuirs qui sont si forts & si bons, qu'il n'y a espee n'y hallebarde qui les puisse perser, tesmoin qu'il en a fait au Roy qui est à present, des casques & cuirasses qui ont eté esprouvez en la presence de [10] sa Majesté, qui n'ont jamais sçeu estre persez, & pareillement ledit Bernardin, & des Suisses aussi courroyeurs, retirez depuis quinze ans au pays de Biard, lesquels acoustrent des peaux de Bœuf en buffle, des chevres en chamoys qui sont aussi beaux & aussi bons que ceux qui viennent d'Allemagne, chose de verité, & par consequent s'en peut-il travailler par toute la France. Autre exēple en la ville de Dourdant, qui depuis quelque annee ce sont accoustumez à faire bas de soye, bas d'estame, & les font aujourd'hui aussi beaux & aussi bõs que ceux qui viennent d'Italie & Angleterre, & en la ville de Senlis, & plusieurs villages aux environs, deux pauvres hommes venant de Flandre, depuis quelque temps, leur ont apris à faire des dentelles, que l'on appelle ouvrages de Flandre, qui aujourd'hui il ne s'en peut voir au mõde de plus belle & mieux faites, & grand[e] quantité, & aussi pareillement de toutes sortes d'ouvrages & manufactures par consequent se peuvent dresser par tout, il n'y a chose du monde que le François ne contreface, & encores le feront mieux quand ils y travailleront avec une belle reigle & discipline, ainsi qu'il se peut faire, par le moyen dudit reiglement.

Que si aisément l'on peut faire manufacturer les draps de soye, & toille d'or & d'argent, plus aisément l'on fera travailler & manufacturer toutes sortes de draps & sarges, & toutes autres marchandises, & peuvent faire travailler &

employer grand nombre de personnes, au grand bien & augmentation du domaine du Roy, & pareillemẽt pour tout le bien public.

[11] Il est grandement necessaire pour le bien & utilité du public, de considerer qu'ordinairement on fait vente de la plus grande partie des laines qui se levent en Languedoc, Provence & Dauphiné, qui se transportent en Italie, là où ils employent lesdites laines, & les font travailler en sarge de Florence, estamets, ras de Milan & autres, qu'apres estant mises en

manufactures on les rapporte vendre & debiter en France, qui est donner à cognoistre l'ignorance des François: car si la reigle & police de la manufacture estoit bien establie en France, on feroit travailler des double-sarges de Florence, tesmoin les draps du seau de Roüen, sarges de Limestres, & autres draperies qui se font en France.

Pour bien faire travailler & manufacturer les ouvrages, il est de besoin dresser des chambres pour chaque corps de mestier, ainsi qu'il est amplement declaré par le reiglement, lesdites chambres estant le vray remede d'amener à bonne fin toutes entreprises qui se travailleront par tout le Royaume.

Il est dit au reiglement qu'il y aura un nombre de marchans & artisans, gens de bien & de bonne reputation, qu'ils ne prendront aucuns salaires n'y esmollument, qui s'employeront pour les pauvres, & vuideront les differens des ouvrages & manufactures, qui viẽdrõt à leur cognoissance: car en toute societé s'il n'y a quelqu'un qui preside, tout ira en confusion, les Justiciers & Officiers des villes ne sont propres à cognoistre les manufactures & ouvrages, est faire Juger les couleurs aux aveugles, il faut des maistres experts pour en decider, estant [12] raisonnable que l'on adjouste autant ou plus de foi aux Jurez & Maistres, & gardes des communautez, que l'on fait à un Sergent qui est creu d'un meffait & dõmage à son simple raport, jusques à trois livres cinq sols, & auront esgard, & empescheront que nuls pauvres desdites communautez n'aillent point mandier, par le moyen desdites Chambres.

Et aussi tous pauvres & gueux qui sont és portes des Eglises, aux coings des ruës, & qui couchent fur les fumiers comme bestes, lesdites Chambres estant establies, c'est le vray moyen d'y empescher, pour raison de la maison publique.

Il ne se trouvera vagabond n'y faineant qui ne soit employé, attendu qu'ils seront descouverts par le moyen desdites Chambres, qui servira de beaucoup pour empescher la perte des enfans de bonne maison, & autres, qui sont ordinairement subornez & desbauchez par le moyen desdits vagabonds qu'on ne peut remarquer ni cognoistre, & ne bougent des bordeaux & mauvaises compagnies, où ils attirent & perdent plusieurs jeunes gens, comme dit est.

Les guerres civiles en partie sont cause que tous serviteurs, ouvriers & autres, ne rendent point l'honneur & l'obeyssance qu'ils doyvent à leurs maistres, & à faute de ce les marchandises & manufactures ne sont faites comme elles doyvent, attendu qu'à present il n'y a nul devoir, si ce n'est par le moyen desdites chambres, qui ordinairement les tiendront sujets, & les apprendront de se rendre capables d'estre maistres, & à faute de discipline ils [13] ne font les ouvrages parfaits.

Par le moyen desdites chambres, les assemblees & confrairies qui ont apporté durant les troubles tant de folies, seront abolies, chose que les feux Roys n'ont sçeu faire, quelque ordonnance & defense qui en ayent esté faites, mêmes lesdites assemblees furent defendues par le feu Roy François en l'an mil cinq cens trente neuf: & par le feu Roy Charles neufiesme, en l'an mil cinq cens soixante, & aujourd'hui lesdites assemblees seront abolies par le moyen dudit reiglement.

Lesdites Chambres establies par toute la France, les ouvrages & manufactures se feront en si belle ordre, que les bons ouvriers des pays estranges se viendront ranger parmy les François, qui sera un bien inestimable, & il n'y aura science au monde qu'on ne recherche pour la mettre en lumiere, & travailler à qui mieux mieux.

Les marchandises & manufactures se feront en perfection, ainsi qu'anciennement elles se souloyẽt faire, & tout a esté aboly par le desordre & confusion, qui a esté par le passé, ce qui ne se peut remedier, si ce n'est par le moyen dudit reiglement, qui se peut faire aisément par lesdites Chambres, & en ce faisant les ouvrages se feront bons, beaux, & durables, qui viendra le tout au grand bien de la Republique, & à meilleur prix, à cause du grand nombre qu'il s'en fera.

L'on peut prendre exemple sur toutes les autres marchandises & manufactures, & que l'on regarde les cuirs, qui sont necessaires aux riches & aux pauvres, le temps passé pour tanner les cuirs, [14] & demeuroyẽt un an ou deux à les tanner & corroyer, & aujourd'hui ils n'y demeurent pas trois mois, de sorte qu'à present quatre ou six paires d'ouvrages n'en vallent pas une du temps passe, qui est un abus infaillible, qui ne se peut remettre, si ce n'est par le moyen desdites Chambres.

Et par cy devant le commerce des vins, sel, pastel, & autres marchandises, amenoit en France beaucoup de thresors, specialement ducats à deux testes, millerais, angelots, & autres especes d'or, & au lieu on nous amene grand nombre de marchandises manufactures, & pour cest effect lesdites chambres estant establies, c'est le vray moyen d'y remedier.

Et pour empescher que les ouvriers & artisans, & autres gens de manufacture ne s'amusent plus à des petits procez ni querelles entr'eux, qui est cause que partie d'iceux se ruynẽt, & par ce moyen lesdites Chambres emprescherõt à telles fautes qui sont dommageables à tout le public, & pareillement osteront partie des yvrogneries qui ruynẽt bien souvent les mesnages & familles.

Les grands Bureaux & Chambres ainsi establies, avec crainte de punition en la maison publique, c'est le moyen de faire fleurir la jeunesse en science, civilité, & obeyssance, & apprendront les ouvrages & manufactures avec belle discipline, mesmes que ceux qui renieront & blasphemeront le nom de Dieu, ils seront rigoureusement punis.

Il y a de la noblesse, & autres qui se plaignent & remonstrent que les draps de soye & passemens, [15] & toille d'or & d'argent les ruinêt, & qu'ils ont fait plus de despense depuis trente ans, que leurs predecesseurs n'en avoyent fait depuis trois cens ans, & plusieurs bourgeois & autres en disent de mesmes, en partie à cause de leurs femmes à qui ils ne peuvent retrancher les habits, & si en veulent faire tous les jours d'avantage.

Le bien qui en adviendra pour le Roy & pour l'Estat, sur ce que sa Majesté pourra faire levees de tel nombre d'hômes de guerre qu'il voudra, par le moyê desdites Châbres, & l'on verra aisémêt toutes les forces qui se peuvêt lever, qui seront grâdes & puissantes, & verra-on pareillement le nombre d'iceux, chose excellente pour la conservation de l'Estat, qui empescheront en un besoin faire levees d'estrangers, qui emportent les thresors hors de France.

Autres instructions qui ont esté obmises aux precedens articles pour faire travailler plusieurs sortes de manufactures, & pour le regard de la draperie, il est cognu à tout le monde qu'elle se fait plus belle & meilleure en France, qu'en tous les endroits de l'Europe, il n'y manque que la pollice de les faire faire de leurs bontez & largeurs, pour le regard des sarges, il en peut travailler en France facilement, à l'exemple de la ville de Sommieres en Languedoc, qui depuis cinq à six ans ils font des sarges larges & fines, aussi belles & meilleures qu'il en vint jamais de Florence, & mesmes dans la ville de Nimes audit pays de Lãguedoc, il se fait des sarges, façon de ras de Millan, & pareillement en la ville de Chartres ont commencé à en faire de bel- [16] les & bonnes, & autres endroits de France.

Pour les draps de soye, il s'en peut faire en plusieurs villes de France, & ainsi qu'ils ont commencé en la ville de Lyon, & Tours, il y a long temps, mesmes en la ville de Paris il y a un maistre nommé Godefroy, qui fait toutes sortes de draps de soye, toille d'or & d'argent, & sans nulle doute en fera des plus belles qu'il en vint jamais des pays estranges, en la ville de Montpelier, depuis trois ou quatre ans ont commencé à faire des velours, satins, taffetas, & autres marchandises de soye, qui donne à cognoistre la facilité à un chacun, & en outre audit Montpelier font des futaines blanches, façonnees de toutes sortes plus beaux & exquis, qu'il en vint jamais de ceux d'Allemaigne & Flandres.

Pour le regard des toilles en la ville de sainct Quentin en Picardie, en la ville de Louviers en Normandie, & autres lieux audit pays, il s'en fait aujourd'huy des plus fines, belles & bonnes que les toilles de Hollande, voila pourquoy ayant en France, lins, chanvres en si grand[e] abondance, l'on peut faire toutes sortes de toilles larges & estroites, façonnees & ouvrees aussi bien qu'au pays de Flandre, leur ostant le cours des leurs, sans difficulté leurs ouvriers viendront vivre & travailler en France, comme ils feront de toutes sortes d'ouvrages, à l'exemple d'aucuns Flamens qui se sont rangez durãt ces troubles en la ville de la Rochelle, qui accoustrẽt aujourd'hui des marroquins plus beaux & meilleurs que ceux mesmes qui viennent de Flandre.

[17] Et depuis quelque temps au pays de Biart, dont il a esté parlé cy devãt, font venir à present de Candu & de Barbarie, par le moyen des marchans de Bayonne, des Buffles & Chamois en poil, qu'ils accoustrent les plus beaux qui n'est pas possible de plus, & à l'exemple d'iceux par tous les ports de mer, en faisant leurs voyages, ils peuvent aporter lesdites peaux, & faire travailler lesdits buffles & chamois en tous endroits de la France, chose facile & sans difficulté.

Autre exemple en la ville de Poictiers, depuis sept ou huit ans, ils acoustrent des peaux de bœuf, vache, chevre, & autres en façon de beuffles & chamois, tres beaux & bons, chose de verité.

Il serait de besoin pour le public, que toutes les villes prinssent imitation à la ville d'Amiens, qui font travailler grand nombre de marchandise qui sont sarges, camelots, toilles & infinis autres marchandises, qui font vivre beaucoup de peuples, & attirent les deniers des estrangers, telles gens sont à louër & les contraires & faineans à mepriser.

Mais l'on pourroit à bon droit comparer aucuns François aux Sauvages, plustost qu'à des hõmes de police: car cõme ils donnẽt leurs richesses pour des siflets & sonnettes, Aussi les François reçoivent des babiolles & marchandises estranges, en eschange de leurs tresors.

Ils peuvent avoir grands moyens & richesses, estant dans un Royaume le plus fertile & abondãt de l'Europe: mais ils ne sçavent user des biens que Dieu leur donne: ils ne considerent point qu'ils demeurent necessiteux, vagabonds, & à rien faire, [18] & par leur nonchalãce & paresse dõner à vivre à la moitié des Royaumes & Provinces voisines de la France, leur faisant faire les ouvrages & manufactures qui aisément se peuvent travailler en France, voyez par experience l'Angleterre que tous les ans, ils nous envoyent plus de mil Navires ou vaisseaux en partie chargez de marchandises manufacturees, qui sont draps de laine, bas d'estames, futaines, bural, & autres marchandises. Et pareillemẽt les pays de Flandre nous envoyẽt leurs tapisseries, paintures, toiles, ouvrages, passemẽt de soye, camelot, sarges, marroquins, & autres marchãdises. Et l'Allemagne semblablemẽt les buffles, chamois, petites futaines, boucassins, boubasins, quinquaillerie, & grand nombre d'autres marchãdises. Pareillement l'Italie, Geneve, & autres Provinces nous aportẽt leurs draps de soye, toile d'or & d'argent, sarges de Florence, & autres marchandises en abõdãce, & pour leur rendre la valeur d'icelles, il semble qu'il serait de besoin n'ayant marchãdises manufacturees, pour cest effect leur bailler en eschãges, les sacs & procez, cartes & dez, & toutes sortes d'autres jeux, qui sont les ouvrages & trafic de la plupart des François, jusques aux Laboureurs des champs, qui en font mestier & marchandise.

Et pour y remedier il est besoin faire travailler les manufactures & ouvrages, pour remettre les pauvres villes & villages ruinees, ce sera avoir trouve la vraye pierre Philosophalle, au lieu de convertir le cuyvre & autres metaux en or & argent, ce serõt des doubles thresors des Indes, pour faire voir & admirer les François à cinq cens lieuës de leur Province.

[19]

AU ROY.

S'il plaist à sa Majesté faire dresser ceste belle & riche Academie, qui sont les ouvrages & manufactures par tout son Royaume, à l'exemple du Sieur de Pluvinel, qui retient & empesche les jeunes Princes & Seigneurs d'aller porter leur argent en Italie, ce sera une œuvre tres-excellent[e], qui demeurera escrit aux Histoires de Frãce à jamais, & sera au grand honneur de sa Majesté, qui apres avoir prins tant de peine d'avoir reduit la France par les armes en bon estat, & qu'apres il y face dresser une si belle & heureuse police, qui donnera exemple à tout le reste du monde, pour y prendre imitation, le tout à la louange de Dieu, & conservation de la chose publique.

[20]
Reglement entre les marchans & artisans concernant l'establissement du commerse de la marchandise, ouvrages, & manufacture d'icelle.

Nos Rois d'heureuse memoire que Dieu absolvë, ont fait plusieurs belles ordonnances sur le fait de la police de ce Royaume, pour contenir chacun en son devoir: mesme sur le cõmerse de la marchandise, ouvrages & manufactures d'icelles: Toutesfois elles ont esté (et sont encores) si mal gardees & entretenues que le commerse est presque du tout pery, & les artisans si ruinez, que les uns ont esté contrains sortir hors ledit Royaume pour vivre, les autres d'aller à la guerre, & suyvre le premier chef qui les a recherchez, dont sont advenues les seditions que nous avons veuës par les villes, & partie de ceux qui sont demeurez en France sont contrains de mãdier leur vie avec leurs femmes & enfans, le tout à faute d'avoir esté employez: Tellement que cest chose pitoyable de voir la multitude des pauvres qui demãdent l'aumosne.

Pour a quoy remedier, il est plus que necessaire de remettre sus lesdits commerse & manufactures, [21] ensemble lesdits mestiers, afin de donner moyen aux marchans de trafiquer, & aux artisans de travailler chacũ de son mestier, & tascher aussi de faire en sorte que les pauvres vallides n'aillent plus mendier, & que les artisans que la faim a exillez de ce Royaume, ayẽt occasion d'y retourner, attendu qu'il n'y a chose en ce monde qui enrichisse plus un pays que les artisans commerse & manufactures de la marchandise.

Et pour ce faire, il plaira au Roy ordonner que tous marchans & artisans seront d'icy en avant tenus & contrains de faire corps de communauté de leur mestier, mesme ceux qui suyvent la Court de sa Majesté, & d'avoir chambre particuliere de chacun art & mestier, en laquelle ils feront enregistrer leurs noms, surnoms, demeures, & vocations, & auront jurez ce chacun mestier comme à Paris, & és autres villes ou les mestiers sont jurez, lesquels ne prendront aucune chose pour leurs vacations en ladite chambre, Mais si le corps de la communauté est fort petit, il n'y aura qu'un juré ou deux en iceluy. Et combien que par les statuts desdits mestiers, soit ordonné que les maistres d'iceux seront jurez l'un apres l'autre à tour de rolle: neãtmoins pour le bien qui reussira de l'establissement dudit reglement les plus anciens & expers de chacun mestier, seront esleuz jurez, & ladite eslection continuera aux plus anciens & capables.

Lesquels jurez feront observer & garder les statuts & ordonnãces de leur mestier, & les deux derniers eleuz d'entre eux seront tenus visiter une fois le mois pour le moins, à tel jour ouvrable qu'ils [22] voudront toutes marchandises & manufactures de leur mestier, & aussi les poix, aulnes, & mesures qu'ils trouveront és boutiques desdits marchans & artisans, & autres lieux ou ils estimerõt y avoir marchandise, & ou on travaillera de leur mestier.

Ayant pouvoir de saisir & faire emporter en la chambre de leur mestier tout ce qu'ils trouveront defectueux, pour être confisque (si besoin est) selon l'advis & ordonnance des Maistres du grand bureau des manufactures & marchandises desdits marchans & artisans, qui sera estably en la ville capitale de chacun diocese, & autres lieux ou il sera necessaire, ainsi qu'il sera dit cy apres. Et pourront lesdits Jurez faire ladicte visitation & saisie, sans prendre aucun officier de Justice: a cause que lesdits officiers consomment tout en frais, & auront lesdits deux Jurez, pour leurs peines, sallaires, & vacations, d'avoir fait lesdites visitations & saisies, ce qui leur fera raisonnablemēt & en saine conscience ordonné par les Maistres dudit grand bureau, à le prendre sur les deniers qui proviendrõt des amendes & confiscations des choses par eux saisies.

Tous lesquels Jurez ne passerõt aucun Maistre de leur mestier, qu'il n'ait demeuré en apprentissage le temps qu'il y doit demeurer, qu'il n'ait fait son chef-d'œuvre & soit capable d'estre maistre, chacun desquels nouveaux maistres paiera à la boete des pauvres de son mestier, ce qui sera ordonné par les Commissaires qui seront deputez pour faire l'establissement du present reglement, appellé avec eux les Jurez de chacun mestier: Au lieu des festins & autres frais qui luy faudroit faire pour estre [23] passé maistre, lesquels serõt tres expressément defendus, sur peine à chacun des contrevenans de cent escus d'amende, tant pour lesdits pauvres, que pour l'entretenement de la chambre dudit mestier: Et ou lesdits mestiers ne sont jurez, se fera le semblable lors que lesdits marchans & artisans voudront estre passez maistres.

S'il advient plainte d'aucun desdicts maistres tenant boutique, ou bien d'un de leurs compagnons ou apprentis, le juré dernier eleu, ou le clerc du mestier si aucun y a, de l'ordonnance verballe des autres jurez, fera commandement verbal aux delinquans en parlant à eux, ou à quelqu'un de leurs logis, de comparoistre en ladicte chambre par devant lesdicts jurez au jour & heure qui leur sera assigné pour rendre raison de ladite plainte, & faire ce que par lesdits jurez sera ordonné, à peine de soixante sols tournois pour chacū desdits maistres, pour les pauvres de leur mestier, & aux cõpagnons & apprentis de telle peine qui sera advise par lesdits Jurez.

Lesquels jurez seront tenus se trouver à certain jour de la semaine par eux prefix à ceux de leur mestier en la chãbre d'icelui, pour ouyr les plaintes qui leur seront faites, & pour donner ordre à ce qui sera necessaire pour ledit mestier, specialement pour empescher qu'il ne s'y commette aucun abus & malversation, & pour punir les malfaicteurs selon leurs demerites suyvant le pouvoir à eux donné par ledit reglement.

Et pour obvier à procez, tous marchans & attisans [sic] de quelque mestier qu'ils soyent, ne pourront [24] à l'advenir intenter procez entre eux pour quelque different que ce soit, à cause de leurs marchandises, ouvrages, & manufactures seulement, sans la faire premieremēt entendre aux jurez de leur mestier, lesquels tascheront de les accorder amiablement sans en rien prendre pour leurs peines, salaires & vacations.

Lesdits jurez ne les pouvant accorder, les renvoyront par devant les maistres du prochain bureau: Ensemble leur advis par escrit contenant l'accord qu'ils auront voulu faire dudit different, à ce que (parties ouyes) ils taschent par tous moyens de les accorder, & s'ils ne le peuvent faire, ils les renvoyeront par devant leur Juge ordinaire, avec l'accord par escrit qu'ils auront voulu faire: lequel Juge avant que retenir la cause, verra ce que lesdits jurez & maistres dudit bureau auront voulu accorder, & aussi la quitance de cent sols tournois que l'appellant dudit arbitrage sera tenu payer à la boete des pauvres de son mestier avant que pouvoir faire appeller partie adverse devant ledit Juge, pour n'avoir voulu entretenir ledit accord, sans laquelle quittance le Juge ne passera outre, sur peine de nullité de tous ses jugemens, afin d'empescher ledit appellant de plaider s'il est possible.

En la chambre commune de la ville ou il y aura bureau & aussi és chambres particulieres desdites communautez, sera mis un tableau en lieu eminēt auquel seront escrits les principaux articles des statuts de chacun mestier, & du present reglement, à ce que personne n'en pretende cause d'ignorance.

Lesdits jurez pourront condamner chacun de- [25] linquant de leur mestier, jusques à cent sols tournois d'amende envers les pauvres de leurdit mestier, avant que pouvoir appeller de leur ordonnance.

Et d'autant que plusieurs marchans, facteurs & commissionnaires tant forains qu'estrangers vendent ordinairement és bonnes villes de ce Royaume, leurs marchandises secrettement & en cachette en leurs chambres, hors le temps de foire, contre les ordonnances ils seront tenus garder, & dans quinze jours apres la publication dudit reglement faire enregistrer en la chambre de leur mestier, qui sera establie au lieu plus proche de leur demeure ordinaire, leurs noms, surnoms, demeures & vocations, ensemble les noms, surnoms, qualitez, & demeures de ceux pour qui ils negotieront, sur peine aux contrevenans de cent escus d'amende envers les pauvres de leur mestier, dont le denonciateur aura le tiers, & de confiscation de leur marchandise.

Deffences seront faites à tous maistres jurez de plus lever sur la communauté de leur mestier, autres deniers que ceux qui sont mentionnez audit reglement, & d'en abuser, comme ils ont fait par le passé sous pretexte de pieté, sur peine du quadruple & de punition corporelle.

Aucun artisan travaillant en draps d'or, d'argent ou de soye ne pourra vendre son ouvrage & marchandise en detail: mais à piece entiere seulement, apres avoir este marquee & scellee d'un scel de plomb, comme les jurez drapiers à Rouen scellēt les draps qui se fōt en ladite ville, & ainsi qu'il sera dit [26] cy apres, sur peine de confiscation de son ouvrage & marchandise, & sera seulement permis aux marchans tenant boutique ouverte de vēdre en detail.

Tous maistres de quelque art ou mestier qu'ils soyent ne pourront pren-dre apprenty, sans le faire entendre aux jurez de leur mestier, lesquels s'informeront des facultez de celuy qui voudra prendre ledit apprenty, & sçau-ront s'il aura le moyen ou non de l'entretenir & de luy apprendre son mestier, à ce qu'il ne perde son temps. Et si aucun maistre fait autrement, il payera cent sols tournois d'amende à la boete des pauvres de son mestier.

Chacun apprenty fera enregistrer son nom, surnom, & le lieu de sa nais-sance en la chambre commune de son mestier, & aussi le jour qu'il entrera en apprentissage, afin qu'on sache au vray lorsqu'il poursuyvra d'estre passé maistre s'il aura demeuré en aprentissage le temps qu'il y devoit demeurer, & sera tenu en faire apparoir aux jurez & maistres dudit mestier par extraict du registre de ladite chambre.

Les compagnons & apprentis de mestier ne pourront abandonner le ser-vice de leurs maistres que le temps par eux promis de servir ne soit accomply, si ce n'est du gré & consentement desdits maistres, sur peine de l'amende en laquelle ils seront condamnez par les jurez de leur mestier, & l'apprenty qui aura laissé son maistre avant qu'avoir achevé son apprêtissage, perdra le temps qu'il l'aura servy, & ne luy sera pour rien compté lorsqu'il voudra estre passe maistre.

[27] En la chambre de chacune cõmunauté y aura un grand coffre fer-mãt à deux clefs, qui aura un trou au milieu de son couvercle, par lequel on mettra dedans tous les deniers que ceux dudit mestier & autres payeront en ladite chambre pour quelque cause que ce soit, apres avoir esté nombrez & comptez en la presence du plus ancien juré, ou du controlleur, qui sera esleu par les maistres du grand Bureau, pour tenir le registre & controlle de tous les deniers desdites Chambres, & auront ledit ancien juré, & iceluy controlleur chacun une clef dudit coffre.

Lequel ne sera ouvert qu'une fois le moys, & publiquement au jour ordi-naire que lesdits Jurez seront assemblez en ladite Chambre pour les affaires de leur mestier, & les deniers qui s'y trouveront seront comptez & nombrez par ledit Controlleur, en presence desdits Jurez, & des maistres du mestier qui s'y voudront trouver, & apres portees par lesdits ancien Juré & Controlleur, aux maistres du grand Bureau, lesquels leur en bailleront descharge, & seront tenus lesdits Juré ancien & Controlleur, tenir registre desdits deniers pour y avoir recours quant besoin sera.

Lesdits Jurez sortant hors de charge, rendront compte de leur administra-tion par devant les maistres du plus proche Bureau, lesquels leur baillerõt telle certification que de raison pour leur descharge.

Sera mis un tableau en lieu eminent de chacune bonne ville ou il y aura Bureau ou Chambres des- [28] dits mestiers pour donner adresse des ruës & lieux ou lesdites Chambres & Bureaux seront establis à ceux qui y auront affaire.

Defenses seront faites à tous Laboureurs de s'abiller d'ores en avant de draps teints en quelque couleur que ce soit, & d'autre sorte que ceux que les autres Laboureurs du pays ont accoustumé porter, sur peine au contrevenãt de cent sols tournois d'amende envers les pauvres de sa paroisse, d'autant que les Laboureurs qui sont à present habillez de couleur mesprisent le labourage.

Et à ce que lesdits Jurez n'ayent procez entr'eux à l'advenir, comme ils ont accoustumé pour leurs mestiers manufactures & marchandises, les maistres du grand Bureau seront arbitres de leurs differens, & l'appellant de leur arbitrage payera cent sols d'amende à la boëte des pauvres de son mestier comme dit est.

Grand Bureau des Marchans & Artisans.

En la ville principale de chacun Diocese, sera estably un grand Bureau des manufactures des marchans & artisans, lequel sera regi & gouverné par certain nombre de notables marchans & maistres artisans d'icelle ville, ainsi qu'il sera advisé par les Cõmissaires qui serõt deputez à faire l'establissement desdits Bureaux & reiglement, lesquels auront honneste moyen de vivre, sans prendre aucun salaire pour exercer ladite charge, attendu que [29] c'est œuvre pie & charitable, ils seront esleus par la pluralité des voix de tous les corps de communauté des marchans & maistres artisans habitans de la ville ou ledit Bureau sera estably, & seront appellez maistres du grand Bureau, apres laquelle eslection ils presteront le serment devant le Juge ordinaire de ladite ville de bien & fidelement exercer ladite charge, sans en prendre aucun emolument, laquelle consistera en ce que s'ensuit.

A faire tenir en union & concorde tous les corps de communauté des marchans & artisans qui seront demeurans en l'estendue de leur charge, & à leur faire garder & entretenir les statuts de chacun mestier, & le present reiglement, sur peine au contrevenant de cent sols tournois d'amende, qu'il sera contraint payer à la boëte des pauvres de son mestier.

Les differens qui surviendront entre les Jurez de chacun mestier, & aussi entre les marchans & maistres artisans, leurs compagnons & aprentifs, lesdits maistres du Bureau tascheront de les accorder, & ne le pouvant faire renvoyeront les parties par devant leur Juge ordinaire, aux conditiõs portees par l'article precedent, conservant le pouvoir des Jurez des mestiers.

Ils esliront l'un d'entr'eux pour tenir le registre & controlles des deniers qui se recevrõt audit Bureau, provenant des Chambres desdites communautez, lesquelles il visitera souvent pour prendre garde qu'il ne se commette aucun abus, tant en la recepte & distribution desdits deniers, que sur les ouvrages & manufactures desdits artisans, sans [30] prendre aucune chose pour son salaire & vocation, attendu que c'est pour le bien public, & pour les pauvres.

Lesdits maistres auront un clerc en chacun Bureau qu'ils esliront & destitueront à leur volonté, quant il y aura occasiõ de ce faire, lequel fera toutes escritures necessaires audit Bureau, & tiendra registre de la recepte & despẽses qui se fera [*sic*] de tous les deniers que lesdits maistres recevront des communautez de quelque art & mestier que ce soit, auquel sera par eux ordonné pour son salaire, ce que de raison, sur les deniers qu'ils recevront.

Ils auront l'intendence sur les personnes qui seront es deux maisons publiques, qu'on dressera en chacune ville ou il y aura Bureau estably, & aussi sur les ouvrages & manufactures qui se feront en icelles, & prendront garde qu'elles soyent suyvant les ordonnances Royaux, sur les peines y contenues, que seront tenus payer ceux qui les feront defectueuses.

Ils seront comme censeurs des mœurs desdits marchans & artisans qui habiteront en l'estendue de leur charge, & denoncerõt à Justice les blasphemateurs du nom de Dieu, & autres malfaicteurs qui viendront à leur cognoissance, pour estre par icelle, & à la diligence du Procureur du Roy aprehendez & punis selon leurs demerites.

Les Jurez de chacun mestier seront tenus leur bailler de moys en moys, un estat vray des pauvres de leur mestier, qui ne pourront gaigner leur vie, auxquels suyvant iceluy, lesdits maistres du Bureau, & iceux Jurez respectivement distribue- [31] ront les deniers qu'ils auront receu [*sic*] desdites communautez, ayant esgard que les corps d'icelles les plus forts subviennent aux plus foibles.

Les maistres de chacun Bureau exerceront leur charges [*sic*] deux ans entiers, & consecutifs, à la fin desquels la moitie d'iceux, & les premiers Receveurs sortiront d'exercice, & au lieu d'eux y en entrera d'autres en pareil nombre, lesquels seront aussi esleuz par la pluralité desdites voix, comme les premiers, & sortant hors de charge ils rendront compte de leur administration audit Bureau par devãt deux de ceux qui auront charge de la police de ladite ville, & des maistres dudit Bureau, qui seront demeurez en exercice.

Et advenant qu'un seul Bureau ne puisse suffire audit Diocese, il en sera estably un ou deux autres aux lieux les plus commodes, qui s'appelleront petits Bureaux, & se refereront audit grand Bureau, à chacun desquels petits bureaux les marchans & artisans demeurans en l'estendue de la charge d'iceluy, feront enregistrer leurs noms, surnoms, demeures & vocations, ainsi qu'il sera cy apres declaré.

Petits Bureaux.

Pour la commodité desdits marchans & artisans, un ou deux petits Bureaux en chacun Diocese, ou le grand Bureau ne pourra suffire, seront establis és villes les plus propres & commodes, ainsi qu'il sera advisé par lesdits Commissaires, appellé avec eux, deux de ceux qui auront [32] charge de la police de ladite ville, chacun desquels Bureaux sera aussi regi & gouverne par tel petit nombre de bons marchans & maistres artisans d'icelle ville, que lesdits Commissaires & ceux de la police adviseront, lesquels seront pareillement esleuz par la pluralité des voix des maistres de chacun art & mestier demeurans audit lieu, & ou les mestiers ne seront jurez par les marchans & artisans tenant boutique.

Et ladite eslection faite, lesdits maistres du Bureau presteront le serment devant leur Juge ordinaire, comme dit est; & auront pareil pouvoir en l'estendue de leur charge, que ceux du grand Bureau en la leur. De laquelle neantmoins ils seront tenus leur rendre raison de trois en trois mois, & lorsqu'ils en seront par eux verbalement sommez & requis.

Ils contraindront tous marchans & artisans demeurant tant en ladite ville qu'es autres villettes & gros bourgs en l'estendue de leur charge, de faire corps de communauté de leur mestier, & d'avoir Jurez en iceluy, & chambre particuliere en la ville ou ledit Bureau sera estably, & de faire enregistrer en icelle leurs noms, surnoms, demeures & vocations, ainsi que les autres dessusdits, sur peine au contrevenant de cent sols tournois d'amende envers les pauvres de son mestier, lesquels Jurez exerceront leur charge avec pareil pouvoir & auctorité que les autres qui demeurent és villes ou les maistres sont jurez, & feront entretenir les statuts de leur mestier, & le present reiglement sur les peines y contenues.

[33]Ils tascheront aussi d'acorder les differens qui adviendront entre les marchans & artisans, & l'appellant de leur arbitrage payera à la boëte des pauvres de son mestier, cẽt sols tournois avãt que pouvoir faire appeller partie adverse devant le Juge ordinaire, & ne les pouvãt accorder serõt par eux renvoyez aux maistres dudit Bureau, qui feront tout ce qu'ils pourront pour les accorder, & ne le pouvant faire les renvoyerõt audit Juge, avec l'accord par escrit qu'ils auront voulu faire, ainsi que dit est.

Les maistres desdits petits Bureaux seront tenus d'envoyer ou porter aux maistres du grand Bureau de moys en moy un estat au vray de tous les deniers, qu'ils auront receu pendant iceluy, & un autre estat de la distribution qu'eux & lesdits Jurez en auront faite aux pauvres desdits mestiers qui seront en l'estendue de leur charge, & aussi de rendre compte auxdits maistres du grand Bureau de leur administration, lorsqu'ils seront hors de charge, & ce presens & appellez deux de ceux de la police, & seront esleus pareil nombre desdits maistres par la pluralité des voix, au lieu de ceux qui sortiront d'exercice.

Tous marchans & artisans de quelque mestier que ce soit, qui auront tenu boutique six moys devant la publication dudit reiglement, & la tiendront encores lors d'icelle publication és villes & lieux ou les mestiers ne sont jurez, demeureront maistres de leur art & mestier, sans faire aucun chef d'œuvre, attendu la preuve qu'ils ont faite de leur suffisance & capacité. Mais ceux qui viendrõt [34] de là en avant estre passez maistres, seront tenus faire chef d'œuvre, & payer à la boëte des pauvres ce qui sera advisé par lesdits Commissaires appellé avec eux les Jurez de chacun mestier, pour les pauvres desdits mestiers qui ne pourront gaigner leur vie, au lieu des festins & autres frais qu'ils feroyent aux Jurez & maistres de leur mestier, lesquels seront à chacun d'eux defendus, sur peine de cent escus d'amende envers les pauvres.

Et pour donner occasion aux bons artisans estrãgers, de se retirer en France pour y travailler & aider à faire lesdites manufactures, il plaira au Roy leur accorder lettres de naturalité, sans payer autre finance que pour la façon & scel d'icelles, & qu'ils jouyront de semblables privileges que les François, apres avoir demeuré an & jour en ce Royaume, dont ils ne pourront sortir pour s'en retourner demeuerer en leur pays sans prendre congé du Magistrat estably au lieu de leur demeure, sur peine au contrevenant de confiscation de ses biens, & seront tenus lesdits estrãgers de se faire enregistrer en la chambre de leur mestier, proche de leur residence dans un moys apres leur arrivee au lieu ou ils voudront s'abituer, sur mesme peine.

Les marchans estrangers qui voudront aussi demeurer en ce Royaume pour y trafiquer, prendront lettres de provision du Roy dans trois moys apres qu'il y seront arrivez, sur peine de confiscation de leur marchandise.

Les commissaires qui seront deputez par le Roy pour establir lesdites Chambres, Bureaux, & maisons publiques, appelleront à ce faire avec eux les [35] plus apparens maistres de chacun mestier, & les uns apres les autres pour ouyr leur plaintes & doleances, auxquels ils defendront d'entreprendre les uns sur les autres, & aussi de plaider l'un contre l'autre, sans avoir premier l'arbitrage des Jurez de leur mestier, & des maistres de leur bureau sur leurs differens, leur enjoignant tres-estroitement d'entretenir les statuts de leurs mestiers, & ledit reiglement sur les peines y contenues.

Et afin de faire travailler lesdits artisans & gaigner la vie à toutes sortes de pauvres mendiens faineans, & autres qui pourront travailler, deux grandes maisons publiques seront dressees en chacune ville, ou il y aura Bureau comme s'ensuit.

Maisons publiques.

En la ville ou sera estably un Bureau des manufactures desdites march-andises, deux maisons seront dressees, esquelles seront logez & mis par con-trainte tous faineans & mendiens valides, qui se trouveront en ladite ville, & és environs d'icelle, pour les faire travailler en toutes sortes d'ouvrages & manufactures de marchandise, & en l'une seront mis les hommes, & en l'autre les femmes, lesquels vivront tous d'une mesme reigle & discipline.

En chacune maison y aura une chapelle ou oratoire, pour y prier Dieu tous les jours, & les maistres & maistresses deputez pour enseigner ceux qui seront esdites maisons, en auront chacun tel nombre en leur charge, qui sera advisé par deux [36] de ceux qui auront charge de la police de ladite ville, & par les maistres dudit Bureau, lesquels auront l'intendence desdites maisons, & tascheront de faire aprendre mestier aux dessusdits pour gaigner leur vie.

Et ou le profit des manufactures que feront ceux qui seront esdites maisons ne sera suffisant pour les nourrir, vestir, & entretenir. Lesdits Sieurs de la police & maistres dudit Bureau y pourvoyront, tant des aumosnes qui seront faites auxdites maisons, que de partie des deniers que lesdits maistres du Bureau recevront des corps desdites communautez par le moyen desdites chambres.

Les peres & meres qui auront jeunes enfans debauchez & à eux desobeissans, les pourront envoyer (si bõ leur semble) esdites maisons, & on leur aprendra à obeir, & quelque honneste discipline, en payant seulement leur nourriture.

Les querelleurs & blasphemateurs du nom de Dieu esdites maisons, y seront punis selon leurs demerites, à ce que les autres y prennent exemple.

Mais pour avoir les estofes & matieres necessaires pour faire travailler lesdits artisans. Seront faites defenses à toutes personnes de transporter hors ce Royaume, les laines, lins, chanvres, fils & fillaces, & toute autre chose qui se peut manufacturer en France, suyvant les ordonnances royaux, & sur les peines y contenues.

Et à l'exemple de la Royne d'Angleterre, & autres Princes voisins de la France, qui ne permettent qu'aucune marchãdise manufacturee entre en leur pays, sera aussi defendu à toute personne de faire [37] entrer audit Royaume, aucune sorte de marchandise estrangere manufacturee, si elle n'est d'invention nouvelle & incogneuë aux Frãçois, sur peine de confiscation d'icelle, & d'amende telle que de raison. Toutesfois sera permis à chacun d'y aporter & faire entrer toutes estofes & matieres propres pour y estre ouvrees & manufacturees;

Et enjoint à tous marchans & maistres artisans demeurans audit Royaume, de s'employer de tout leur pouvoir à dresser les ateliers & mestiers necessaires és lieux les plus commodes qu'ils pourront choisir, & à recouvrer les estofes propres pour faire lesdits ouvrages & manufactures.

Sera pareillement fait deffense à tous passementiers de faire aucun passement & frange, ou il y ait or ou argent, si ce n'est pour le service du Roy, ou des Princes & Princesses, & par expres commãdement de sa Majesté, sur peine de confiscation d'iceux, & de cinquante escus d'amende, & à tous marchans d'acheter & vendre lesdits passemens & franges, apres le temps prefix qu'il leur sera baillé aux peines que dessus.

Tous draps & ouvrages d'or, d'argent, de soye, & de laine, & autres marchandises & denrees que besoin sera, qui seront d'icy en avant ouvrees & manufacturees en France. Seront marquees & visitees par lesdits Jurez, avant
qu'elles soyent exposees en vente, pour eviter que nul ne soit trompé ny abusé,
sur peine de confiscation d'icelles.

Sera aussi enjoint tres estroitement à tous tissiers & ouvriers, en draps d'or,
d'argent, de soye, & de laine, de les faire de la bonté largeur & longueur qu'ils
doyvent estre par lesdites ordonnan- [38] ces, sur les peines y contenues, de
ne faire la liziere des draps de laine, plus large d'un doigt, & de mettre chacun d'eux la marque au bout de la piece de leur ouvrage, de differente estofe
& couleur de ladite piece, sur peine de confiscation des ouvrages non marquees, à ce que ceux qui les auront faits soyent cogneus & punis selon lesdites
ordonnances.

Et afin que les marchans drapiers qui acheteront d'oresnavant lesdits
draps, n'ayent excuse sur lesdits tissiers & ouvriers, leur sera semblablement
fait defense d'acheter ne vendre aucuns draps, s'ils ne sont marquez comme
dit est, & ainsi qu'ils doyvent estre par lesdites ordonnances.

Deffenses seront aussi faites à tous marchãs François, trafiquans en pays
estrange, de vendre ou eschanger leurs marchandises & denrees, à perles &
pierreries, ains à or & argent, ou estofes propres pour estre manufacturees ou
bien à denrees necessaires en France, d'autant qu'on y a aporté une si grande
quantité de perles, qu'il n'y a bourgeoise ne femme de mediocre qualité qui ne
porte chaine, collier, ou bracelet de perles, ce qui est en partie cause du grãd
luxe que nous voyõs en ce Royaume, au grand prejudice & dommage d'iceluy,
d'autant que par ce moyen les estrangers en emportent l'or & l'argent.

Et pour le grand benefice que tous lesdits marchans & artisans recevront
du Roy par l'establissement dudit reiglement, ils donneront à sa Majesté pour
une fois quelque petite gratification, ainsi qu'il sera advisé sur les lieux par
lesdits Commis- [39] saires, appellé avec eux l'ancien juré de chacun mestier,
& ou il n'y aura Jurez, quatre bons bourgeois du lieu, à ce que la taxe qui en
sera par eux faite soit si raisonnable, que lesdits marchãs & maistres artisans
la payent tres volontiers, ainsi que plusieurs d'iceux se sont ja offerts.

Lesquels deniers seront employez tant à l'establissement desdites manufactures, qu'à ce qu'il plaira à sa Majesté ordonner.

Toutes lesquelles choses contenues audit reiglement, estant fondees sur la
raison & sur les ordonnances Royaux, il plaira au Roy ordonner par Edit,
que ledit reiglement sera publié & inviolablement gardé, sur les peines y contenues, attendu que c'est le bien public, & qu'aucun n'a interest audit establissement, mesme les Juges ordinaires n'y en ont point, d'autant que le pouvoir

qui est attribué aux Jurez de chacun mestier, & aux maistres desdits Bureaux, n'est que comme arbitres des differens qui adviendront entre marchans & artisans, à cause de leurs mestiers manufactures & marchandises seulement, sans prendre cognoissance de leurs cedulles & obligations par escrit, & aussi que celuy qui se sentira grevé de leur arbitrage, en pourra tousjours appeler devãt son Juge, en payãt seulement cent sols tournois à la boëte des pauvres de son mestier, qui n'est que pour tascher de retenir de plaider, & garder qu'ils ne se desbauchent de leur mestier & vocation.

Et d'autant que c'est le bien public & le moyen d'enrichir la France, specialement le menu peuple qui est royné [sic], le Clergé & la Noblesse doivent avec [40] le tiers Estat embrasser si estroitement c'est affaire qu'il vienne à sa perfection.

Ce faisant le Roy coupera chemin à infinis abus & malversations, retranchera le luxe desordonné, ramenera les artisans que la necessité à exilez de ce royaume, contraindra les vagabons & faineans à travailler, fera que les pauvres seront nourris, & que la France fleurira plus que jamais, non seulement en marchãdise & manufactures d'icelle: mais aussi en tous arts & mestiers à l'honneur & gloire de Dieu, & de sa Majesté, & au grand contentemẽt de tous ses bons subjets.

Beau-semblant supplie Messieurs de l'assemblee de le vouloir ouyr sur les propositions qu'il a à leur faire.

DE PAR LE ROY.

Sa Majesté à permis & permet à Barthelemy de Laffemas, dit Beau-semblant, son premier tailleur, & varlet de chambre ordinaire, de faire Imprimer par tel Imprimeur que bon luy semblera, un discours intitulé Reiglement general pour l'establissement des manufactures en ce Royaume. *Avec deffenses à tous autres Imprimeurs d'Imprimer ledit Reiglement, sinon celuy ou ceux que voudra ledit Beau-semblant, à peine de cinq cens escus d'amende, & à ceste fin est mandé au Prevost de Paris, Bailly de Rouen, leurs Lieutenans & autres Justiciers qu'il appartiendra. De le faire jouyr de la presente permiβion sans aucun empeschement. Fait à Rouen le quatorziéme jour de Decembre mil cinq cens quatre vingts saize.*

Signe,
HENRY. DE NEUFVILLE.

[1]

Response aux difficultez proposees à l'encontre du Reglement general touchant le manufactures.

Aucuns qui n'ont pu concevoir toutes les raisons ny le bien de ceste police, ils en donnent des sentences, comme font les Juges qui donnent leur jugement sans ouyr les parties: qui m'a occasionné leur faire response de chaque difficulté, ainsi qu'il sera dict cy apres.

PREMIERE OBJECTION.

Toutes polices qui amenent nouveautez ne sont point necessaires au public, ayant tant de belles & anciennes lois & coustumes en France.

RESPONSE.

Ceux qui donnent ces raisons sont plus propres à controller, que non point pour y apporter ce qui seroit de leur devoir: ce Reglement est pour le bien public, & trouveront que ce [2] n'est point nouveauté, & que sont les vrayes & anciennes lois & coustumes, sçavoir est, laisser le mal & reprendre le bien, remettre les ruines en bastimens neufs, faire cognoistre le mal que nous ont fait les estrãgers: & travailler chacun en sa vocation, n'entreprendre point l'un sur l'autre, ne demeurer point oisifs ni vacabons, & faire vivre les pauvres: empescher les yvrõgneries qui se font des deniers qui doivent estre employez en œuvres pieuses: & les monopoles qui se font par les cõmunautez: remettre le bien en lumiere qui est caché & perdu: toutes ces raisons sont les anciennes loix & coustumes & non point nouveautez: Ce reglement n'est que pour les faire observer attendu la necessité du cas qui le requiert, la longueur du temps & les troubles & guerres ont faict rõpre & abastardir toutes les bonnes loix & coustumes du passé, & par ce moyen la confusion & le mal s'est engendré en toutes sortes de vacations: Il est donc necessaire pour le repos public chercher ce remede de reglemẽt pour conserver lesdictes anciennes coustumes & oster & retrancher les nouveautez qui se sont mis parmy les peuples par le moyen des abus, que l'on ne peut par autre voye retrancher.

II. OBJECTION

Que ce Reglement ne peut estre estably à present à cause de la pauvreté & incommodité, pour raison des troubles qui ne sont encores apaisez par tout le Royaume.

RESPONCE.

Il est besoin de remonstrer à telles gens, [q]u'ils [3] communiquent avec personnes capables pour cognoistre la facilité de l'establir, & le bien ou le mal qui peut empescher cest effect, sans nulle doubte l'on verra que cest

establissement est si necessaire pour tout le general, qu'il ne se trouvera crea-
ture telle qu'elle soit y dõner empeschement, si ne sont estrãgers, pour raison
que les monopoles, vols & brigandages qu'ils ont faict au passé par leurs ruses
& inventions sur le pauvre peuple de France, qui en meurent par les hostels-
dieux & ailleurs de misere: Et d'autant qu'ils se voyent descouverts ils tascheront par tous les moyẽs d'y vouloir nuire, mais la raison & le grand bien qu'il en
adviendra empeschera tous lesdicts monopoleurs d'avoir ny bouche ny raison
pour cõtredire à ce bien general: si le peuple de France peut avoir recognu
le mal que leur ont faict lesdicts estrangers, il sera facile à leur faire veoir le
chemin de leur pays: Ils sont assez cognus par les grands thresors qu'ils possedent & manient tous les jours aux despens de tout le peuple qui est ruyné &
perdu, comme dict est cy dessus.

III. OBJECTION.

Que l'execution dudict Reglement ne se peut faire qu'avec un grand amas
& maguasins de marchandises & deniers pour dresser ladicte manufacture.

RESPONCE.

L'on fera cognoistre à ceux qui ne peuvent cõprendre la facilité de ceste
manufacture, qu'elle se peut establir par les habitans des villes, & par les [4]
marchands qui trafiquent en icelles, & mesmes des deniers qui se portent ez
pays estranges, ainsi qu'il est porté par ledit Reglement.

IIII OBJECTION.

Les gens riches & qui ont des moyens de vivre n'ont que faire de travailler,
& mesmes les gens de qualité ne se doivent point employer à la manufacture
ny ez arts mechaniques, & qu'on ne tient point en reputation ceux qui s'y
employent.

RESPONCE.

Les Royaumes & provinces bien reglez, & mesmes les principalles villes
d'Italie, où les nobles & les plus riches font travailler aux manufactures, & sont
commis à la police, avec telle grade & respect que nul n'est employé avec eux
à ladite police qui ne soient gens de bonne reputation, jusques à s'informer si
les biens qu'ils possedent sont venus de bonne acquisition; Qui est pour mon-
trer à la noblesse & aux riches François que le commerce & police doit estre
observé par les grands, & non point en user de mepris.

V OBJECTION.

Que lesdictes manufactures de toutes sortes d'ouvrages establies, les
laboureurs quitteroient leurs labourages pour s'y employer, chose qui serait
dommageable à tout le peuple.

RESPONCE.

Ceste difficulté est bien foible attendu que le [5] Reglement sera tel que chacun fera sa vacation, les marchands feront la marchandise, les artisans feront leurs ouvrages, & les laboureurs le labourage, les villes & bourgs seront reglez: les uns feront les draps de soye, les autres la drapperie de laine, & autres feront les toiles & ainsi toutes les autres marchandises iront par ordre, en telle façon que les uns & les autres vivront avec police, qui sera facile & sans difficulté: Et aussi que les artisans ne pourront prendre des apprentifs que suivant l'ordonnance, & par ce moyen l'on n'empeschera point les laboureurs du labourage: mesmes que plusieus [sic] laboureurs pourront faire les soyes escrues, filer & travailler aux laines & plusieurs autres petites negoces d'ouvrages, ce qui leur donnera moyen de payer les tailles, & faire de mieux en mieux leurs labourages.

VI. OBJECTION.

Que les marchandises manufacturees ne venant ainsi que à la coustumee des pays estranges, seroient trop cheres, qui feroit prejudice au public.

RESPONCE.

Nulle marchandise ne sera chere, pourveu que les deniers ne tombent ez mains des estrangers. A l'exemple de celuy qui faict bastir, & qui despend dix ou vingt mil escus à son bastiment, lesquels ne sont point deniers perdus ny jetez hors du Royaume, car c'est bailler à gaigner au public & faire vivre des pauvres: Et ainsi les manufactures establies avec police, toutes sortes de marchan- [6] dises & ouvrages se feront & se vendront à meilleur pris à cause du grand nombre qu'il s'en fera, ainsi qu'il a esté dict.

VII OBJECTION.

Que l'establissement des Chambres en ce Royaume feroient faire des assemblees qui seroient prejudiciables au public.

RESPONCE.

Ceste raison est tres-mal fondee, & prise tout au contraire, à cause du bien inestimable qui en peut advenir, les assemblees se font par le moyen des confrairies & non point par les Chambres, & ce seront lesdictes Chambres qui feront abolir les assemblees: Et que pour cet effect que les habilles hommes marchans & artisans soyent appelez pour en donner leur advis, on trouvera que c'est le vray remede d'un repos public, & le moyẽ de recognoistre le roy & les superieurs, & pareillement le vrai moyen de travailler & faire gaigner la vie à toutes sortes de gens, & empescher les pauvres de mandier ainsi qu'il a esté dict. Ceux qui meurent de grande necessité, oisifs, comme bestes brutes donnent assez à cognoistre le mal que toute la France reçoit d'empescher le moyen de faire vivre un chacun.

VIII OBJECTION.

Que ce Reglement a esté mis en lumiere il y a long temps, & que c'estoit des hõmes qui entreprenoient faire eux mesmes les ouvrages, & qui venoient d'estrange pays.

[7]

RESPONCE.

Ceux qui auparavant ont voulu dresser les manufactures, c'estoit gens estrangers & qui cherchoient à faire leur proffit particulier, & entreprenoiẽt faire travailler mil ou deux mil personnes sous leur charge & domination, dressant les atteliers en un endroict & rien aux autres, faire gaigner & petitement vivre aucuns, & tout le reste demeurer à rien faire: & apres qu'ils eussent faict un grand proffit, ils eussent emporte les deniers hors du Royaume.

Les moyens qui se dressent à present sont tout contraires, pour raison que au lieu qu'ils eussent faict travailler mille personnes, lon fera voir que deux millions seront employez, & tous les entrepreneurs se seront François, & les estrangers qui viendront seront sous leur charge. Il ne se trouvera ville ny bourg dans tout le Royaume qui ne se ressente de ce bien: Car au lieu d'une piece de marchandise qui se faict à present en France, il s'en fera dix ou vingt, & par ainsi le peuple vivra, & leur donnera moyen de payer les tailles au Roy, & le domaine de sa Majesté s'accroistra au bien & contentement de tout son peuple: ce serõt des forces qui feront craindre & redouter le Roy de ses ennemis, pour autant que les manufactures conserveront en France l'or & l'argent, & y en feront apporter par les estrangers: C'est le moyen de remettre les ruynes generalles qui perdent la chose publique par un desreglement & mauvais ordre qui est en iceluy.

Sur les moyens de dresser les ouvrages par tout [8] le Royaume, le principal article est de faire la drapperie de laine: Il est de besoin que toutes sortes de gens qui auront des moyens secourent ceux qui sont pauvres, pour avoir des bestes à laine, à fin d'en nourrir une grande quantité aux villages, ainsi que l'on faisoit auparavant les troubles. Il n'est de besoing en dire d'avantage, chacun cognoist assez le bien qui en peut advenir, pour raison du grand nombre de peuple qui peuvent vivre soubs ceste manufacture de laine.

Aucuns articles qui ont esté obmis au Reglement general,

De la maniere de planter les meuriers & nourrir le vers à soye.

Aux pays de Languedoc, & aux Sevenes tirant sur les montaignes, ils font à present une si grande quantité de soyes, qu'ils les ont en telle abondance que nous avons en France le lin, & la chanvre, ceux du pays tesmoigneront à Messieurs de l'Assemblee, qu'il est verité. Ceste raison & moyen facile doit induire toutes sortes de gens à faire le semblable, c'est une manne que Dieu nous envoye, pour faire vivre une infinité de pauvres.

Plusieurs qui ne peuvent cognoistre la facilité de faire les draps de soye, pensent qu'il n'y a que les Italiens, Genevois, & Luquoys qui soyent propres à faire lesdicts draps de soye, les Ambassadeurs du Roy qui ont esté en ces pays là, tesmoignerõt que les ouvriers qui font aujourd'huy lesdits draps de soye, à Gênes, Luques, & Naples, & autres lieux, se sont partie des François qui depuis vingt ou trente ans sont sortis de France: Quant aux taintures desdites soyes, elles se font aujourd'huy à Paris, Tours, & Lion, plus belles qu'ils ne se firent jamais en Italie.

[9] Quelques uns mettent en avant que les vers ne se peuvent nourrir en France, à cause du pays qui est froid, se sont gens qui en parlent par fantaisie, & non point par raison: d'autant que lesdits vers font leur couvee au commencemẽt de l'Esté, lorsque les meuriers jettent leur feuille & font leur opperation depuis qu'ils commencent à couver, & ont fait chacun leur soye, ayant refait leur grene, ils meurent: le tout se fait dedans un mois, soit en pays chaud ou froid, c'est tousjours au commẽcement des chaleurs, les moyens de les nourrir est facile, & principallement en ce qu'il ny a qu'un mois de l'annee, & en apres on s'amuse à faire accoustrer les soyes.

Et pour exẽple à S. Chaumont & à S. Romain en Lyonnois, villes scituees en pays froid & ez montagnes, il s'y faict pour le jourd'huy des soyes escrües si belles & si fines qu'ils sont preferables à celles de Messine.

Mesmes en l'Abbaye de Poissy en l'Isle de France les Religieuses nourrissent des vers, & ont plante des meuriers, dont ils recueillent des soyes tresbelles & bonnes: Qui sera pour response à ceux qui disent que la soye ne se peut faire qu'ez pays chaults.

Pour le regard des meuriers ce sont arbres beaux & fort excellens en leur fueille, nulle vermine ne si engendre, ny aucunes choses ne les gastent, & ont leur fueilles belles & nettes, en outre qu'ils sont bonnes [*sic*] à nourrir les vers, ils sont propres à couvrir & à faire des allees: ils sont faciles à venir, le moyen est qu'il faut prendre les meures toutes [10] pourries tombant de l'arbre, & en frotter de vieilles cordes, & les enterrer dans un verger bien labouré, les petites pepiniers sortiront en abondãce pour les replanter en apres aux endroits où on verra bon estre, car dés qu'ils ont trois à quatre ans, ils jettent la fueille qui commence à servir & nourrir lesdits vers: les meuriers blancs sont beaucoup plus propres que les noirs, pour raison que la fueille en est plus douce & delicate, tout le surplus de la nourriture desdits vers, est facile à sçavoir à un chacun.

Autre moyen pour faire venir les meuriers, lon peut coupper des grosses branches, & les scier en petits tronçons, & iceux planter en terre, cela fera rejetter infinis petits rejettons qui se pourrõt replanter aux lieux necessaires.

Il est de besoin en passant dire un mot des marchans de chevaux de Paris, & d'ailleurs, & les accomparer aux marchans de draps de soye: car ils sont tousjours apres à trouver des escus, & autres especes d'or, pour r'emplir la bourse des marchãs de Flandre, & Allemaigne, speciallement à Paris qui espuisent tous les ans beaucoup de deniers: si les deffenses sont faites d'entrer en France les manufactures estrangeres, l'on payera lesdits chevaux en eschange de danrees, outre que lon peut avoir le moyen de nourrir des jumens en tant de beaux villages, fermes, & marests par tous les endroits du Royaume, & mesmes en France ou lon fait le labourage avec les chevaux, on peut facilement labourer avec des jumens qui apporteront des petits qui seront meilleurs & de plus long [p. 11] service que ne sont les chevaux de Flandre & d'Allemaigne, & aussi les harasts qui se peuvent dresser en tant de beaux endroits, le tout pour servir d'instruction & memoire aux bons & sages mesnagers.

AU ROY.

SIRE,

Barthelemy de Laffemas, dit Beau-semblant, premier tailleur & varlet de châbre de vostre Majesté, vous remonstre tres humblement que depuis long temps il a travaillé à dresser un reiglement general, pour establir les manufactures & ouvrages en votre Royaume, & par ce moyen faire vivre les pauvres, & les employer ainsi qu'il est specifié par ce petit livre cy attaché. A ces causes il vous plaira le faire voir à Nosseigneurs de vostre Conseil, & de l'Assemblee, attendu qu'il s'agit pour le biě de vostre estat & utilité de vos subjets, & le suppliant priera Dieu pour vostre grandeur & Royalle Majesté.

*Renvoyé ausdits sieurs de l'Assemblee pour voir adjuger
de l'utilité qui peut provenir dudict reiglement,
& en donner advis à sa Majesté, afin d'en
ordonner ce qu'il verra estre à faire par
raison. Fait à Rouen le dixseptiesme
jour de Janvier mil cinq
cens nonante sept.*

EXTRAICT DU REIGLEMENT GENERAL FAIT EN
l'Assemblee tenuë à Rouen,
par commandement du Roy.

Que l'entree du fil, drap, & passemens d'or & d'argent, ensemble de toutes sortes de marchandises de soyes, & laines manufacturees hors le Royaume, soyent deffendues en iceluy, & que les soyes & laines cruës soyent deschargees des imposts & droicts de doüane qu'elles payẽt, & que les monopolles soyent empeschez, & deffenses de transporter les laines & autres estoffes non manufacturees: sera par sa Majesté fait declaration, que ceux qui y viendront & travailleront continuellement durant rrois [*sic*] ans, jouyront des mesmes privileges que les François naturels, sans qu'il soit besoin obtenir aucunes lettres de naturalité.

Signé le Blanc Greffier de l'assemblee.

Le present extraict a esté delivré par commandement
de Meßieurs de l'Assemblee
à Beau-semblant.

AU LECTEUR.

Apres que j'ay communiqué & baillé coppie de ce Reglement à nos Seigneurs de l'Assemblee & autres, aucuns se sont voulus prevalloir & donné louange, qu'ils ont mis en avant l'establissement des manufactures, j'en laisse le jugement de ce faict à tous ceux qu'il plaira voir le discours. Le subjet que j'ay pris de ce faire, est dedans la lettre du Roy au commencement de ce livre, & feray voir que j'ay entrepris faire ceste remonstrance, dez l'annee mil cinq cens quatre vingts cinq. Faict par moi

Barthelemy de Laffemas natif de
Beau-semblant en Dauphiné.

General regulation for the establishment of manufactures in this kingdom to contain the cost of silk fabric and other merchandise that harms and ruins the state, which is the true way of restoring France to her splendor, provide work for the poor, and keep them from begging for a living.

With an extract of the opinion which the Lords of the Assembly held in Rouen have sent to his Majesty, that the entrance of all sorts of gold thread and woolens manufactured outside the kingdom be prohibited here, and that levies on woolens and raw silk be suppressed.

Along with the means of producing silks throughout France.

[By Barthélemy de Laffemas.]
Paris: C. de Monstr'oeil et Jean Richer, 1597.
By privilege of the king.

[3]

TO THE KING

SIRE,

Having had the honor of being your servant for thirty years, and having served you in the capacity of tailor and manservant, and since then as merchant in your silver service, the length of time and the trade I have done with several foreign merchants has given me the experience to discover the secret and hidden evil that silk cloth, gold and silver fabric, and other merchandise introduce into your state, coming from Italy, Flanders, England, and other countries; and for this purpose, having discussed it with numerous persons, it is a very certain thing that if the course of these abuses were halted, it would be a sort of thanks offered to God for the blessings he has so bestowed on your realm that it seems he has appointed it to have authority and command over all others, having so constituted it and provided it with all that is necessary for a man's life, and in such abundance, that it can do without all his neighbors, and none can do without it. As an example we need to consider the wealth and means that can come from distant countries, the established policy and manufacture with respect to grains, wines, salt, pastel, taxes,[5] and many kinds of cloth, which used to supply all of the Orient, which can still be done with workshops of the same manufactures being set up, and also with several other kinds of merchandise which are traded in foreign countries which cannot do without, and which will be the true treasures of the Indies to fill France with coin and wealth, preventing us from seeking them in foreign countries, which can be made and fashioned in France, to the benefit of your subjects: this has led me, and I have had the boldness, to have you hear the means that seem proper to prevent such abuses. And insofar, SIRE, as I have neither the eloquence nor the effrontery to speak directly to your Majesty of the remedy that must be applied to them, this has led me to importune you with this little book in the form of a general regulation where I have set down what I am presenting to you, which you will kindly show to your Assembly, and I shall pray the Creator,

SIRE,

That you may never lack for health and happiness, by him who was born to die.

Your most humble, obedient and faithful servant,

LAFFEMAS, called Beau-Semblant

[5]

To regulate well, maintain and bring prosperity to the state*, its head must know the members, thus Republics much be maintained in such a condition that the Prince may be aided, the poor assisted and succored, and each according to his station, given that guilds cannot subsist nor sustain themselves without the power of the sovereign, the virtue of the prince, and the authority of the magistrate.

It is thus expedient to suppress and cease the misappropriations that are committed, that is the abuses, deceit, monopolies, assemblies, and other overindulgences and drunkenness, which by this means are abolished, as shall be declared, and easily, by a general regulation for the public's benefit and utility and the preservation of the state.

Before taking up the benefit to be found in said regulation, we need to take up the monopolies and misfortunes introduced here by silk, gold and silver fabric, and other such merchandise coming from foreign countries, which is in part the ruin of the state, as we shall see, and which the most ignorant of people will be able to see.

Said silks, gold and silver fabric which foreigners bring in have taken away a hundred and five hundred thousands of crowns[6] at a time, which have permitted them to fund franchises and great associations which have ruined and ravaged every province in the kingdom, and if the French were as bold in manufacturing as they are in litigation, they would prevent said foreigners from creating such franchises and associations, exchanges and displacements that are draining the gold and silver of France.

It seems that said franchisers, and those who have invented the customs house in Lyon, have predicted or desired France's misfortune; they gave the king to understand that his domain would recover two or three hundred thousand crowns from it, but they did not say that they were taking them from his purse or that of his poor subjects, and by means of their ruses and inventions, for every five thousand crowns which they gave the king, they were drawing ten million outside of France.

Judge if you please whether the customs house established by the Duke of Savoy in Suze, at the frontier of his country, every year earns him large quantities of coin, thanks to the silk cloth, gold and silver fabric and other such merchandise that come to Lyon, I will have you consider whether they bring monies from Italy to pay said customs, and whether it is not the clear coin of France.

And by the industry of those who have sent such quantities of silk cloth manufactured in France, they have rendered a great service to the enemies of the king and of the state: for they have drawn treasures outside of France which are said to be the sinews of war, that is why the king and his people are devoid of means, we have seen a time when more gold and silver would have been found in simple despoiled villages than today could be found in the entire realm, thanks to the great treasures which said silk cloths and others have drawn out of France, amounting to three times greater sums of monies than all the armies have cost.

An example of the above is that all the merchants who deal in silk cloth throughout France, who are numerous, witness the city of Paris, we have seen that there were only five or six silk merchants dealing in Lyon, and at present their numbers are infinite, and all the cities of France thus supplied with said silk merchants, they are like commissioners or salesmen of those who send us said silk cloth from Italy and elsewhere, for the reason that every day and hour they are after gold and silver on all sides, and seek all the good purses in quest of silver, and employ all their friends and influence to assemble great masses of monies to take to Lyon or to Italy and elsewhere, which is a true means of completely despoiling the state, if God in his mercy does not halt the course of this evil invention, which brings only the ruin of the French.

Another greatly damaging abuse, having to do with the permission which is given to allow the fabrication in the city of Paris and elsewhere of so much gold and silver braid that we might as well allow them to haul the finances of France in a wagon into the sea, given that this is work lost to people, for whom no profit returns, and similarly that these are fabrics that should be worn only by kings and princes, all this for want of a good rule and policy, which can be done with that of silk cloth by means of said regulation.

Just consider the example of the silk stockings that enter France every year; there will be more than fifty thousand persons who wear them, more likely a half more than less, were they to cost only four crowns on average, and everyone can use up four pair a year, this article alone would come to eight hundred thousand crowns, and who could know for sure if there might not be even more.

So it is that silk stockings come to such a tidy sum of monies taken out of France, gold, silver and silk cloth will cost twenty times more, taking into account the great number that are worn everywhere in France, great and small, down to the men and women of the bourgeoisie, and others who wear them all the time, to the great detriment of the public, insofar as we could have the means of making wearing apparel in France, and by this means would provide work to the poor; for they remain idle for want of our giving them the means, and perish withall from poverty or otherwise.

If princes and princesses want woven cloth of gold and silver and other rare fabrics, they can be manufactured and made in France, fine and good ones with no difficulty, and we can easily bring in raw silk from Persia and the Orient, and even in exchange for other merchandise, without draining the gold and silver from France.

Besides the fact that with time there will be mulberry trees planted about France to feed silkworms, as in Languedoc, which they have them in great number, even the lord of Saint Privat,[7] a gentleman of that country, who made nurseries for said mulberry trees, of which he has planted in the purvey, even in Provence, Orange, and the county of Avignon, more than ten million, besides those they already had; these are easy trees to raise, and bring great profits, both from the wood, which can be cut every five years, or from the leaves for feeding said worms, which make a good deal of silk; a given mulberry has brought its owner over a crown, and the common ones are sharecropped for twenty or thirty sols per year, there are similarly mulberry trees in Touraine which make fine, good silks, indeed the best that can be found; this memoir will serve as instruction to many who can plant said mulberry trees, the land is well-suited to it in several parts of France, on which mulberry trees the worms will feed, which will employ several households which will benefit from it, that is a true and certain fact.

Or take this lesson for leather from the city of Nerac in Gascony: there is a master currier named Bernardin who produces leathers that are so strong and good that no sword or halberd can pierce them, witness that he has made some for the present king, helmets and armor cuirasses that have been tested in his Majesty's presence, which have never been pierced, and similarly said Bernardin, and also Swiss curriers, withdrawn for the last fifteen years into the region of Biard,[8] who produce cowhide as buffalo hide,[9] goats as chamois that are as fine and good as those that come from Germany, a known fact, and consequently can be so prepared in France. Another example in the city of Dourdan, which for a few years has become accustomed to making silk stockings, wool knit stockings, and making them today as fine and good as those that come from Italy and England, and in the city of Senlis and several villages nearby, two poor men coming from Flanders have recently taught them to make lace that are called *courages de Flandre*, than which nothing finer or better made can be found anywhere, and in great quantity, and also similarly all sorts of handwork and manufacturing can consequently be set up everywhere; there is nothing on earth which the French cannot counterfeit, and will even do it better when they work at it with proper rule and discipline, such as can be done by means of said regulation.

As easily as we can manufacture silk, gold and silver fabric, we can even more easily make and manufacture all sorts of cloth and serges and all other kinds of merchandise, and can make them and employ a large number of persons to the great benefit and augmentation of the king's domain, and similarly for the public benefit.

It is extremely important for the public benefit and utility to consider that ordinarily we sell most of our woollens, which are produced in Languedoc, Provence and Dauphiné, are transported into Italy, where said woollens are used, and fashioned into Florence serge, muslins, Milan velvet and others, which afterward manufactured are taken to be sold and detailed in France, which is to manifest the ignorance of the French; for if the rule and policy of manufacturing had been established in France, we would be making Florentine double-serges, witness the cloth under seal of Rouen, serges of Limestre,[10] and other cloths that are made in France.

In order to well make and manufacture handwork, chambers have to be set up for each guild, as is amply set forth by the regulation, said chambers being the true remedy for bringing to fruition all enterprises put into operation throughout the realm.

It is said in the regulation that there will be a number of merchants and craftsmen, good men of good reputation, that they will accept no pay or emolument, who will work for the poor, and resolve disputes over workshops and manufacturing of which they are apprised; for in every society, if there is no one to preside, everything will be confused, the judges and officers of the cities are not qualified to look into manufacturing and workshops, which is to have the blind deciding on colors: what is required is master experts to decide, it being reasonable that as much or more faith be placed in the officers and masters and guards of the guilds as one places in a sergeant who is believed in a case of misdeed or damage on his report alone up to three livres five sols, and will keep watch and prevent any of the poor in said guilds from going begging, by means of said chambers.

And also all the poor and wretched who stand in church doors, at street corners, and lie on dunghills like animals, said chambers being established, this is the true means of preventing this, for reason of the public house.[11]

No vagabond nor idler will be found who will not be put to work, given that they will be found out by means of said chambers, which will help a great deal to prevent the loss of children of good families,[12] and others, who are usually subordinated and debauched by the means of said vagabonds who can be neither located nor known, and never leave the brothels and bad company where they attract and despoil many young men, as it is stated.

The civil wars are partly the cause that all servants, workers and others, fail to give the honor and obedience they owe to their masters, and for want of these products and manufacturing being done as they should, given that at present there is no duty to do so, if not by means of said chambers, which ordinarily will hold them subject, and teach them to become cable of being masters, and for lack of discipline they do not do perfect work.

By means of said chambers, the assemblies or fraternities which were responsible during the troubles for such madness will be abolished, which the late kings were unable to do, whatever decrees and prohibitions were issued; even said assemblies were forbidden by the late king Francis in 1539[13] and by the late king Charles IX in 1560, and now said assemblies will be abolished by the means of said regulation.

Said chambers once established throughout France, the workshops and manufacturing will be run in such fine order that the good workers of foreign countries will come of their own accord to work alongside the French, which will be an inestimable benefit, and there will be no knowledge in the world that will not be sought out to bring it to light, and vie for who can perform the best work.

Products and manufactured goods will be done to perfection, as they used to be, and it was all done away with by disorder and confusion, which is all past and cannot be remedied if not by means of said regulation, which can easily be done by said chambers, and in so doing the products will be good, fine, and durable, and all will be to the great benefit of the republic, and at lower cost, thanks to the large number that will be produced.

We can take our example from all the other products and manufactured goods, and look at the leathers, which are a necessity for the rich and the poor, the time spent tanning leathers, and waiting a year or two to tan and curry them, and today they do not wait three months, so that now four to six pairs of articles cost less than one in the past, which is an infallible and irremediable abuse, if not by means of said chambers.

And previously the trade in wines, salt, pastel and other goods brought much treasure into France, particularly doubloons, *millerais*,[14] *angelots*,[15] and other gold specie, and instead they bring us a large number of manufactured goods, and for this effect said chambers being established, that is the true means of remedying it.

And to prevent workers and craftsmen and other manufacturing personnel from dabbling in petty lawsuits and quarrels amongst themselves, which is the reason some of them go broke, and by this means said chambers will prevent such errors which are damaging the public as a whole, and similarly they will do away with some of the drunken bouts that often ruin households and families.

Large bureaus and chambers thus established, with fear of punishment in a public house, this is the means of making youth thrive in knowledge, civility, and obedience, and they will learn handwork and manufacturing with fine discipline, just as those who deny and blaspheme the name of God will be rigorously punished.

There are nobles and others who complain and remonstrate that silk cloth and braid and gold and silver wovens are ruining them, and that they have spent more in the last thirty years than their forebears had in three hundred years, and many bourgeois and others make the same claims, in part because of their wives, whose clothing they cannot cut back on, and who on the contrary want ever more.

The benefit that will result for the king and state, so as to permit his Majesty to raise as many men of war as he wishes by means of said chambers, and it will easily be seen all the forces that can be raised, which will be great and powerful, and we shall similarly see their number, an excellent thing for the preservation of the state, which will prevent in need the raising of foreigner troops, who will remove treasures from France.

Other instructions which have been omitted from the preceding articles to create work for several kinds of manufactures, and with regard to the making of cloth: it is known to all that it is made finer and better in France than anywhere in Europe, all that is wanting is the policy to have them made of quality and width, with respect to serges, they can easily be produced in France, following the example of Sommières in Languedoc, where for five or six years they have been making broad, delicate serges, as fine and better than we ever got from Florence, and even in the city of Nîmes in said region of Languedoc serges are made, done like Milan velvets, and as well in the city of Chartres they have begun to make fine and good ones, as in other places in France.

As for silk cloth, it can be made in several cities in France, and thus they have begun in the city of Lyon, and Tours, long since, even in the city of Paris there is a master named Godefroy who makes all sorts of silk cloth, gold and silver wovens, and without any doubt he will make finer ones than ever came to us from foreign countries; in the city of Montpellier they began three or four years ago to make velvets, satins, taffetas, and other silk articles, which puts on display the abilities of each man, and besides in said Montpellier they make white fustians, made in every way finer and more exquisitely than any we ever got from Germany and Flanders.

As for the cloths in the city of Saint-Quentin in Picardy, the city of Louviers in Normandy, and other places in said country, there are today being manufactures that are finer, lovelier and better than the cloths of Holland, that is why, having linen and hemp in such abundance in France, we can make all sorts of broad and narrow cloths, fashioned and handworked as well as in the land of Flanders; by removing the rate[16] of theirs, their workers will with no difficulty come to live and work in France, as will they do for all sorts of handwork, following the example of some Flemish who have taken their places during these troubles in the city of La Rochelle, who today finish finer and better moroccos than themselves who come from Flanders.

And for some time in the region of aforementioned Biart they are now importing from Candu and the Barbary Coast, through the merchants of Bayonne, buffalo and chamois skins which they dress so fine it cannot be done better, and following their example, by travelling they can bring such skins through all seaports, and prepare buffalo and chamois everywhere in France, something which is easy and without difficulty.

Another example in the city of Poitiers: for seven or eight years they have been dressing steer and cow hides, goatskins and others in the style of buffalo or chamois, very fine and good, this is true.

It is needful for the public that all cities do like the city of Amiens, where they craft a large number of articles, which are serges, *camelots*,[17] canvasses and countless other items, that provide a living for many peoples, and attract foreigners' monies; such men are to be praised and their opposites, the idle, to be scorned.

But one could rightly compare some Frenchmen to savages rather than to civilized men, for as they give their wealth for whistles and bells, so do the French receive baubles and strange articles in exchange for their treasures.

They can have great means and wealth, being in a kingdom which is the most fertile and productive in Europe; but they do not know how to make use of the benefits God gives them; they do not consider that they remain in misery, vagabonds, and idle, and by their carelessness and laziness provide a living to half the neighboring realms and provinces of France, having them supply the handwork and manufactured goods which can easily be made in France: see from the experience of England that every year they send us more than a thousand ships or vessels partly bearing manufactured goods such as woollen cloth, muslin stockings, fustians, ratinés, and other products. And similarly the regions of Flanders send us their tapestries, paintings, canvasses, handwork, silk braid, *camelot*, serges, moroccos, and other items. And Germany similarly, buffalo, chamois, fine fustians, fustians for linings, *boubasins*,[18] ironmongery, and many other items. Similarly Italy, Geneva, and other provinces bring us their silk cloth, gold and silver wovens, Florentine serges, and other items in abundance, and to render them their value, it seems we should need, having no manufactured goods, to send them back in exchange the lawsuits, cards and dice, and all sorts of games, which are the handwork and trade item of most of the French, even the field workers, who make a trade and merchandise of it.

And to remedy this we need to make work for manufacturing and handwork, to redress the poor, ruined cities and towns: this will be to have found the true philosopher's stone, instead of converting copper and other metals into gold and silver it will be the double treasures of the Indies to get the French to see and admire at five hundred leagues from their province.

TO THE KING[19]

If it please his Majesty to set up this fine and rich Academy constituted by the handwork and manufactures throughout his realm, as did Sieur de Pluvinel,[20] who restrains and prevents young princes and lords from carrying their silver into Italy, it will be an even more excellent deed that will remain written forever in the histories of France, and bring great honor to his Majesty, who after taking such care to reduce France in good condition by arms, and afterwards he should set up such a fine and fortunate policy which will set an example for everyone else to follow, all to the praise of God and the conservation of the republic*.

Regulation among merchants and craftsmen concerning the establishment of trade in goods and their manufacture.

Our kings of happy memory whom God absolve have made several excellent decrees relating to the policy of this realm, to hold everyone within his duty; even to trade and merchandise, goods and their manufacture. Nevertheless they have been (and still are) so poorly observed and maintained that trade has almost completely perished, and craftsmen so impoverished that some have been forced to leave said kingdom to live, others to go to war,[21] and follow the first chief who sought them out, whence the seditions that we have seen in the cities, and some of those who have remained in France are forced to beg their living with their wives and children, all for want of employment. To such a point that it is a pitiable thing to see the multitude of the poor begging alms.

To remedy this situation, it is more than necessary to go back to said trade and manufacturing, as well as said trades, so as to provide means, to merchants to deal, and to craftsmen to work each in his trade, and try also to bring it about that the able poor should not go begging, and that craftsmen who have been exiled from this kingdom by hunger have the opportunity to return, given that there is nothing in the world that more enriches a country than craftsmen, trade and manufacturing of merchandise.

And to achieve this, it shall please the king to order that all merchants and craftsmen will henceforth be held and constrained to join in a guild of their trade, even those who follow his Majesty's court, and to have a separate chamber for each art and trade, in which they will have listed their names, surnames, residences, and vocations, and will have guild officers in each trade as in Paris and in other cities where trades have guilds, who will take nothing for their wages in said chamber. But if the guild membership is quite small, there will be but one officer or two in it. And although by the statutes of said trades, be it ordered that their masters will serve as officers, by turns nevertheless, for the benefit that will succeed in the establishment of said regulation the senior and expert men in each trade will be elected officers, and said election shall continue on to the most senior and skilled.

The which officers will see to it that the statutes and decrees of their trade are kept and observed, and the two last elected among them shall be required to inspect at least once a month, on whatever working day they wish, all the goods and workshops of their trade, and also the weights, alders, and measures they find in said shops of said merchants and craftsmen, and other places where they will judge there is merchandise, and where work is being done in their trade. Having power to seize and remove to the chamber of their trade anything they find defective to be confiscated (if need be) according to

the sentiment and prescription of the masters of the grand bureau of manufacturing and merchandising of said merchants and craftsmen which will be
established in the capital city of each diocese, and other places where it is necessary, as shall be stated hereafter. And said officers shall be empowered to
make said inspection without taking along any officer of justice, for such officers consume everything in fees, and said two officers for their pains, wages,
and time, for having performed said inspections and seizures, will have what
will be reasonably and in good conscience ordered by the masters of said
grand bureau, to take from the monies produced by fines and confiscations of
the things they have seized.

All such officers will pass no master into their trade unless he has remained
in apprenticeship for the time required of him, has created his masterwork,
and is able to be master, each of which new masters shall pay into his trade's
poor box the sum stipulated by the commissioners who are sent to carry out
the establishment of the present regulation, having called together with them
the officers of each trade, in lieu of the feasts and other costs that he would
have to cover to become master, which will be very explicitly forbidden, on
pain to each offender of one hundred crowns penalty, as well for said poor as
for the maintenance of the chamber of said trade. And where said trades have
no officers, the same shall be done when said merchants and craftsmen shall
wish to be passed masters.

If a complaint should arise from any of said masters holding shop, or from
one of their companions or apprentices, the most recently elected officer, or
the clerk of the trade if there is none, from the verbal decree of the other officers, shall make a verbal command to the delinquents, speaking to them, or
to one of their lodgings, to appear in said chamber before said officers on the
appointed day and hour to give reason for said complaint, and do what shall
be ordered by said officers, on pain of sixty *sols tournois*[22] for each said master,
for the poor of their trade, and to the companions and apprentices of such
penalty as shall be determined by said officers.

The which officers shall be required to find a certain day of the week which
they shall set for those of their trade in its chamber, to hear the complaints
that are brought to them, and give order as to what shall be necessary for said
trade, especially to prevent any abuse or misappropriation being committed,
and to punish the malefactors according to their faults according to the power
conferred on them by said regulation.

And to avert any lawsuit, all merchants and craftsmen of whatever trade
shall be unable in the future to bring a suit against them for whatever dispute
they may have because of their merchandise, handwork, and manufactures
alone, without first having it heard by the officers of their trade, the which

will try to reconcile them amicably without taking anything for their pains, wages or time.

Said officers, being unable to reconcile them, shall send them to appear before the masters of the next bureau, together with their written opinion containing the agreement they would have wished to conclude with said dispute, so they (the opponents having been heard) may try by all means to reconcile them, and if they cannot, they shall send them to appear before their regular judge, with the written agreement they should like to have made; the which judge before retaining the case shall see what said officers and masters of said bureau have wished to conclude, and also the receipt for the hundred sols tournois which the appellant of said arbitration shall be required to pay to his trade's poor box before he can appeal in opposition before said judge, for not having wished to entertain said agreement, without which receipt the judge shall not proceed, on pain of nullification of all his judgments, so as to prevent if possible said appellant from appealing.

In the common chamber of the city where are also the bureau and in the individual chambers of said guilds there shall be a table in a prominent place on which shall be listed the principal articles of the statutes of each trade, and the present regulation, in order than no one pretend to be unaware of them.

Said officers may find against each delinquent of their trade, up to one hundred sols tournois in fines on behalf of the poor of their said trade, before he may appeal their decree.

And insofar as some merchants, salesmen or commissioners both outsiders and foreigners sell regularly in the good cities of this realm their merchandise secretly and hidden in their chambers, outside the time of fair, against the decrees, they shall be required to respect, and a fortnight after the publication of said regulation to register in the chamber of their trade, which shall be established in the place closest to their usual dwelling, their names, surnames, residences and vocations, along with the surnames, qualities, and residences of those for whom they will deal, on pain to the offender of a fine of one hundred crowns in behalf of the poor of their trade, the informer of which will have one third, and the confiscation of their merchandise.

It shall be forbidden to all master officers ever to levy on the guild of their trade any other moneys than those mentioned in said regulation, and to abuse it, as they have in the past, under pretext of piety, on pain of quadruple fine and corporal punishment.

No craftsman working in gold, silver or silk cloth shall be able to sell his handwork and merchandise item by item, but solely by whole piece, after being marked and sealed with lead, the way the weaver officers of Rouen seal the cloth made in that city, and as it shall be stated below, on pain of the confiscation of his handiwork and merchandise, and only merchants keeping open shop shall be permitted to sell by the item.

All masters, of whatever art or trade they be, cannot take an apprentice without having him heard by the officers of the trade, the which shall inquire into the faculties of the one who would take said apprentice, and shall find out whether he will have the means or not to support him and to teach him his trade, so he shall not waste his time. And if any master does otherwise, he shall pay one hundred sols tournois fine to his trade's poor box.

Each apprentice shall register his name, surname, and place of birth in the common chamber of his trade, and also the day on which he begins his apprenticeship, so it can be truly known when he shall apply to be passed master whether he has remained in apprenticeship the requisite time, and shall be required to give evidence of it to the officers of said trade by certificate from the register of said chamber.

Their companions and apprentices of the trade may not abandon the service of their masters until the time they promised to serve is fulfilled, unless it be by the agreement and consent of said masters, on pain of the fine to which they will be sentenced by the officers of their trade, and the apprentice who has left his master before completing his apprenticeship shall lose the time he has served, and nothing of it shall be counted when he wishes to be passed master.

In the chamber of each guild there shall be a large chest with two keys which shall have a hole in the middle of its lid by which shall be placed therein all the coins that those of said trade and others shall pay into said chamber for whatever cause, after having been numbered and counted in the presence of the eldest officer, or the controller, who shall be elected by the masters of the grand bureau to keep the register and control of all the monies of said chambers, and said eldest officer and this controller shall each hold a key to said chest.

The which shall be opened but once a month and publically on the regular day on which said officers shall be assembled in said chamber for the affairs of their trade, and the monies that are found therein shall be counted and numbered by said controller in the presence of said officers, and the masters of the trade who wish to be present, and after brought forth by said eldest officer and controller to the masters of the grand bureau, the which shall deliver to them a receipt, and said eldest officer and controller shall be required to keep a list of said monies so as to have recourse to them when there is need.

The said officers leaving their charge shall give account of their administration before the masters of the nearest bureau, the which shall deliver to them such certification as is suited for their release.

There shall be placed a table in a prominent place in each large city where there is a bureau or chamber of said trades to list the address of the streets and places where said chambers and bureaus are established for those who have dealings with them.

It shall be forbidden to all laborers to dress henceforward in tinted cloth of whatever color and other sort than those which other laborers of the country are accustomed to wearing, on pain to the offender of a fine of one hundred sols tournois on behalf of the poor of his parish, insofar as the laborers who are now dressed in color scorn the tilling of the land.

And so that said officers should have no suit between them in the future, as they are accustomed by their trade, manufacturing and goods, the masters of the grand bureau shall be the arbiters of their disputes, and the appellant of their arbitrage shall pay a fine of one hundred sols to the poor box of his trade as it is stated.

Grand Bureau of Merchants and Craftsmen

In the principal city of each diocese there shall be established a grand manufacturing bureau of merchants and craftsmen, which shall be managed and governed by a certain number of notable merchants and master craftsmen of such city, as it shall be determined by the commissioners who will be sent to create the establishment of said bureaus and regulation, the which shall have an honest means of living without taking any wages to the execution of said charge, given that it is a pious and charitable deed, they shall be elected by a plurality of the votes of all the guilds of merchants and master craftsmen who live in the city where said bureau is established, and shall be called masters of the grand bureau, after which election they shall take an oath before the regular judge of said city to well and faithfully execute said charge, without taking any emolument for it, which shall consist in the following.

In keeping in union and harmony all the guilds of merchants and craftsmen who live in the purvey of their charge, and make them keep and maintain the statutes of each trade, and above all the present regulation, on pain to the offender of a fine of one hundred sols tournois, which he will be required to pay to his trade's poor box.

Said masters of the bureau will try to reconcile the disputes that arise between the officers of each trade, and also among the merchants and master craftsmen, their companions and apprentices, and if they cannot shall send the adversaries to appear before their regular judge, under the conditions laid out in the preceding article, preserving the power of the officers of the trades.

They shall elect one among themselves to keep the register and controls of the last to have been received in said bureau, coming from chambers of said guilds, the which he shall inspect often lest any abuse be committed, either in the receipt and distribution of said monies or in the articles and manufactures of said craftsmen, without taking anything for his wages and time, given that it is for the public benefit, and for the poor.

Said masters shall have an amanuenses in each bureau whom they shall elect and remove at their pleasure, when there is occasion for doing so, who shall do all the writing necessary for said bureau, and keep a register of receipts and expenses of all the monies which said masters shall receive from the guilds of whatever art and trade, to whom shall be ordered what is reasonable for his wages from the monies they shall receive.

They will have the management of the persons who will be in the two public work houses that shall be set up in each city where there is a bureau established, and also over the handwork and manufactures performed therein, and shall take care that they be in keeping with royal decrees, on the pains there contained, which those shall be required to pay who make them defective.

They shall be like censors of the morals of said merchants and craftsmen who live within the purview of their charge, and shall accuse before justice blasphemers of the name of God and other malefactors who come to their knowledge, so that they may be, by the diligence of the king's prosecutor, apprehended and punished according to their faults.

The officers of each trade shall be required to deliver to them each month a true state of the poor in their trade, who are unable to earn a living, to whom, in accordance with it, said masters of the bureau and these officers respectively shall distribute the monies they have received from said guilds, taking care that the strongest guilds among them shall subsidize the weakest.

The masters of each bureau shall exercise their charges for two full years, consecutive, at the end of which half of them, and the first receivers, shall cease their function, and in their place an equal number shall enter, who also shall be elected by the plurality of said votes, as the first, and leaving their functions they shall give account of their administration to said bureau before two of those responsible for the policy of said city, and the masters of said bureau who have remained in office.

And should it occur that a single bureau is insufficient for the diocese, another or two others shall be established in the most convenient places, which shall be called petty bureaus, and they shall refer to said grand bureau, in each of which petty bureaus the merchants and craftsmen living within the purview of its charge shall register their names, surnames, residences and vocations, as shall be set forth below.

Petty Bureaux

For the convenience of said merchants and craftsmen, one or two petty bureaus in each diocese where the grand bureau is not sufficient shall be established in the most suitable or convenient cities, as shall be determined by said commissioners, called with them, two from those responsible for the policy in said city, each of which bureaus shall also be managed and governed by such small number of good merchants and master craftsmen of this city as said commissioners and those of the policy shall determine, which shall similarly be elected by a plurality of votes of the masters of each art and trade living in said place, and where the trades are not sworn by shopkeeping merchants and craftsmen.

And said election done, said masters of the bureau shall take a vow before their regular judge, as is stated; and they shall have similar power within the purview of their charge as those of the grand bureau in theirs. Of which nevertheless they shall be required to give them account every three months, and when they are verbally summoned and required by them.

They shall require all merchants and craftsmen living both in said city and in other small cities and large towns within the purview of their charge, to constitute a guild of their trade and have officers in it, and a separate chamber in the city where said bureau is established, and have registered therein their names, surnames, residences and vocations, as the aforesaid others, on pain to the offender of a fine of one hundred sols tournois on behalf of the poor of his trade, the which officers shall exercise their charge with the same power and authority as the others who live in the cities where the masters are sworn, and shall maintain the statutes of their trade, and the present regulation, on the pains contained therein.

They shall try as well to reconcile the disputes that may arise between the merchants and craftsmen, and the appellant of their arbitration shall pay into the trade's poor box one hundred sols tournois before he can call his adversary before the regular judge, and being unable to reconcile them, they shall be sent to the masters of said bureau, who shall do what they can to reconcile them, and if they cannot they shall send them to said judge, with the written agreement they would like to have made, as is stated.

The masters of said petty bureaus shall be required to send or bear to the masters of the grand bureau every month a true state of all the monies they have received in that time, and another state of the distribution that they and said officers have made to the poor of said trades that are within the purview of their charge, and also give account to said masters of the grand bureau of their administration, when they are out of office, and with present and called two of those of the policy, and they shall be elected an equal number of said masters by the plurality of votes, in the place of those who are leaving office.

All merchants and craftsmen of whatever trade who have kept shop for six months before the publication of said regulation, and still keep shop at the time of publication in the cities and places where the trades are not sworn, shall remain masters in their art and trade without presenting a masterpiece, given the proof that they have given of their adequacy and ability. But those who come forward there to be passed masters shall be required to present a masterpiece, and pay to the poor box what shall be determined by said commissioners called together with the officials of each trade, for the poor of said trades who cannot earn their living, in lieu of the feasts and other expenses they would make for the officials and masters of their trade, the which shall be forbidden to each of them, on pain of a fine of one hundred sols tournois on behalf of the poor.

And to provide opportunity to good foreign craftsmen to relocate to France to work here and help operate such manufacturing, it shall please the king to grant them letters of naturalization without other cost than for the drawing up and seal of such, and they shall enjoy the same privileges as the French after remaining a year and a day in this kingdom, which they may not exit to return to live in their country without taking leave of the magistrate established in the place of their residence, on pain to the offender of confiscation of his property, and said foreigners shall be required to register at the chamber of their trade near their residence within a month after their arrival in the place where they wish to settle, upon the same penalty.

Foreign merchants who wish also to remain to trade in this kingdom shall seek letters of appointment from the king within three months after their arrival, on pain of confiscation of their merchandise.

The commissioners who are dispatched by the king to establish said chambers, bureaus and public work houses, shall call the most affluent masters of each trade to do this with them, and the ones after the others to hear their protests and grievances, whom they shall forbid to encroach on each other, and also to plead against each other, without first having the arbitration of the officials of their trade and the masters of their bureau on their disputes, enjoining them very strictly to maintain the statutes of their trades, and said regulation, on the pains contained therein.

And in order to provide work for said craftsmen and earn a living for all sorts of poor, idle beggars and others who can work, two large public work houses shall be set up in each city where there is a bureau, as follows.

Public Work Houses

In the city where a bureau of manufactures of said goods shall be established, two houses shall be set up, in which shall be lodged and forcefully placed all the able idle and beggars to be found in said city and its environs, to make them work on all sorts of handwork and production of merchandise, and men shall be put in one and women in the other, all of whom shall live under the same rule and discipline.

In each house there shall be a chapel and an oratory for praying God every day, and the masters and mistresses dispatched to teach them who are in said houses shall each have a set number in their charge, which shall be determined by two of those who are responsible for the policy in said city, and by the masters of said bureau, who shall also have the management of said houses, and shall attempt to make the above learn a trade to earn their living.

And where the profit from manufacturing made by those who are in said houses is not sufficient to feed, clothe, and maintain them, said lords of the policy and masters of said bureau shall provide for it both by alms given to said houses, and by part of the monies which said bureau masters shall receive from said guilds by means of said chambers.

The fathers and mothers who have debauched or disobedient young children may send them (if they so desire) to said houses, and they will be taught to obey, and some honest discipline, by paying just for their food.

Quarrelers and blasphemers of God's name in said houses will be punished according to their faults, so others will learn by their example.

But to have the fabrics and materials necessary to give work to said craftsmen, it shall be forbidden to all persons to transport out of the kingdom any wool, linen, hemp, thread and tow, and any other thing that can be manufactured in France, according to the royal decrees, on the pains contained therein.

And following the example of the queen of England and other princes neighboring France who allow no manufactured merchandise to enter their country, it shall also be forbidden to any person to bring into said kingdom any sort of foreign manufactured merchandise unless it be of new invention and unknown to the French, on pain of its confiscation and an appropriate fine. And merchants and master craftsmen living in said realm are enjoined to attempt with all their power to set up the workshops and trades needed in the most convenient places they may choose, and to recover the fabrics proper for the fabrication of said articles and workshops.

It shall likewise be forbidden to all manufacturers of soft goods to make any braid and fringe containing gold or silver, unless it be for the king's service, or that of princes and princesses, and by express command of his Majesty, on pain of confiscation of same, and a fine of fifty crowns, and for all merchants to buy or sell said braids and fringes after the preset time that will be indicated to them, on the pains listed above.

All cloth and gold, silver and silk handwork, and of wool, and other merchandise and commodities as shall be needed, which shall henceforth be fabricated and manufactured in France, shall be marked and inspected by said officials before they are exposed for sale, to avoid anyone being deceived or abused, on pain of confiscation of same.

All weavers and workers in gold, silver, silk, and woollen cloths, shall be enjoined to make them of the quality, width and length they must be by said decrees, on the pains therein contained, not to make any woollen selvage wider than a finger, and to place on each of them the mark of the piece of their handwork, of different fabric and color of said piece, on pain of confiscation of the unmarked items, in order that those who made them be known and punished according to said decrees.

And so that the cloth merchants who henceforth buy said cloth have no excuse for said weavers and workers, they likewise shall be forbidden to buy or sell any cloth that is not marked as specified, and as they must be by said decrees.

It shall further be forbidden to all French merchants dealing in foreign lands to sell or exchange their merchandise and commodities for pearls and precious stones, as for gold and silver, or fabrics proper for being manufactured or for commodities necessary in France, insofar as such a great quantity of pearls has been imported that there is no bourgeoise nor woman of mediocre condition who does not wear a chain, necklace or bracelet of pearls, which is in part the cause of the great luxury we see in this kingdom, to the great prejudice and harm of same, especially since by this means foreigners take gold and silver out.

And for the great benefit which all said merchants and craftsmen shall receive from the king through the establishment of said regulation, they shall give his Majesty for one time some small gratification, as shall be determined locally by said commissioners, called together with the eldest officer of each trade, and where there are no officers, four good bourgeois of the place, so that the tax they will pay shall be so fair that said merchants and master craftsmen will pay it quite willingly, as several of them have already offered to do.

The which monies shall be used both for the establishment of said manufacturing and for what it pleases his Majesty to command.

All those things contained in said regulation, being founded on reason and on the royal decrees, it shall please the king to command by decree that said regulation be published and inviolably preserved, on the pains contained within, given that it is the public benefit, and that no one has a vested interest in said establishment, even the regular judges have none, insofar as the power that is attributed to the officers of each trade, and to the masters of said bureaus, is only as arbitrators of the disputes that may arise among merchants and craftsmen because of their trades, manufactures and merchandise alone, taking no cognizance of their written notations and obligations, and also that he who feels harmed by their arbitration can always appeal before his judge, merely by paying one hundred sols tournois into his trade's poor box, which is only intended to restrain him from pleading, and keep them from straying from their trade and vocation.

And insofar as it is the public benefit and the means of increasing the wealth of France, especially the humble folk which is impoverished, the clergy and the nobility must with the third estate embrace this matter so closely that it may come to perfection.

By this means the king will cut off the path to numberless abuses and misappropriations, diminish disordered luxury, bring craftsmen whom need has exiled from this kingdom, will require vagabonds and idlers to work, see that the poor are fed, and that France shall flourish more than ever, not only in merchandise and its manufacturing, but also in all arts and trades to the honor and glory of God, and of his Majesty, and to the great contentment of all his good subjects.

Beau-semblant entreats the lords of the assembly to hear him on the propositions he has to make to them.

BY ORDER OF THE KING

His Majesty has allowed and allows Barthélemy de Laffemas called Beau-semblant, his first tailor and regular manservant, to have printed by whatever printer he wishes a discourse entitled *General Regulation for the Establishment of Workshops in this Kingdom*. With prohibition to all other printers to print said regulation, if not he or those whom Beau-semblant might wish, on pain of a fine of one hundred crowns, and to this end notice command is made to the Provost of Paris, bailiff of Rouen, their lieutenants and appropriate officers of justice. He may enjoy the present permission without any constraint. Done in Rouen the fourteenth day of December 1596.

Signed,
HENRY DE NEUFVILLE

Response to the difficulties proposed with respect to the general regulation concerning manufacturing.

Some who have been unable to conceive all the reasons or the benefit of this policy hand down sentences on it, as do judges who give their judgment without hearing the adversaries, which has prompted me to give them a reply to each objection, as shall be stated below.

First objection.

Policies that introduce novelties are unneeded by the public, there being so many excellent and ancient laws and customs in France.

Reply.

Those who give these reasons are better suited for controlling than for contributing what their duty should require; this regulation is for the public benefit, and they will find it is nothing new, and that these are the true and ancient laws and customs, to wit, renouncing the bad and resuming the good, restoring ruins as new buildings, making known the harm that foreigners have done to us; and each one working at his vocation, not encroaching on each another, not remaining idlers nor vagabonds, and providing a living for the poor; preventing the drinking committed with coin that ought to be in pious works, debauchery, and monopolies organized by the guilds, shining light on the good that is hidden and lost: all these reasons are the ancient laws and customs and not novelties. This regulation is only to see that they are observed, given the necessity of the case which requires it, the length of time and disturbances and wars that have breached and corrupted all the good laws and customs of the past, and by that means confusion and harm has been fomented in all sorts of professions. It is thus necessary for the public tranquility to seek this remedy of regulation to conserve said ancient customs and suppress and remove the novelties that have arisen among peoples by means of abuses that cannot be diminished by other means.

Second objection.

That no regulation can be established at present because of poverty and inconvenience, because of the disturbances that have not yet been quieted throughout the realm.

Reply.

We should tell such people that they are communicating with persons capable of understanding the facility of establishing it and the benefit or harm that can prevent that effect; without a doubt we shall see that this establishment is so necessary overall that there will be no one at all to obstruct it, unless it be foreigners, because of the monopolies, thefts and banditry they have perpetrated in the past by their ruses and inventions upon the poor French people who therefore die of misery in hospitals and elsewhere. And to the degree they see themselves discovered they will attempt by all means to do harm, but reason and the great benefit that will come of it will prevent all said monopolists from having either tongue or cause for contradicting this general benefit; if the people of France can recognize the harm that said foreigners have done them, they will easily see their country's path. They are well enough known by the great treasures they possess and manipulate daily at the expense of the whole people which is destitute and ruined, as is stated above.

Third objection.

That the execution of said regulation can be accomplished only with a great store and reserve of merchandise and funds to effect said manufacturing.

Reply.

We will make it known to those who cannot understand the facility of this manufacturing that it can be established by the residents of the cities and by the merchants who trade in these, and even the facility of the funds that are borne off to foreign lands, as is indicated in said regulation.

Fourth objection.

The wealthy who have the means of living have no desire to work, and people of quality must not participate in manufacturing nor in the mechanical arts,[23] and those who do so are not held in high esteem.

Reply.

Well-regulated kingdoms and provinces, and even the principal cities of Italy, where the nobles and wealthiest put people to work in manufactures and are committed to the policy, with such rank and respect that none is employed with them for said policy who are not people of good reputation, to the point of inquiring whether the things they possess were honestly acquired; which is to show the nobility and the wealthy French that trade and the policy must be observed by the great, and not be scorned by them.

Fifth objection.

That said manufacturing of all sorts of articles once established, field hands would desert their plows to work there, something which would harm everyone's interest.

Reply.

This difficulty is quite weak given that the regulation will be such that every man will tend to his profession, merchants will do merchandise, craftsmen will make their items, and field hands the ploughing; the cities and towns will be regulated: some will make silk cloth, others woolen drapery, still others will make canvas and so all other merchandise will go in good order, such that all will live with a policy, which will be easy and without difficulty. And also craftsmen will be able to take apprentices only in keeping with the decree, and by this means that field workers will not be kept from their ploughing, and some farm workers even will be able to make raw silk, spin and prepare wools, and some others exercise small trades in handmade goods, which will offer them the means of paying the tailles and perform their ploughing better and better.

Sixth objection.

That manufactured goods not coming as usual from foreign lands, would be too costly, which would be detrimental to the public.

Reply.

No merchandise will be costly, provided the monies do not fall into foreigners' hands. As is the case with the man who builds, and who spends ten or twelve thousand crowns on his building, which is not money lost nor cast out of the realm, for it allows the public to earn and provides the poor with a living. And thus with manufactures established under policy, all sorts of merchandise and handwork will be made and sold more cheaply because of the great quantity that will be made, as has been said.

Seventh objection.

That the establishment of chambers in this kingdom would give rise to assemblies that would be detrimental to the public.

Reply.

This reason is very ill-founded, and is all backward, because of the inestimable benefit that can come from it, the assemblies are created by fraternities and not by the chambers, and it is said chambers that will bring an end to assemblies. And in order for this to happen, if able merchants and artisans should be called upon to state their opinion, it will be found that this is the true remedy for public tranquillity, and the means of recognizing the king and superiors, and equally the true means of helping all sorts of people work and earn a living, and preventing the poor from begging, as has been stated. Those who die from dire necessity, idle, like dumb beasts, make clear enough the damage to all of France of preventing each man from having the means of living.

Eighth objection.

That this regulation was long ago brought to light, that it was men who undertook to make articles themselves, and who came from a foreign country.

Reply.

Those who formerly tried to set up manufacturing were foreign people and who were trying to make their own profit, and undertook to put to work a thousand or two thousand persons under their authority and domination, setting up manufactures in one place and nothing in others, to allow some to earn enough money to scrape by, and the rest to remain with nothing to do; and after they had made a big profit, they took the funds with them out of the realm.

The means that are being set up now are just the opposite, for the reason that instead of providing work for a thousand persons, we shall see that two million will be employed, and all the entrepreneurs will become Frenchmen, and the foreigners who come will be under their authority. There will be no city or town in the entire kingdom unaffected by this benefit. For in place of every piece of merchandise now made in France, there will be ten or twenty made, and thus the people will live and it will give them the means of paying tailles to the king, and His Majesty's domain will grow, to the benefit and contentment of all his people; these will be strengths that will cause the king's enemies to fear and dread him, insofar as the workshops will keep the gold and silver in France and cause foreigners to bring it in. This is the means of recovering from the general disasters that break the republic* by a deregulation and disorder that it entails.

On the means of setting up manufactures throughout the realm, the principal item to produce is wool cloth. We need for all sorts of people who have the means to aid those who are poor to keep sheep so as to feed a large quantity in the villages, as we did before the troubles. There is no need to say more about it; everyone knows the benefit that can come of it, because of the large number of people who can live under this production of wool.

Certain items which were omitted from the general regulation.

On the manner of planting mulberry trees and feeding silkworms.

In the region of Languedoc and in the Cévennes on the mountains flanks, they presently make such a quantity of silk, that they have them in such abundance as we have linen and hemp in France; those from that area will testify to the lords of the Assembly that this is true. This reason and the easy means should induce all sorts of people to do likewise; it is a manna which God sends us to provide a living to numberless of the poor.

Some who cannot know the facility of making silk cloth think that only the Italians, Genevans, and Lucans are suited to making silk cloth; the king's ambassadors who have been in those countries will testify that the workers who are now making said cloth in Genoa, Lucca and Naples and elsewhere are a group of Frenchmen who left France twenty or thirty years ago. As for the dyeing of such silk, they are now made in Paris, Tours, and Lyon, finer than they ever were in Italy.

Some maintain that the worms cannot be fed in France because it is a cold country; these are people who speak arbitrarily and not reasonably, insofar as said worms lay their eggs at the beginning of summer, when the mulberry trees are sprouting leaves, and they produce from the time they begin to lay, and have each spun their silk, having renewed their generation, they die: it is all over within a month, whether the region be cold or hot, it is always at the beginning of the hot season; the means of feeding them are easy, and principally in that there is only one month in the year, after which you can take your time preparing the silk.

And for example in St. Chaumont and St. Romain in the region of Lyon, cities situated in a cold and mountainous regions, such fine and lovely raw silks are being produced today that they are preferable to those of Messina.[24]

Even at the convent of Poissy in Île de France the nuns feed worms, and have planted mulberries, from which they harvest lovely, fine silks. This shall serve as reply to those who say that silk can only be produced in warm countries.

For the eye, mulberries are handsome trees with quite excellent trees leaves; no vermin attacks grow on them nor does anything else spoil them, and they have fine, clear leaves; besides the fact that they are good for feeding silkworms, they are well suited to providing cover and constructing avenues. They are easy to grow; the means is to take the rotten mulberries falling from the tree and rub them with old rope, and bury them in a well-tilled orchard; the little shoots will emerge in abundance to be replanted subsequently in places that one judges favorable, for once they are three or four years old, they sprout leaves that begin to serve and feed said worms; white mulberry trees are much better suited than black, because the leaf is more tender and delicate; all the surplus of the food of said worms, this is easy for anyone to see [?].

Another means of growing mulberry trees: one can cut large branches, saw them into small segments, and plant these in the ground; this will create numberless small shoots that could be replanted in the needed places.

A word needs to be said in passing about horse traders in Paris and else-where, to compare them to silk cloth merchants: for they are always seeking crowns and other gold coin to fill the purse of the merchants of Flanders and Germany, and especially in Paris, who every year press out a good deal of money; if it is forbidden to bring foreign manufactured products into France, we will pay said horses in exchange for supplies, besides the fact that one can have the means of feeding mares in so many villages, farms and fens in every part of the realm, and even in France where ploughing is done with horses one can easily plough with mares which will bring forth young which will be better and serve longer than the horses of Flanders and Germany, and also the stud farms which can be set up in so many fine places, all to serve as instruction and model for good and wise farmers.

To the King

Sire,

Barthélemy de Laffemas, called Beau-semblant, your Majesty's first tailor and manservant, points out very humbly that he has long toiled at drawing up a general regulation to establish workshops and manufacturing in your king-dom, and by this means to provide a living to the poor and employ them as is specified in the little book here attached. FOR THESE REASONS it will please you to present it to the lords of your Council and of the Assembly, given that it is for the benefit of your state and the utility of your subjects, and the supplicant will pray God for your grandeur and royal majesty.

Forwarded to said lords of the Assembly
so they may judge of the usefulness that may result from said regulation
and advise his Majesty so he may
command what seems best for him to do.
Done in Rouen the seventeenth day of January
one thousand five hundred ninety-seven.

Extract of the general regulation
made at the Assembly held in Rouen
by the king's commandment.

Barthelemy de Laffemas native of
Beau-semblant in Dauphiné.

That the import of thread, cloth, and gold and silk braid, along with all sorts of silk and woollen merchandise manufactured outside the realm, be forbidden within it, and that raw silks and wools be relieved of the taxes and customs they pay, and monopolies be prevented, and it be forbidden to transport woollens and other non-manufactured fibers may it be declared by his Majesty; that those who come and work continually for three years, shall enjoy the same privileges as native Frenchmen, without requirement that they obtain any sort of naturalisation.

Signed Le Blanc, registrar of the Assembly.

The present extract was delivered by
order of their Honors the Assemblymen
to Beau-semblant.

To the reader,

After I communicated and dispatched copies of this regulation to the lords of the Assembly and others, some have pretended to take advantage and given praise that they put forward the establishment of manufacturing; I leave the judgment of this fact to all those whom it pleases to read the discourse. The reason I have used for doing so is in the letter to the king at the beginning of this book, and will show that I undertook to make this remonstrance as early as the year fifteen hundred eighty-five. Signed by me,

Barthélemy de Laffemas, native of
Beau-semblant in Dauphiné

Notes

1 'Est reglement d'un estat et communauté, soit monarchique, aristocratique, ou democratique, en denrées, habits, commerce, et autres choses concernants le bien de tous. Il vient du Grec politéia, extraict de polis, Cité, par ce que la Cité a esté le premier subject de tel reglement [...].' (Jean Nicot, *Trésor de la langue française tant ancienne que moderne* [1606]).
2 'C'est la façon de quelque ouvrage faicte à la main' (ibid.)
3 'Il se prend quelquefois pour toute sorte d'Estat, de Gouvernement' (*Dictionnaire de l'Académie*, 1694).
4 'Il se dit dans le corps des artisans de ceux qui sont préposez pour faire observer les statuts & reglemens à ceux de leur mestier' (ibid.): 'It is said in trade guilds of those who are designated to apply the statutes and regulations to those of their trade.'
5 Specifically *tailles*, royal taxes on the third estate.
6 *Écus*, a silver coin usually worth three pounds (*livres*) or 60 *sols*.
7 As there are several places bearing this name in Languedoc, the exact reference is uncertain; but as he says, the raising of silkworms was widespread through the region.

8 Near Poitiers, in central-western France.

9 Buffalo is 'strong and thick, and being well prepared serves as defensive weapon' (*Dictionnaire de Trévoux*, 1742).

10 In Tuscany.

11 It becomes clear below that *maison publique* or public house means a sort of combination poorhouse/prison.

12 Reputedly sometimes kidnapped by the poor.

13 François I (1494–1547).

14 Exact meaning not determined.

15 A medieval gold coin, equivalent to an *écu* (crown).

16 That is, undercutting the price.

17 'A kind of fabric made ordinarily of goat hair mixed with wool, silk, etc.' (*Dictionnaire de l'Académie*, 1694).
    Espece d'estoffe faite ordinairement de poil de chevre & meslée de laine, de soye, &c

18 'Silk fabric, the making of which was brought from Milan to France. It is also called a futian with two undersides' (*Dictionnaire de l'Académie*, 1762).

19 Henry IV, king of Navarre, who became king of France in 1589 by surrendering his Protestant allegiance.

20 An allusion to the riding academy set up by Antoine de Pluvinel (1555?–1620) in 1594.

21 The first to jobs abroad, the second to sign up as mercenary soldiers (or to get the signing bonus).

22 An archaic term to distinguish the coin from a *sol parisis*, which could have a higher value.

23 This principle, called *dérogation*, meant that 'a gentleman who becomes a merchant, [tax] farmer, or sergeant loses his nobility' (*Dictionnaire de Furetière*, arciel 'Déroger').

24 In Sicily.

Chapter 3

LEONHARD FRONSPERGER (1520–CA. 1575) AS AN EARLY APOLOGY OF THE MARKET ECONOMY

Rainer Klump and Lars Pilz

Introduction

At the annual Autumn Fair of 1564 in Frankfurt on the Main the printed catalogue of books presented – the very first of its kind – contained a chapter on '*German Books on the Holy Bible by the Protestant Theologists*' ('*Deutsche Buecher inn heiliger Schrifft / der Protestierenden Theologen*').[1] In this chapter a booklet is listed with the title '*On the Praise of Self-Interest*'[2] ('*Von dem Lob deß Eigen Nutzen*'[3]). The front page of the booklet depicts self-interest as a person whose chest is emblazoned with the striking claim: '*Everything in my bag*' ('*Alles in mein Sack*'). The author does not belong to the leading Protestant theologists of the time, but rather has a reputation as an experienced writer on warfare. His name is Leonhard Fronsperger[4], a citizen of the Free Imperial City of Ulm, located in the Upper German part of the Holy Roman Empire. The work is dedicated to the connection between the strife for individual benefit, in particular in economic activities, but also in social and political affairs, and the common good of a society as a whole. It anticipates, by at least 150 years if not longer, two famous theoretical concepts in economic analysis and social ethics that were developed in the eighteenth century by Bernard Mandeville and Adam Smith.

This early praise of self-interested behaviour and its positive impact on the common good has been overlooked even in the German-language literature, with very few exceptions. There may be various reasons for the lack of recognition: Fronsperger only wrote this one work on the subject, his authorship is asserted but not finally proven, he wrote in the German language, and there has never been a translation into English or French. However, all these aspects should not obscure the fact that he belonged to a relatively small group of writers in Northern Italy and Upper Germany who developed a revolutionary new concept of selfish human behaviour and its consequences as early as the sixteenth century. The rediscovery of Fronsperger's work has only started a decade ago, but there are still some mysteries to solve concerning its origins and repercussions.[5] And we are sure that the first English translation of the text will very much contribute to a higher international awareness of this unique German contribution to the theory of economic thought.

In the following we will extend and complement our earlier research on Fronsperger and his book[6]. After a short summary of the *'Praise of Self-Interest'* we will discuss in more detail the question of Fronsperger's actual authorship and the multitude of his literary references. Subsequently we analyze whether and to what extent the text was influenced by the Reformation and by new contemporary views on human behaviour. Finally, we will compare Fronsperger's analysis of self-interested actions in the second half of the sixteenth century in the German Empire with views of two well-known writers from the eighteenth century in the Netherlands and Great Britain: Bernard de Mandeville and his *'Fable of the Bees'* (1714) and Adam Smith, author of the *'The Theory of Moral Sentiments'* (1759) as well as *'The Wealth of Nations'* (1776).

A Short Summary of the *'Praise of Self-Interest'*

Fronsperger's book on self-interest is written in sixteenth-century German. The translation of the original text into modern English has given occasion to intensive discussions amongst the editorial team for this volume in regards the actual meaning of words or expressions and of its adequate lingustic transfer. These discussions have helped open our eyes for the stylistic particularities in the book that we will document in the following chapter. But the new edition and its translation have also made it much easier to understand the internal structure of the text and to summarize its content.

The book starts with a self-presentation of self-interest on the front page that already presents the central thesis of the whole text – namely the fact that self-interest is not considered fairly, but blamed as a source of evil despite its important contribution to the common good:

I am known as Self-Interest,
well known to all ranks of society high and low.
But not as bad as I am made out to be
when the matter is considered clearly.

Much good is brought by me to some,
But people do not generally grant me praise.

The central thesis is repeated in the preface where the author explains that
the unfair condemnation of self-interest as well as the unfair praise of the
common good in the usual public discourse have called for a revision:

> Self-interest has had to let itself be disgraced and reviled by everybody,
> but most commonly by those who have received great riches, honour
> and goods from and through it. In turn, the Common Good is exalted
> and praised, as if no one had ever lost a heller[7], or had incurred any
> damage or shortcomings because of it.

The main text is then split into 22 chapters. *Chapter 1* takes up the central
thesis, now again from the perspective of self-interest itself:

> … in the following I shall prove with meaningful and illustrative argu-
> ments that not only am I not as evil as my ungrateful children think,
> but also that through me the whole world is maintained and preserved
> in good public order, shape and peace; and was maintained from the
> beginning; and could not be maintained without me.

Chapter 2 mentions wine as a well-known example how something good may
become evil by consuming too much of it.

> But if wine, the noble creation, is used too heavily and excessively, who
> wants to tell every now and then of the great disadvantages, misfortunes
> and unfortunate damage it causes people and their bodies, souls, hon-
> our and wealth?

And if all things (or attitudes) commonly considered good are always in dan-
ger of misuse, one should also accept that things with a traditionally bad
reputation can be very beneficial if used properly:

> And so it is with all things in this whole wide world: nothing is ever so
> good that it couldn't also cause damage and detriment in numerous
> ways through abuse or excessive use. On the other hand, nothing is so
> bad that it couldn't principally serve a useful and good purpose when
> used skilfully and right. And this I want to bring to light clearer.

Chapter 3 takes flattery, what may in some instances be better than telling the truth, as another example how a behaviour with an immoral reputation might in the end, if used in the right way, become very beneficial:

> However, if you look at the matter at its core, flattery may, when used correctly and well, bring good; whereas the truth can lead to bad things. Yes, this may sound highly surprising, but flattery and truth do not stand in each other's way.

Chapter 4 is dedicated to folly which had already been praised, in particular by Erasmus of Rotterdam, as a human attitude that may have valuable implications despite its bad reputation, whereas self-interest had thus far not received any positive evaluation:

> Even the Goddess Folly – if she can indee be understood to be a goddess – found someone who would undertake her praise, although she was once despised and mocked. However, she was praised and affirmed by the erudite and unsurpassably eloquent Erasmus of Rotterdam, so that now one is of the opinion and believes, that she is of great use to mankind and its wit and therefore is not so sparsely praised.
>
> But not only am I not praised by anyone; I am also also reviled, despised and scorned by all humanity, even by those who are attracted to me and who love me.

After complaining about its bad reputation in *Chapter 5* self-interest now praises itself for its good deeds.

> Therefore, to ensure that everyone is of keen mind and can understand my praise, I intend to compensate for this daily humiliation, by praising myself and saying something about my good deeds …

The good deeds due to self-interest are further elaborated in the following chapters. *Chapter 6* treats the example of marriage motivated by self-interest, while *Chapter 7* explores how self-interest affects other areas of human life, such as friendship and marriage.

> I also wanted to show that I not only cause and initiate matrimonial friendship, but all friendships in general. I am aware that this is no small factor in my praises…

Chapter 8 extends the analysis by economic, social and political aspects. It starts with an interesting distinction between '*Nahrung*' – an untranslatable idiosyncratic term which stands for the economic sphere – and '*Regierung*' – a term that might be translated by '*governance*' or '*government*' which includes political and religious authorities. In a modern economic terminology, one might say that the former provides private goods for individual consumption, while the latter is responsible for securing public goods for the whole community. Referring to the traditional division of medieval society into three distinct estates, namely nobility, clergy and peasants, the first two are related to the aspects of '*government*' while the peasants, unsurprisingly, together with the merchants and artisans are responsible for the supply of *Nahrung*:

> It is well-known that all human life and public order (*Policey*) are pre-served chiefly through two things: firstly, food and *Nahrung*; secondly, temporal [secular] authority…
>
> *Nahrung* covers not only food and drink, but also clothing, housing, medicine and what[ever else] people require.
>
> The world is divided into spiritual and temporal [secular] government [Ger. *Regierung*], that is the perception of God and observance of prayer, and the protection of the secular order [as princes, Kings and rulers do]. That's why in ancient times the human governance and social structures (Ger. *menschliche Policey*) were skilfully divided into three.
>
> Namely, into the Emperor, Pope and Farmers [as a collective third estate] … the Pope [the Church] shall pray; the Emperor [the State] shall protect, and the farmer shall work.

Chapter 9 further explores the role of self-interest for the promotion of private goods in agriculture, trade and craftsmanship. Self-Interest concludes:

> Food, drink, clothing, houses, and everything else making up the necessities for human life: all this you receive through my grace; because if Self-Interest did not exist, you would have to want for all of this. How deeply would you want for it, because you couldn't live without it.

Chapter 10 then deals in more detail with clergy and nobility. Fronsperger sees the main motivation for individuals to rule and to reign over others in their self-interest and not in their original interest in the common good:

If I, Self-Interest did not exist, one would have to search to the end of the world (in order to recruit a pope, bishop, or someone else of this order; or emperor, king, prince or other peer) and one would have to force him with the sword or threaten him with incarceration.

However, in these present times (for this you should be grateful) no great pressure is required; instead so much is achieved through my help and assistance. Therefore these offices and honours are not only accepted gladly, but also being strived for with life and limb, with great diligence and all sorts of practices and tricks ...

These methods include all sorts of military conflicts that Fronsperger had experienced sufficiently himself:

... one can experience every day how wars and turmoil among people stem from the governance and powers of their rulers.

As an interim conclusion, we learn in *Chapter 11* that the common good per se (or more precisely, the interest in pursuing the common good) should not be regarded as a meaningful motivation for individual behaviour in whatever sphere of action:

There is no Common Good, and I am certain that no one has ever seen it, no matter how much one has blabbered or written about it, or still does.

In fact, I go as far as saying that you won't find a spark of Common Good on this earth; amongst any social rank, status and orders, no matter where you turn to look for it.

In order to explain how the pursuit of self-interest is ultimately very successful in promoting the common good (so that one must distinguish the common good as an individual motivation from the common good as the result of individual action), *Chapter 12* recalls earlier scholarly debates on this topic:

If one truly wanted to discuss the Common Good properly, one would have to contemplate it even more deeply and broadly. ...

... Thus, I won't shy away from detailing my argument (which was formed by closely examining the work of other scholars).

The important starting point for further analysis is Fronsperger's observation that all human actions, whether on the level of individuals or on the level of whole countries, are interconnected:

the Lord the Creator, through His eternal wisdom directed all things in a manner that every country requires the others. No country is completely self-sufficient, and no human can live without the others' help.

Chapter 13 describes mutual dependences among individuals using the metaphor of a chain that links their actions:

> ... human interactions are like links in a chain which are entangled; therefore one person is directly connected to another, just as though you had someone beneath you and pulled him towards you, then the whole chain would follow with all its links. So that whatever business you have with others you will find that other activities inevitably follow suit, all according to a greater order.

> The Lord in His eternal wisdom has arranged everything just so that people would have a reason to talk to each other, and to love each other, because they would see that nobody can achieve anything without the others.

> ... every person is created for the benefit of others, and no one is created just for themselves.

Given this interconnectedness, self-interest not only promotes the well-being of the individual, but automatically also the well-being of others.

Based on this chain-link paradigm *Chapter 14* defends the provocative thesis that all goods in the world are finally common:

> From this follows that just as the whole world shares one grand scheme of [political and economic] order (*Policey*) and nature ... that all goods in the world are held in common

This should not be understood in the sense of a perfect equality in the distribution of goods, assets or skills. Quite on the contrary, Fronsperger is a vivid defender of inequality, but he sees this inequality as the final reason for the need of individual interactions that lead to a harmony of interests, in which the common good is realized:

> ... true equality will never be found either in Heaven nor on earth. Instead all creatures will experience inequality and will be pitted against each other in competition and opposition. But through this inequality and opposing forces the greatest equality will emerge in turn, and sweetest harmony and unity, which no tongue can speak of or praise

highly enough … just like an organ which has many sorts of pipes, long and short; big and small; none of which are sounding equal and alike. But from all these uneven voices rises the sweetest musical harmony.

Chapter 15 describes the specialization of tasks and their interconnectedness using the example of the administration of a large royal court.

> … Here matters are or should be the same as in (managing) a large royal court or noble estate, where one is responsible for handling the lord's money [i.e. income and expenses]; another for his silver ware; a third one for his clothes and jewels; the fourth for his wine and grain; the fifth for food; no one must embezzle or misappropriate any of these goods but manage with them properly. Even though they have the goods within their power, they get little joy from them; because they know that not only will they have to return them to their lord when asked to do so, but they also have to produce accounts for how they have kept, maintained and managed them … .

Here too, it is self-interest in the fulfilment of the individual task that contributes in the best possible way to the overall good. In this perspective, the traditional understanding of a common good per se should be abandoned and replaced by a praise of the positive forces of self-interest:

> All this goes against common good as it has been described here and cannot co-exist with it; instead it actually pertains to me (Self-Interest)…

With *Chapter 16* the tone of the text changes. The references to classical and contemporary philosophers are significantly replaced with hints to the Bible. In this new perspective *Chapter 16* comes back on the question what the true common good should be. The chain-link metaphor, in which the diversity of people, abilities and tasks is supposed to motivate action according to the individual self-interest and at the same time bind these actions together in the common interest of all, now also receives a religious backing. Since the various human qualities are given by God, it is a Christian duty to use them in the best way, but this means following the guidance of self-interest:

> True Common Good as outlined above means that all things in the world, whether power, artistic talent or material possessions should be and are received to be held in common and on behalf of others; and one should help out the other, offering his hand to praise and serve God the Creator, work and toil and pay his dues; just as Jesus Christ the son of

God and redeemer of the world, and true teacher and founder of the Common Good, clearly and explicitly demonstrated everywhere in his divine teachings …

Chapter 17 recalls the biblical Parable of the Entrusted Bags of Gold from Matthew 25, 14–29, in order to prove that God does not tolerate idleness in the use of the goods that he gives. Those servants will be praised who have earned a return with their gold, while the servant who has only buried the treasure will be severely scolded by Christ. And the individual use of a good or ability will also benefit all other people:

> From this parable it is clear that God wants us to do good with His offerings. He dislikes idleness, but wants us to serve our neighbour…

Chapter 18 summarizes and repeats the central thesis from *Chapter 11* that self-interest is the source of the true common good, but still lacks the adequate reputation for its fundamental value in all human activities:

> People speak about the Common Good, but yet no one knows it; no one has ever seen or recognised it. Still everyone scolds me, even though the whole world is preserved and governed by me. I have not received much gratitude or praise, even though I cause and do much good for the people. And if there is, or if there ever were, a Common Good on this earth, then it has originated from me; therefore, I can be rightly called its father.

Chapter 19 reconfirms that self-interest is the true driving force in human life as it is the main motivation for human action:

> I truly influence everything: through me the field is tilled for the nourishment of the people. Towns and castles have been built by Self-Interest. For the shelter and protection of the common people, for the maintenance of public order and control – through Self-Interest worldly and spiritual authority is instated. Nothing is created without Self-Interest; it is through Self-Interest that merchants travel foreign countries; activities from which all people benefit. Self-Interest has incentivised craftsmen and artisans, to invent, improve and manufacture those things in life that people need and which let them thrive; and nothing that people require is too small or insignificant for self-interest to create. Self-Interest creates everything and makes sure that this earth lacks nothing.

Chapter 20 then makes two qualifications to the unlimited praise of self-interest. First, there is no need to condemn those who directly and explicitly strive for the common good, as long as it is widely accepted that self-interest is the more general motivation of individual behaviour:

> ... it is my sincere advice: leave the two of us [Self-Interest and the Common Good] together, just as it has been since the beginning of the world. Keep striving for the best, using all your ability and might; diligently work towards the Common Good as much as you can, because I am not that egoistic, actually – even though I am Self-Interest itself. Not that I would desire to try and make you reject the Common Good; for I have to admit that God takes pleasure in it ... But at the same time you should also let me, Self-Interest, be; and should refrain from trying to drive me away. I am not easily driven away; I am too deeply rooted and have been for a long time; from the beginning of the world ... .

Secondly, coming back to what has already been outlined in the *Chapters 2* and *3*, the author warns that badly used self-interest can also cause harm:

> I, myself, am not so bad. There is no need to curse at me, because as you have heard above, through me the world is preserved in essence and nature. And even though sometimes damage or disadvantage is caused by me – and I am not so desperate for praise to deny this – the harm is caused by bad improper use, as it is the case with many other things as well.

This naturally leads to the question of what guidance can be given for an appropriate use of self-interest. This question is answered in *Chapter 21*. Fronsperger postulates that individuals who follow their self-interest should not do so at the expense of others. With a reference to Cicero, he goes on to remind us that this general principle has already become part of the natural and written laws for all people:

> Cicero has written: It is justifiable that a person strives for its own self-interest more fervently than for their neighbour's good. On the other hand, nature prevents that one person's wealth and capabilities are increased by harming or robbing others. This is not only a principle of natural law, that all people adhere to justice and honour with everything they own and do. It is also codified in the written laws of all peoples and is a common principle of governance that no one should harm another person for their own Self-Interest.

But what should motivate the selfish person to obey these laws? Chapter 22 is then full of references to the Gospel to illustrate that it is ultimately the expectation of an eternal life that motivates people not to harm others. In view of the unlimited lifetime of 'spiritual goods' that one can accumulate through a godly life, the selfish pursuit of the accumulation of 'wordly goods' becomes much less important:

> … you will have learnt how the Lord in the Holy Scripture commands us to refrain from temporal and worldly strife for riches, forbidding the misuse of the goods He has given us. And therefore, we have to seek spiritual over worldly goods, and we should not succumb to misusing the force of Self-Interest and be excessively avaricious and greedy, lest we miss out on the eternal goods … Because we really only live in this earthly valley of tears for a short and transitory time, we should righteously follow God's commands and live piously and neighbourly with others, to ensure the blessedness of our souls; so that we may, following this transient life, gain eternal salvation (hopefully given to us by God). Amen.

Is Fronsperger the Actual Author?

In the preface of the work, Fronsperger reports that the original idea of writing a text on self-interest arose in discussions with a good friend of his, Oswald Gut, a *Doctor iuris utriusque* (Doctor of both laws) and chancellor of the Margraviate of Baden between 1530 and 1554[8]:

> … About this world view, custom and tradition I once spoke to a gentleman and friend of mine known by the name of Doctor Oswald Gut (may God rest his soul), then chancellor to the Margrave [*of Baden-Durlach*] and still alive. He had a thirst for history and old tales; among other things we dwelled and spent much time on the topic of Common Good, and we considered and concluded that the matter had almost never been examined closely; but that instead always and throughout the history of the world, it was self-interest alone which was scrutinised …

In view of this remark, some have assumed that almost the entire booklet was written by the Margravial chancellor[9] or that at least large parts of the work were written by Gut with Fronsperger only adding some notes and insertions.[10] An indication of at least joint authorship is found in the obvious break in the text between *Chapters 15* and *16*. In the first part of the text one finds virtually no reference to the Bible, but many references to classical authors

and philosophers; the later part, on the other hand, is full of biblical quota-
tions. Before drawing a conclusion about the actual authorship, we would like
to recall the biographies of the two protagonists.

Leonhard Fronsperger was most probably born in Bavaria in 1520. He
was of the Lutheran faith and, after marrying a local woman and buying a
house, became a citizen of the Free Imperial City of Ulm in 1548, where he
died in 1575.[11] Ulm, situated on the Danube in Upper Germany, where the
Reformation had been introduced in 1524,[12] was one of the most important
imperial cities at the time, along with Augsburg and Nuremberg, and an
important trading hub for textiles. Fronsperger had joined the imperial army
at a young age, originally as a lancer. After serving as a master-at-arms in a
campaign in southern France and as a field judge in the Turkish War of 1566,
he received a lifetime rent as an imperial pensionary and was appointed a
military councillor by the council of the city of Ulm. On May 23, 1575 he
met with a fatal accident while inspecting riflemen at the city fortifications.

Given his professional background, it is not surprising that Fronsperger
became and remained known primarily as an author on military matters.
Apart from smaller writings on price tables in the wine and grain trade[13]
and a tract on urban building regulations[14], most of his texts written since
1555 dealt with a wide range of warfare issues. He wrote about martial law[15]
and military strategy[16] as well as about artillery[17] and the construction of fortifications[18]. In 1573 he combined his war-related works into a three-volume
'War Book'[19] ('Kriegsbuch'), into which he also integrated contributions by other
contemporary authors. Until today, this extensive work can be found in many
libraries throughout Europe. Since the theme of self-interest and the way it
is presented in a satirical poem are only loosely related to his other works,
doubts about Fronsperger's authorship are justified, and they were already
nurtured by the author himself.

Compared to Fronsperger, even less is known about Oswald Gut, the
chancellor of Margrave Ernst I. of Baden-Durlach. From his epitaph in
the Schloßkirche (castle church) of Pforzheim we only learn that Gut died on
March 28, 1554.[20] The Margrave was known for his religious tolerance,
which enabled the spread of Reformed ideas in his territory. However, he
himself remained Catholic until his death in 1552, as did all his most important administrators, including Oswald Gut, who apparently feared that an
official confession of the new faith might trigger uncalculated conflicts with
the emperor. The introduction of the Reformation in its Lutheran form in
the Margraviate did not take place until 1556 under a new Margrave and
after the death of Gut.[21] The city of Pforzheim, capital of the Margraviate
in Gut's time, is also known as the home of Johannes Reuchlin (1455–1522),
one of the most important humanist scholars of his time and uncle of Philipp

Melanchthon (1497–1560), who himself had attended school in Pforzheim for a year and later became one of the leading Reformist writers. We know that Gut was granted a peerage by Emperor Charles V at the Imperial Diet in Augsburg in 1530 and that Philipp Melanchthon fought for official recognition of the Protestant cause in the Empire on that same occasion, but we have no indication that the two were in closer contact.

Nor are any details known about the beginnings of the friendship between Gut and Fronsperger or the exact modalities of their communication. But Gut, who had begun work on the text, must have known Fronsperger's intention to publish a book on warfare, probably the '*Fünff Bücher von Kriegß Regiment vnd Ordnung*' which finally came out in 1555.

> my good chancellor set out to write about the difference between Self-Interest and the Common Good. Whilst intending to do so he asked me – as I was about to put my military manual (*Kriegsordnung*) into print again – whether I was willing to help complete the little volume which he had started, so that it could be put in print.

Oswald Gut died, however, without having finished the text on self-interest.

> I willingly offered him my services; yet shortly afterwards the aforementioned chancellor was struck by God with weakness, died and passed away in Christ.

Fronsperger felt obliged to fulfill the will of his friend, finished the text and brought it to publication ten years later.

> Since this time many gentlemen and friends have reminded me of my willing promise; and I thus declare myself responsible for having to fulfil it.

It is possible that Oswald Gut, with his academic knowledge of classical philosophy, contributed mainly to the first part of the book, while Fronsperger, who was well acquainted with Luther's new translation of the Bible, contributed much to the second part. Moreover, in later chapters, the literary form of the satirical poem with self-interest speaking in the first person is abandoned several times with the author(s) switching to lengthy elaborations and explanations, reminiscent of Fronsperger's other writings. However, looking at the book as a whole, we find a high degree of consistency in the content and see no convincing reasons why Fronsperger's ultimate responsibility for the text should be cast into doubt, even acknowledging Oswald Gut's strong and lasting influence. Had the work been largely completed by the time of Oswald Gut's death, it could have been published much earlier. But ten years passed before the booklet finally came out. The long period of time suggests a considerable effort on Fronsperger's part to put the contents and results of the conversations with his friend into a written form. This also explains why Fronsperger published the book on self-interest exclusively under his own name and only mentioned Oswald Gut in the preface. In his own words, Fronsperger added further content to Gut's original ideas, and it is impossible to quantify how great these additions are:

> Even though this purpose – in this case to commence with printing – was difficult to fulfil in this transient world, I nevertheless did not dare neglect it. I wanted to preserve the blessed good name of the chancellor and provide an immortal and praiseworthy memory. Therefore took up the task; to carry it out in good order. I ventured to achieve this as well as I could given my humbly intellectual capacities, especially given the scope and purpose of the work, and the space afforded to elaborate on this important matter.

Finally, it should also be noted that Fronsperger, as a citizen of Ulm, must have been familiar with issues of trade, payments and innovations, because Ulm was, after all, an important center of the trans-European textile trade,[22] much more so than the small city of Pforzheim. Moreover, his military experience probably meant that he was not only confronted with a number of economic problems, such as the procurement and administration of funds or the logistics of feeding a large army. The military system of the time produced constant technical improvements, which were massively promoted by the competing princely warlords.[23] For this reason, Niccolò Machiavelli, only a generation older than Fronsperger and famous as a political philosopher, also became known as the author of a widely known book on the *'Art of War'*.[24]

Like his other works, Fronsperger had *'On the Praise of Self-Interest'* published by Sigmund Feyerabend and Simon Hüter in Frankfurt on the Main. Feyerabend, who was born in Heidelberg and acquired citizenship in Frankfurt in 1559, founded the book printers' and publishers' association *'Companei'*, which Simon Hüter joined in autumn 1562.[25] Under Feyerabend's leadership, the *'Companei'* quickly became one of the city's most successful publishing houses, whose works were distinguished above all by their outstanding illustrations. The success can be attributed to Feyerabend's great entrepreneurial spirit, but also to his sometimes ruthless business conduct. It is known, for example, that he was sentenced to several days imprisonment for illegally reprinting a number of popular works, including Luther's translation of the Bible. Feyerabend's entrepreneurial skills made him one of the largest publishers in Germany in the 1560s and 1570s and Frankfurt one of the European centers of book printing and trading.[26]

What Are the Literary Sources?

For a book presented at the Frankfurt Fair in the section on theological writings, the literary form is rather unusual. Fronsperger, at least in the first part of the book, lets self-interest (*'Eigen Nutzen'* or *'Eigennutz'*) take on the role of the first-person narrator. This characterizes the literary genre of the satirical *encomium*, a peculiar form of poetry in which a vice is ironically praised in order to indirectly portray and criticize its social ills. The traditional encomium is a classical form of poetry praising a famous and honourable person. In the era of the Renaissance humanists, the traditional genre was transformed into a satirical criticism and therefore enjoyed great popularity.[27] The satirical examination of a politically and theologically problematic topic enabled the author to express dissenting opinions without appearing to endorse deviant or subversive attitudes themselves, which would have had legal consequences.[28]

By reflecting on the origin and effect of human vices in the form of a satirical encomium, Fronsperger followed important predecessors. One reference that is not explicitly mentioned in the text is Sebastian Brant's '*Ship of Fools*' ('*Narrenschiff*')[29] from 1494, the most successful book in the German language before the Reformation. In *Chapter 1*, Fronsperger refers to the Roman poet Horace, who was also known as a writer of satirical texts:

> Because as Horace said, all things have a certain measure, and when this measure is overstepped, they become a vice.

Chapter 3 mentions two other classical poets: the Roman Terence, who was known in Fronsperger's time as the author of numerous comedies, and the Greek Lucian of Samosata, who had the reputation of being the best satirical author in the ancient world. Both are presented as proponents the art of flattery:

> This is why Terence said: Friends are won through flattery, truth gives birth to hate.

> I wish you had read the erudite Lucian's beautiful and delicate book on how flattery is the highest art

And in *Chapter 4*, reference is made to three different authors[30]:

> At the same time, I have been more than a little bewildered at what
> could be the reason that nothing on earth is so disdainful that it hasn't
> found someone who has bestowed praise upon it: Erasmus and his folly;
> Ulrich von Hutten and the fever; even baldness – such a disdainful
> thing! And the drunkenness during our times, praised through fables of
> the virtuous poet Aesopus.

The nod towards Ulrich von Hutten (1488–1523), one of the main representatives of the German Renaissance humanists at the beginning of the sixteenth
century, refers to the *'Gesprächbüchlein'* (*'Little Book of Conversation'*) published in
1521. In this little book, Hutten engaged in a satirical discussion with his son
about the benefits and harms of fever, in which also fever itself takes an active
part.[31] The Greek poet Aesop was famous for his fables in which he gave
human features to animals or inanimate objects. A famous and beautifully
illustrated collection of Aesop's tales in German had been published in Ulm
as early as 1476. Also well-known in the sixteenth century was the edition of
Aesop's Fables published by Sebastian Brant in Strasbourg in 1501.[32] And a
famous proverb taken from of Aesop's fables is quoted in *Chapter 9*:

> A single swallow does not make a summer, as the proverb says.

The most important reference for Fronsperger, however, is Erasmus of
Rotterdam (1466/69–1536) and his *'In Praise of Folly'* (*'Moriae encomium'*)[33] of
1509. Erasmus, who along with Johannes Reuchlin is considered the most
influential humanist intellectual at the time of the Reformation, was born in
the Netherlands but spent most of his time after 1514 until his death in the
Southwest of the German Empire as a professor at the Universities of Basel
and Freiburg, not far from Pforzheim and Ulm. And so it is not surprising
that the first German translation of Erasmus's *'Praise of Folly'* was printed and
published in Ulm in 1534. This translated edition was the work of Sebastian
Franck (1499–1543), a controversial Protestant theologian and citizen of Ulm
between 1534 and 1539. Franck also wrote the *'Paradoxa'*, a collection of paradoxical propositions from the Bible and other sources intended to make the
reader aware of the inner meaning (*'inneres Wort'*) that cannot be found outside the individual. In *Chapter 1*, Fronsperger quotes one of the proverbs from
the *'Paradoxa'*:[34]

> … Just as in recent times (the saying goes 'The Lord's Gospel would not
> be so hard to follow if there was no Self-Interest'.

A possible reference to Franck's collection of proverbs '*Sprichwörter, Schöne, Weise und Herrliche Clugreden, und Hoffsprüch*', published in 1541, can be found in *Chapter 5*:[35]

> A common and traditional saying goes that he who praises himself approvingly and righteously will not be praised by anyone else and has bad neighbours.

In *Chapter 3* we find a reference to '*Sileni Alcibiades*', an earlier book by Erasmus (1517), which is meant to underline that self-interest, like everything else, has two sides, one good and one evil:

> … there are two sides to all things in the world; just as was the case with the *Sileni Alcibiadis*. And everything can bring forth good or evil, depending on whether used for evil or for good, as has been stated above …

The entire *Chapter 4* of the booklet is then devoted to the '*Godess Folly*' and her praise by Erasmus. Compared to Erasmus, however, Fronsperger's treatment of the literary genre is less severe. He begins with an ironic portrayal of self-interest; but as the booklet progresses, he changes the narrative perspective and replaces the first-person narrator with a detached third-person narrator who provides a descriptive and reflective account of society. Erasmus is twice explicitly rebuked by Fronsperger for attributing responsibility for many forms of human behaviour to folly rather than self-interest.[36] First, self-interest complains in *Chapter 4*.

> Erasmus did not treat me fairly, since he – not unlike some of my other ungrateful children – bestowed upon the aforementioned Goddess of Folly almost all the praise (which should have been mine and had been unjustly taken from me).

Second, discussing the motivation of political and religious leaders to take responsibility, *Chapter 10* states, with explicit reference to Erasmus' encomium:

> And although the distinguished man Erasmus of Rotterdam has stated in his delicate and artful book on the *Praise of Folly* that folly was a reason for good deed, nobody considered the high burden and weight that these high posts of ruling bring with them, and thus would be much eschewed. It is possible that this is partly due to folly; but I, Self-Interest, am the proximate reason, and therefore this praise should first and foremost go to me.

However, if one takes into account their common philosophical antecedents, Erasmus' concept of self-love (*'philautia'*), which is widely developed in '*In Praise of Folly*', and Fronsperger's concept of self-interest are closely related.[37] Aristotle had explicitly discussed self-love in the '*Nicomachean Ethics*'[38] refraining from an exclusively negative social connotation. He condemned those who are obsessed with the pursuit of money, fame or sensual pleasure, but also recognised another form of self-love that can be observed in those who strive for morality, justice and wisdom. This form is to be understood as a valued trait of human being. After Aristotle, it was Cicero who, in his three books '*De officiis*' ('*On Duties*') – important references for both Erasmus and Fronsperger – treated *'philautia'* as one of the central motivations for people's actions. Cicero speaks of '*suum commodum*' or '*sua utilitas*' when he talks about individual interest or self-love. He presents them as useful as long as the interests of others are not violated. He also states that a political community would not be able to survive if everybody only acted according to their individual benefit, neglecting the common interest. In the first German translation of Cicero's book by Johann von Schwarzenberg and Johann Neuber, printed in Augsburg in 1531, '*sua utilitas*' and '*suum commodum*' were both translated as '*eignen nutz*'[39]. In other German writings of the first half of the sixteenth century, the same term stands for selfishness or egoism and is widely considered to be similar to Aristotle's negative form of self-love.[40] Egoism was understood as a negative behaviour of people in a society, whereas people and governments should strive to achieve the common good. Fronsperger's book challenges this view. Referring to Cicero and especially to '*Laelius de amiticia*' , '*De legibus*' and '*De officiis*', Fronsperger reintroduces the Aristotelian position that self-love or self-interest is neither a negative nor a positive quality of human beings, but merely the driving force behind human actions. As he explains in *Chapter 7*:

> When Cicero demonstrated the necessity of friendship, he gave plenty of evidence that Self-Interest is the true origin (of seeking friendships).

And as we mentioned above, in *Chapter 21* Fronsperger explicitly refers to Cicero for the proposition that self-interest will lead to positive outcomes, provided the necessary regulating and framing devices are taken into account:

> Cicero has written: It is justifiable that a person strives for its own self-interest more fervently than for their neighbour's good. On the other hand, nature prevents that one person's wealth and capabilities are increased by harming or robbing others. This is not only a principle of natural law, that all people adhere to justice and honour with everything

they own and do. It is also codified in the written laws of all peoples and is a common principle of governance that no one should harm another person for their own Self-Interest.

Chapter 17 deals in detail with Seneca, another Latin Stoic philosopher, and his book '*On Benefits*' (*De Beneficiis*). Here Fronsperger finds further justification for selfish behaviour. It becomes a duty for every human being to make the best use of all talents and goods that are given by God for time:

> Thus speaks Seneca: You should live your life, as if you owned nothing, but only were a manager and steward of the things given to you by God. This is fully in line with Christian teaching.

This quotation corresponds to a reference to Audius (or Audaeus) in *Chapter 14*, an early Christian ascetic and sharp critic of the extravagance of priests and bishops:

> … as Audius said: There should be such an equality and communality among people that everyone knows that nothing he owns, in fact everything he has, be this his title of nobility, power, wealth, reason, wisdom, strength, craft and talent and other worldly goods, has been given him by God so that he can serve and help his neighbours and thus play his part in establishing and keeping God's chosen order (*Policey*) … One should manage one's worldly goods not like one owned them, but rather as a steward held accountable by God

In both original versions of the passages above we find the German term '*Schaffner*', which is translated in English by '*steward*'. The term also appears in a side note of *Chapter 14*, which says: '*We are all stewards*'. It should be noted that '*Schaffner*' is the original German translation of the biblical word and Greek expression οἰκονόμος, which has been Latinized as '*oeconomus*', meaning '*economist*' or '*house or estate manager*'. This context also helps to identify the source of the reference in *Chapter 13* to '*Brison, the Greek*' and the origin of the '*chain-link*' metaphor, which is so important for the understanding of the social benefits of self-interested behaviour in Fronsperger's perspective:

> No one on earth would ever be so high or mighty that they would not occasionally need the help of the lowest and depraved. In fact, the need is so great that one cannot do without them. Therefore [the Greek philosopher] Bryson rightly said that human interactions are like links in a chain…

Several Greek writers and philosophers with the name Brison (Bryson) are known. Fronsperger refers neither to Bryson of Achaia nor to Bryson of Herakleia, but to a (much younger) neo-Pythagorean philosopher of that same name who probably lived in Alexandria or Rome in the first century AC.[41] His text '*Oikonomikos*' on the principles of good house management was preserved only in two original Greek fragments, one of which contains the '*chain-link*' metaphor of economic interdependence.[42] The fragments were included in a Latin collection of Greek writings compiled by Johannes Stobaios in the fifth century, which became an important reference for medieval Islamic economic thinking. The first German translation of Stobaios' collection by Georg Frölich, which also contains the text fragment from the '*Oikonomikos*' was published in Basel in 1551.[43] In Bryson's view, every economic activity is dependent on a variety of preliminary work and framework conditions provided by others. All these activities interlock like links in a chain. If a link in the chain is broken or missing, the function of the chain is rendered impossible. As an example, Bryson refers to a single craft that is an an art in itself, but also needs the arts of other crafts for its implementation and productivity.[44] Fronsperger takes this example and reproduces it almost word-for-word in *Chapter 13* of the '*Praise of Self-Interest*':

> If someone cultivates a field, does he not first need the craft and product of the carpenters and blacksmiths? And before them the art of the smelters, who in turn need the miners? Now for the miners, in order for them to stay at work, they need to cover themselves and have shelter, which is why they need the weavers and the builders. It's one thing for another; one craft requires the other. And so if you sought out the truth and researched it properly you would find that all things are connected.

Finally, it should be noted that Fronsperger also quotes some proverbs and sayings that must have been common in Upper Germany at the time of his writing. Two of them, which are included in the first *Chapter* of the '*Praise of Self-Interest*', are also found in the '*Florilegium Politicum*', a collection of proverbs published in 1630 by Christoph Lehmann (1568–1638), an administrator of the of City of Speyer:

> ... Self-Interest, you are bad dress.[45]

> Self-interest, concealed envy, and childish advice destroyed Troy and many other big city.[46]

How Important Was the Influence of the Reformation?

Fronsperger's text ends prayerfully with '*Amen*' and was classified at the Frankfurt Fair as a book written by a Protestant theologian. One would therefore expect some direct references to the Reformation, which spread to most parts of Central and Northern Europe after 1517. Interestingly, however, this is not the case. Neither Martin Luther nor any other leading Protestant theologian or philosopher are explicitly mentioned, while the Pope is presented as the typical representative of the clergy in *Chapter 8* and *Chapter 10* without any critical remark. It is not clear whether this is due to Oswald Gut's co-authorship – who was a Catholic – or to a more general distancing of the Lutheran Fronsperger, who had served in the imperial army, from the principles of Protestantism.

In the first part of the book, references to important Christian texts are rare. Only in *Chapter 5* one reads:

> … Saint Augustine the great teacher said that he who doesn't think highly of himself is cruel [to himself]. Therefore, to ensure that everyone is of keen mind and can understand my praise, I intend to compensate for this daily humiliation…

But from *Chapter 16* onwards, a series of references to biblical passages follow that deal with wealth and poverty from Christian perspective. In *Chapter 15*, Fronsperger takes up one of the most well-known sentences of the New Testament, which is mentioned in Mark 10:25, Matthew 19:24 as well as Luke 18:25:

> It is easier for a camel to go through the eye of a needle than for a rich man to enter the kingdom of God.

But then he adds his own interpretation:

> Now, I will acknowledge that many people interpret this text *verbatim*, meaning that those who want to be perfect, have to sell all that is theirs and follow Jesus Christ … . However, in my opinion the meaning is more spiritual than physical; referring to the act of spiritually loving God and thy neighbour, rather than doing everything for your neighbour and suffer in consequence; or having no own posessions. [The purpose is] to unite all things and efforts in a common cause, for the praise of God and the love of one's neighbour.

Chapter 17 quotes the parable of the entrusted bags (or talents) from Matthew 25:14–29 and the last two chapters of the book are full of references to biblical parables dealing with the accumulation of worldly versus heavenly goods, such as the parable of the rich grain farmer (Luke 12:16–21), the parable of the rich man and Lazarus (Luke 16: 19–26) or the parable of the poor widow (Luke 21). But Fronsperger's conclusion is again a special one:

> ... God wants us to recognise the favours and blessings He has bestowed upon us. We shouldn't waste or use them up in our arms' work.

This interpretation is not in line with the statements of Martin Luther or some other authoritative Protestant reformers on self-interest and wealth. A central component of Martin Luther's theology was the assumption that for a true Christian, original sin cannot be overcome by good deeds, but only by the grace of God. The expression of the individual's sinfulness is self-love, which manifests the detachment from God and must be replaced by God's love in order to attain salvation. Luther demands that human action be guided by the model of *'love your neighbor (as yourself)'*, behind which concern for one's own material well-being must take a back seat. True love of your neighbour can only be found where it is practised with all one's heart and religious conviction. The good Christian must therefore overcome self-love in order to attain salvation through God.[47] Consequently, every person who acts out of self-interest is rejected.[48]

The impact of Luther's teachings on early modern political and social theory can be seen, for example, in the work of Johannes Ferrarius (1486–1558), the first rector of the Protestant University of Marburg.[49] His work *'Von dem Gemeinen nutze'* (*'On the Common Good'*)[50], published as early as 1533, represents a viewpoint in post-Reformation Protestant literature directly opposed to Fronsperger. He pleads emphatically for the common good:

> And is therefore the common good called / that in this case no one should see on his own thing alone / but stand up for them / that one's neighbor is thereby not only not hindered / but also (where it seizes the need) demanded.[51]

And he particularly emphasizes the idea of charity propagated by Luther:

> ... even those who did not grow up in the community shall see on the common prosperity ... / So seek their use / that they may not forget the neighbor / or at least never want to harm him.[52]

In Ulm after the Reformation, Luther's views competed with the teachings of Ulrich Zwingli, which spread from Switzerland to Upper Germany, and later those of Zwingli's disciple Johannes Calvin. Since Max Weber's studies in the sociology of religion[53], Calvinism has been regarded as the form of Protestantism that supports individuals in maximizing their self-interest in order to achieve economic success. However, it should not be forgotten that the Calvinist attitude is also oriented towards divine salvation, i.e. it does not pursue self-interest as an end in itself. Economic success ultimately has no other objective than a religious, completely immaterial self-assurance. The pursuit of self-interest is by no means aimed at increasing the overall welfare of society, and every form of material luxury and worldly pleasures is rejected.[54] According to Calvin, economic success serves the individual above all as an indicator of right faith and its recognition by God.[55]

Fronsperger's explanation of how political communities function on the basis of self-interest is only loosely connected to any kind of religious objective. Even though he does not question the validity of religious promises of salvation in heaven, for him much of human happiness must already be sought and found on earth. Only rarely he seems concerned not to fall into complete contradiction with Protestant theology and then, as at the end of *Chapter 16*, tries to integrate some elements of charity into his practical recommendations for human action:

> But what this actually means is the state of being prepared; to help preserve the Lord's great order (*Policey*) to His praise and glory, with everything given to us by the Lord, be it body, reason, arts and crafts, honour and material possessions.

The reference to God reveals the two main reasons for Fronsperger's optimism that self-interested behaviour will actually contribute to the common good. First, he firmly believes that self-interest, by nature and by God's will, leads people to communicate and cooperate with each other, so that respect and love for each other will develop out of an awareness of interdependence. In *Chapter 13* he explains this:

> The Lord in His eternal wisdom has arranged everything just so that people would have a reason to talk to each other, and to love each other, because they would see that nobody can achieve anything without the others.

Secondly, Fronsperger is convinced, as a quotation from *Chapter 19* shows, that Christians have strong egoistic incentives to do good because it gives them access to eternal life.

> ... in my opinion even the Lord is praised through Self-Interest. Because how many good works do you think would be done by people, if Self-Interest did not exist, hoping to go to Heaven and gain eternal life? / ... .

In the concluding *Chapter 22*, Fronsperger then denies a conflict between individual self-interest and Christian values, as long as self-interest is not abused, especially in the form of greed.

> ... the Lord in the Holy Scripture commands us to refrain from temporal and worldly strife for riches, forbidding the misuse of the goods He has given us. And therefore, we have to seek spiritual over worldly goods, and we should not succumb to misusing the force of Self-Interest and be excessively avaricious and greedy,

What Drives the New View on Human Behaviour?

Fronsperger's conception of human behaviour is no longer bound to religious norms, but is determined by '*human affection*' ('*menschliche affection*') and '*natural desire*' ('*natürliche begirligkeit*').[56] This '*realistic*' view commenced at the beginning of the sixteenth century and became the basis for important philosophical and political thinkers of the seventeenth and eighteenth centuries, including Thomas Hobbes, Baruch de Spinoza, Giambattista Vico and Jean-Jacques Rousseau.[57] Before Fronsperger, it was above all the Florentine Niccolò Machiavelli (1469–1527) who did pioneering work. In chapter XV of his book '*The Prince*' ('*Il Principe*') – written in 1513, printed in 1532 and already placed on the index of books banned by the Vatican in 1557 – the famous distinction between '*the real truth of the matter*' and '*the conceit of it*' appears. Just as Machiavelli criticizes that: [58]

> ... many have pictured republics and principalities, which in fact have never been known or seen because how one lives is so far distant from how one ought to live

Fronsperger presents the concept of the common good in *Chapter 1* as a chimera:

... no one has ever seen, recognised, or known the Common Good, or knows where it has come from, or which shape it takes.

There is no evidence that Fronsperger knew Machiavelli's work, although both wrote extensively on the art of war. Nevertheless, their *'realist'* views on the causes of human behaviour are remarkably similar. While the notion of self-interest (or a related term) is not used by Machiavelli, it plays a central role in the thought of another influential contemporary Florentine writer, Francesco Guicciardini (1483–1540). In his *'Maxims'* (*'Ricordi'*), written between 1512 and 1530, he declared:

In this world of ours, the men who do well are those who always have their own interest in mind and measure all their actions accordingly.[59]

A central implication of Fronsperger's new view, already outlined in *Chapter 1*, is the impact of individual self-interest on the overall welfare or common good

... in the following I shall prove with meaningful and illustrative arguments that not only am I not as evil as my ungrateful children think, but also that through me the whole world is maintained and preserved in good public order, shape and peace; and was maintained from the beginning; and could not be maintained without me.

Fronsperger tries to prove that individuals' actions based on self-interest do not lead to chaotic social structures but, on the contrary, contribute toward stable social institutions and the common good. This is the essence of his analyses of the reasons for marriage and friendship as well as for market transactions and international trade.

The understanding of self-interest as an essential part of human nature and as a driving force for the common good links Fronsperger's work to the debates on the relationship between the pursuit of commercial interests and the common welfare that took place in the powerful trading cities north and south of the Alps in the sixteenth century. In the Upper German Free City of Augsburg, the humanist and politician Conrad Peutinger (1465–1547) had already been thinking about the role of commercial self-interest for the common good more than thirty years before Fronsperger, albeit in a different form and with a different focus. When he addressed the problem of trade monopolies in an expertise for the Diet of Speyer in 1530, he argued that a merchants pursuing their own profit, taking on hardships and risks to supply the domestic market with exotic goods positively contributed to the common good.[60] In 1588, Giovanni Botero (1544–1617), born in Piedmont in northern Italy, published '*On the Magnificence and Greatness of Cities*', which became the first economic bestseller of modern times, with forty editions by 1850.[61] He names trade and profit ('*commodità*' and '*utilità*') as the most important driving force for the successful development of cities and regards them as essential elements of human nature.[62]

Such writings confirm that the (commercial) utility of an action or object was considered to be of very central value in the urban communities.[63] Urban elites, especially the economically successful merchants, advocated a new moral philosophy that included a new approach to self-interest. In the Upper German imperial cities, which had all introduced the Reformation during the first half of the sixteenth century, we find a very intensive reception of Cicero's writings on practical philosophy and especially his three books '*De officiis*' ('*On duties*') during this period. After several annotated editions of '*De officiis*' by Erasmus between 1515 and 1528, there was a whole series of new editions, commentaries, translations – including the first German translation of 1531 – and pamphlets being published within the Protestant communities.[64] The debates in these publications sought to clarify the extent to which the moral aspect of individual actions was determined by metaphysical rules of theological ethics ('*lex divina*') or rather by practical principles of human nature ('*lex natura*'). The realisation that both existed already paved the way for a steady expansion of the non-metaphysical approach, which became important above all for a new self-awareness of the ruling Lutheran elites in economic and political matters.

Philipp Melanchthon (1497–1560), the leading Protestant philosopher of his time and promoter of a comprehensive educational system in Lutheran congregations, included '*De officis*' in the compulsory reading list ('*rationes studiorum*') for secondary schools.[65] And it is astonishing that one does not find a direct reference to Melanchthon in the '*Praise of Self-Interest*'. There is only one hidden link to Melanchthon's main dogmatic work '*Loci communes*', whose first edition appeared in 1521, followed by expanded new editions in 1535, 1544 and 1559. *Chapter 11* deals with Alexander the Great and later with Sulla, Marius and Pompeius and their motivation by '*their own honour, glory and self-interest*'. In the '*Loci communes*' of 1521, Alexander the Great is presented by Melanchthon as an example of a human driven by individual passio*ns*.[66] And in the extended edition of 1559, the '*Loci Praecipui Theologici*', one reads about Sulla, Marius and others who fulfilled their public duties not for the glory of God or out of altruism, but out of self-interest.[67]

Politically, Melanchthon had become the most important negotiator of the Protestant princes and cities with Emperor Charles V at the Imperial Diet in Augsburg in 1530, where the Augsburg Confession was formulated. At the same Diet Oswald Gut received his nobilitation. One can take as a hidden reference to this important event that in the *1ˢᵗ Chapter* of the '*Praise of Self-Interest*' a famous statement of George Frederick, the Margrave of Ansbach and Bayreuth at the Diet is quoted:[68]

> The Lord's Gospel would not be so hard to follow if there was no Self-Interest.

Melanchthon's doctrine of affects and its significance for his economic ethics has been examined in detail by Bauer[69] and Biehler[70]. An important aspect is Melanchthon's assumption that human affects are and can be regulated either by other (and stronger) affects or by a legal order. Therefore, he advocated not only private property, but also private exchange regulated by contracts, which ensured the equality ('*aequitas*') of the trading partners.[71] This idea of a legally regulated '*social and economic communication*'[72] is closely related to Fronsperger's chain-link metaphor in describing the benefits of trade.

It is therefore not surprising to observe Fronsperger claiming in *Chapter 21* self-interest to be morally acceptable as long as it respected the natural laws of humanity, including the basic rules of Christian life as well as the written laws which form the basis of good governance for any community. Within this framework, self-interested behaviour could be recognized as a positive contribution to the common good. With his optimism about the generally positive effects of self-interest, Fronsperger also opposes demands for radical social justice and a classless society, such as those raised by some in the Peasant Wars after the Reformation[73]. For him, the pursuit of poverty called for in the Bible does not mean material poverty, but spiritual poverty. For logical reasons, he considers it of little use to give one's worldly possessions to the poor, as he explains in *Chapter 16:*

> … If one gave everything to the poor, the poor would become rich, and the givers would become poor and in turn would seek assistance. So that the same poor to which they had given would also have to sell their goods and give them to the poor, who had before been rich.

And in *Chapter 14* he clearly condemns, as Melanchthon did,[74] all efforts of the '*common mob*' to achieve an equal distribution of wealth:

> … but did not truly understand the concept and instead acted out of Self-Interest and pounced on the goods and wrongly attempted to introduce communal ownership of goods by force and make everything equal; even if equality of some sorts could somehow have been achieved,

it would not have been allowed, because God does not want things to be owned in common property and did not arrange things this way ...

In the city of Ulm, Fronsperger's home, two goals dominated urban politics throughout the early modern period: the consolidation and expansion of urban autonomy on the one hand, and safeguarding prosperity and commercial interests on the other.[75] When the construction of Ulm's new town hall was completed in 1540, a series of paintings adorned the exterior walls of the building, illustrating the sources of good government.[76] Many of these paintings were inspired by illustrations in a comprehensive German edition of Cicero's works ('Der Teutsch Cicero'), published in 1534 by Johann von Schwarzenberg, which included his German translation of 'De officiis' from 1531.[77] They also contained a painted juxtaposition of the common good ('Gemeiner Nutz') and self-interest ('Eigen Nutz'), the latter acquiring a clearly negative connotation in the inscriptions, similar to tyranny and falsehood.[78] This shows the orthodox Lutheran view of Cicero's moral philosophy and good city government.

When Fronsperger, who must have known about these paintings on the Ulm town hall, published the 'Praise of Self-Interest' in 1564, the political conditions in the Free Imperial City had changed considerably. In 1548, the year when Fronsperger became citizen of Ulm, Emperor Charles V suspended the old constitution, which had established a balance of power between merchants and craftsmen, and introduced a new constitution that clearly favoured the economically more successful merchants in the city council over the craftsmen and their traditional guilts. The guilds were even suspended for some years.[79] In light of these changes, Fronsperger's book, with its positive connotations of self-interested behaviour, can be seen as an apology of a power shift that clearly privileged the more self-interested groups which had also become the new ruling elite.[80]

How Does 'Praise of Self-Interest' Compare to 'The Fable of the Bees'?

At first glance, the 'Praise of Self-Interest' has much in common with 'The Fable of the Bees' by Bernhard Mandeville (1670–1733), which is usually regarded as an apology of the socially beneficial consequences of self-interest.[81] Mandeville, a Dutch-born physician and writer, had become known in London at the beginning of the eighteenth century as the author of several satirical pamphlets.[82] His poem 'The Grumbling Hive: or, Knaves turn'd Honest', published in 1705, had immediate success and was soon out of print. In 1714, the poem was supplemented with a detailed commentary and published as a book entitled

'*The Fable of the Bees: or, Private Vices, Publick Benefits*'. Both the earlier printed version of the poem and the book were very well known in England and widely distributed on the market because of their very low price, but also because of a high number of illegal reprints. Between 1723 and 1732, numerous new editions of the book were published.[83]

It is not known that Mandeville – who wrote 150 year later – knew Fronsperger's booklet on self-interest. However, it cannot be ruled out that some of the Dutch writers who shaped Mandeville's economic thinking knew the text. Trade links and interpersonal connections between the Netherlands and Frankfurt, where the '*Praise of Self-Interest*' was published and presented at the internationally attended book fair, were particularly intense toward the end of the sixteenth and the beginning of the seventeenth centuries. It would therefore not be surprising if one day a copy of the book were discovered in a Dutch private library.

The satirical tone of both texts is, of course, similar, even if the main stylistic reference point for Mandeville is the novel '*Don Quixote*' by Miguel de Cervantes (1547–1616), which appeared in two parts in 1605 and 1615,[84] rather than Erasmus' '*Moriae encomium*'. In the '*Fable*', Mandeville uses the metaphor of a beehive that thrives as a community only because its members are encouraged to act according to their individual vanities, vices, envy and extravagance. As a result, the hive develops into a rich and powerful society. Science, commerce and the arts flourish, but so do vice and injustice. This leads to a catharsis that transforms the bee society into a community centered on modesty, justice and honesty; however, the social reorganisation leads to a collapse. In the end, the bees survive, having moved their hive to a hollow tree, but they must lead an existence of higher risk and lower standard of living than before. Mandeville comments on the moral of his fable with his famous sentence that private vice leads to public benefits.

> Then leave Complaints: Fools only strive
> To make a Great and Honest Hive
> T'enjoy the World's Conveniences
> Be fam'd in War, yet live the Ease,
> Without great Vices, is a vain
> EUTOPIA seated in the Brain.
> Fraud, Luxury and Pride must live,
> while we the Benefits receive (…).[85]

Mandeville is not the first in the history of philosophy to compare human society to a beehive. Plato had already used this allegory in the *Politeia*. For him, the drone was an example of a vicious and immoral member of society, a purely negative element within the hive, comparable to a thief or a beggar who lives at the expense of others. For Mandeville, however, as for other British writers of his time, the bee stands out as the symbol for industrious and purposeful work. What was once considered a vice now plays a key role in increasing the prosperity of society as a whole. Mandeville provides the example, among others, that the policeman, the judge or the blacksmith would lose their jobs if there were no more crime. He does not deny the existence of affects and emotions, but they could endanger economic success:

> Pity, tho' it is the most gentle and the least mischievous of all our Passions, is yet as much a Frailty of our Nature, as Anger, Pride, or Fear. The weakest Minds have generally the greatest Share of it, for which Reason none are more Compassionate than Women and Children.[86]

The satirical style of the 'Fable' leaves it open whether Mandeville is confronting his readers with a serious analysis of society or whether the text is to be understood as an ironical exaggeration. The creation of ambiguity through the use of irony was a common contemporary writing strategy that Mandeville had already used in his earlier pamphlets: it served to entertain the audience, but it also helped to avoid censorship and denunciation. It is obvious that Mandeville's aim with the original satirical poem – like Fronsperger's – was to entertain his readers, as he emphasised in the preface:

> 'If you ask me, why I have done all this, cui bono? and what Good these Notions will produce? truly, besides the Reader's Diversion, I believe none at all (...).'

However, with the addition of numerous notes, supplements and explanations in later editions, the 'Fable' turned more and more into a genuine contribution to contemporary philosophical and political debates. It is undeniable that at least the opponents of Mandeville's positions took them very seriously and seriously tried to argue and refute them.

   In its thematic elusiveness, Mandeville's philosophical approach certainly shows a lack of systematization. His observations – like Fronsperger's – were never integrated into a broader theoretical framework. Nevertheless, there are some remarkable traces of Mandeville's intellectual predecessors and inspirers. Verburg (2015, 665 Fn1) summarises them as follows: '... the naturalistic idea that man is ruled by his passions, anti-rationalism (reason as an instrument played upon by the passions, not the arbiter between right and wrong), Dutch political theory (Johan and Pieter de la Court's views on the political conditions of harmony of interests), sensationalistic psychology such as Hobbes' (claiming that man was egoistic), and the French moral tradition of Montaigne, Nicole, La Rochefoucauld, and Bayle (emphasising that, instead of having to rely on force, the passions could be manipulated into the service of order and prosperity).' Luban condenses these roots even further, seeing Mandeville as influenced simultaneously by a moralist and a materialist tradition: 'Part of Mandeville's achievement was to take the rich moral psychology of the French tradition—with its depiction of the subtle and varied manifestations of human egoism in the social world—and transpose it from seventeenth – century court society to eighteenth-century commercial society, thereby using it to explain emerging forms of economic behaviour.'[87] The fusion of these very contrasting approaches would then also explain the apparent inconsistencies and even contradictions in Mandeville's work, but also its innovative features.

Mandeville explicitly saw himself as a successor to the French philosopher Michel de Montaigne (1533–1592):

Twas said of Montagne, that he was pretty well vers'd in the Defects of Mankind, but unacquainted with the Excellencies of human Nature. If I fare no worse, I shall think my self well used.[88]

Montaigne's Essays,[89] published in 1571 and thus almost at the same time as the 'Praise of Self-Interest', with their subtle and sceptical thoughts on human nature, had a lasting influence especially on the French thinkers of the seventieth century, usually referred to as Neo-Augustinians and/or Jansenites. Hengstmengel (2016) identified three intrinsicly Augustinian motives in the 'Fable'. The first one is the distinction between worldly happiness, which is derived from temporary goods, and true happiness (in God), which can only be fully achieved in the afterlife and depends on divine grace. The second motif refers to the original sin, which had made fallen man a slave of passions that ceaselessly crave satisfaction during life on earth. The third motif is the thought that it is God who can transform evil into good. The second motif in particular was elaborated in great detail by the French moralists. They did not refer directly to self-love ('amour-propre') as the strongest driving force of human behaviour, but emphasised the key role of the individual's desire for esteem and recognition by others. Only the desire to be loved by others can explain why intrinsically egoistic individuals can exhibit explicitly non-egoistic behaviours such as religions ascetism, charitism, martial valour or even suicide. All virtuous-looking individual behaviour is just selfishness in disguise, motivated by the desire for social recognition.

> The Greediness we have after the Esteem of others, and the Raptures
> we enjoy in the Thoughts of being liked, and perhaps admired, are
> Equivalents that overpay the Conquest of the strongest Passions.[90]

The moralistic tradition of the '*Fable*' is thus concerned with human motives
rather than with human behaviour. It refers to the social norm that can determine how others value them. 'Thus the moralist account of human nature
can only be turned into a social theory if it is supplemented by a sociohistori-
cal account of the values governing self-love.'[91]

The materialist tradition, on the other hand, which represents a new form
of Epicureanism, is more concerned with human behaviour than with human
motives. The desire for esteem is no longer central, but only one of the preferences that an individual can develop. 'These preferences prescribe specific
and intuitive behaviours that are balanced through some calculus of want-
satisfaction.'[92] It remains a question of empirical observation – rather than
moral judgements – to find out what exactly these preferences are. Of course,
the materialist approach goes hand in hand with the successful economic
development in the Netherlands and in England immediately before and during Mandeville's lifetime, the emergence of a trading society. It was the time
when amenities and luxury goods became available to an ever larger part of
society. This led to a new conception of man in which the pursuit of desires
beyond basic needs was freed from natural limits. The de la Court brothers were among those who had analyzed this process and its economic and
political dynamics in the Dutch provinces, while Mandeville felt the need
to defend the results of increasing commercial activity in England after the
Glorious Revolution.[93] In a commercial society much larger and more diverse
than the Upper German urban societies of Fronsperger's time, admiration
and prestige are sought through wealth, creating a strong mixture of vanity
and greed. The accumulation of material possessions, driven by pride and
vanity, means that the smooth functioning of the system and the mechanisms
of control depend on the '*proper functioning*' of greed in its various forms and
at different levels of the system.[94] On a much larger scale, this is not so different from Fronsperger's idea of regulating self-interest through frameworks. If
religious norms no longer play as eminent a role as they once did, they must
be supplemented all the more by moral rules. Interestingly, the legal framework explicitly mentioned by Fronsperger does not play an important role for
Mandeville.

Given the existence of these two somehow contradictory traditions, it is
not surprising that throughout his work Mandeville emphasized the constant interactions and tensions between the empirically relevant motivational
structure (the disruptive, selfish, and innovative passions or preferences) and

the morally relevant institutional structures (normative rules and constraints) through which benefit is derived from people's passionate impulses. Only if private actions and their public consequences can be judged by different moral standards the paradoxical claim that private vices lead to public virtues remains tenable. What remains unresolved, then, is the question of the origin of social norms. Mandeville does not follow Thomas Hobbes (1588–1679) in a philosophical speculation about the emergence of a social contract that would put an end to the struggle of self-interested individuals by transferring all power to government.[95] Rather, he sees an ongoing task in striking a balance between the (rapidly growing and diversifying) individual passions and the (far less dynamic) public norms, so that the forces that transform evil into good under the conditions of a commercial society can operate. Interestingly, Mandeville sees this task in the hands of '*Good Politicians by dextrous Management*' (Mandeville 1723, 57), concluding the first volume of his book:

> … with repeating the seeming Paradox, … that Private Vice by the dextrous Management of a skilful Politician may be turned into Publick Benefits.[96]

As the lively debate between Jacob Viner and Friedrich August von Hayek has shown, it is not clear what this ultimately means. In the '*Fable*' there are references both to interventionist policies, as they were common in the seventeenth and eighteenth century mercantilism across Europe, and to the unintended emergence of a '*spontaneous*' institutional order for the good functioning of markets.

Even though the original idea of transforming vices into virtues is rooted in the revival of Augustinian theology by the French moralists, Mandeville gives it a clear anti-religious meaning in the end, motivated by the economic development of his time. This is most evident when he at the end of the '*Fable*' has Cleomenes talk about money in a dialogue with Horatio. One can see his analysis as a more modern version of the '*chain-link metaphor*' that Fronsperger took from Bryson's '*Oikonomikos*' to explain the necessities and advantages of bilateral exchanges of all kinds. For Mandeville, this is money:

> … so absolutely necessary to the Order, Oeconomy, and the very Existence of the Civil Society; for as this is entirely built upon the Variety of our Wants, so the whole Superstructure is made up of the reciprocal Services, which Men do to each other … To expect, that others should serve us for nothing, is unreasonable; therefore all Commerce, that Men can have together, must be a continual bartering of one thing for another. The Seller, who transfers the Property of a Thing, has his own

Interest as much at Heart as the Buyer, who purchases that Property; and, if you want or like a thing, the Owner of it, whatever Stock of Provision he may have of the same, or how greatly soever you may stand in need of it, will never part with it, but for a Consideration, which he likes better, than he does the thing you want. Which way shall I per-suade a Man to serve me, when the Service, I can repay him in, is such as he does not want or care for? ... Money obviates and takes away all those Difficulties, by being an acceptable Reward for all the Services Men can do to one another.[97]

In developed commercial societies money as a universal medium of exchange, not created by nature but introduced by human action, has taken over the role previously played by honor and pride as moral norms for the behaviour of self-interested individuals. At this point, Mandeville finally leaves the realm of theological traditions and paves the way for an assessment of what drives economic success in an environment of ever-increasing and even unlimited preferences:

> ... nothing is more universally charming than Money; it suits with every Station; the high, the low, the wealthy, and the poor, ...[98]

How Does Fronsperger Compare to Adam Smith?

Finally, we will examine how Fronsperger and his '*Praise of Self-Interest*' com-pare to Adam Smith (1723–1790), the author of '*The Theory of Moral Sentiments*' (1759) and '*The Wealth of Nations*' (1776), who wrote 200 and more years after Fronsperger.[99] We see no reason to distinguish artificially between Smith' two most important texts or even to construct an '*Adam Smith Problem*' in the sense of Oncken (1897). Rather, we see them as complementary for understanding how Smith saw the impact of individual self-interested behaviour on economic and social development.[100] We will show that, although the literary forms are quite different, Smith's reflections on the socially beneficial effects of individ-ual selfish activity, provided they take place within the framework of appro-priate formal and informal institutions, are much closer to Fronsperger's than Mandeville's satirical analysis of self-interest.[101] As a reason for this striking similarity, we point out some common intellectual roots.

Again, we have found no evidence that Adam Smith knew Fronsperger's works. Interestingly, however, the University of Glasgow, where Smith stud-ied and taught, owned a copy of Fronsperger's book on warfare since 1807. Originally, this copy probably belonged to Henry Pemberton (1694–1771), a contemporary of Smith's who played an important role in popularising Newtonian philosophy in Britain.[102] Montes (2006) has documented the influence of Newtonian thought on Smith's understanding of the dynamics of social relations. Isaac Newton (1643–1727) had argued that all natural processes do follow regularities and a certain order that can be observed and understood by the human mind. The existence of God could be recognized by human observers not through the existence of miracles, but through the recognition of this structured system of natural laws which all processes are subjected to. Based on the idea that nature is strictly ordered according to immutable laws allowing the prediction of future events, the philosophers of the Scottish Enlightenment, including Adam Smith, were convinced that human behaviour and social processes must also be based on these strict laws.

> … the Scots philosophers turned … to building a science of human nature as the foundation for all other scientific knowledge. Reason would come only after belief, sentiment and experience. This was a philosophy which suited the needs of a small nation eager to grapple with its practical problems and to find a place in the world.[103]

David Hume (1711–1776) became the main representative of this philosophical tradition in Scotland. For Hume, sympathy, understood as the emotional affect of the individual towards others, was a basic prerequisite for making man a social being.

> We can form no wish, which has not a reference to society. A perfect solitude is, perhaps, the greatest punishment we can suffer. Every pleasure languishes when enjoyed a-part from company, and every pain becomes more cruel and intolerable. Whatever other passions we may be actuated by; pride, ambition, avarice, curiosity, revenge or lust; the soul or animating principle of them all is sympathy.[104]

Hume's philosophy had a lasting influence on the view of human beings that underpinned Adam Smith's thinking. '*The Theory of Moral Sentiments*', Smith's main text on moral philosophy begins with a sentence that sees man as interested in both himself and in the welfare of others:

> How selfish soever man may be supposed, there are evidently some principles in his nature, which interests him in the fortune of others, and render their happiness necessary to him, though he derives nothing from it except the pleasure of seeing it.[105]

Smith assumes that people have a persistent tendency to share suffering and joy with others, and that understanding the affects or feelings of others leads to interpersonal acceptance, goodwill and social cooperation. Following Hume, Smith calls this empathy of the people '*sympathy*'. Of course, this feeling may vary from person to person, but the desire of each person to be respected and liked in the eyes of others leads the individual to act according to the social norms of decency. Ideally, the individual behaves in society as an '*impartial spectator*' who seeks to understand and analyse the affects of others in terms of their social consequences. In doing so, Smith distinguishes between three different forms of affects, the selfish passions, the social passions and the unsocial passions.[106] Selfish passions are those feelings or affects that are related to an individual's personal situation, such as joy, sadness or boredom. These passions do not necessarily affect others and are understandable and widely accepted. Equally understandable and accepted by society are social passions such as generosity, compassion or kindness, as they strengthen human relationships. The most interesting affects are unsocial passions, as they embody individual actions that affect others in a negative way and develop a perpetrator-victim relationship. In this case, Smith's impartial spectator might have sympathy for both sides and also understand the sentiments that might have led the perpetrator to act, but the sympathy with the perpetrator is not as intense as sympathy with the victim. Out of this intensity comes a sense of justice and morality in society. Since all individuals are driven by the affect of self-love, they strive to act according to society's norms of justice and morality in order to be respected and held in high regard in the eyes of others. The more respected a person is, the higher the position in society, the more the affect of self-love is satisfied.

The view of the individual as driven by sympathy and benevolence towards others in '*The Theory of Moral Sentiments*' can be contrasted with the description of the human character in '*The Wealth of Nations*':

> Every man, as long as he does not violate the laws of justice, is left perfectly free to pursue his own interest his own way, and to bring both his industry and capital into competition with those of any other man, or order of men.[107]

The two statements can be seen as two sides of the same coin. They complement each other if, like Fronsperger, one considers the '*laws of justice*' as well as the '*principles in human nature*' as means that necessarily frame the forces of '*selfishness*' or '*self-interest*' in such a way that they can contribute to the common good. What is missing, however, in Smith's conception compared to Fronsperger's is an explicit reference to religious norms. In '*The Wealth of*

Nations', Smith describes how the pursuit of self-interest becomes the driving force of transaction in a diversified economy:

> It is not from the benevolence of the butcher, the brewer, or the baker that we expect our dinner, but from their regard to their own interest. We address ourselves, not to their humanity but to their self-love, and never talk to them of our own necessities but of their advantages. [108]

Two centuries ago, Fronsperger had already seen the same forces at work in *Chapter 9* of the '*Praise of Self-Interest*':

> To start off I shall therefore ask: Is it possible to determine or say you could or would find a single farmer who cultivated and drove the plough into his field purely for the Common Good, if Self-Interest had not caused and driven him to it in the first place? …

> It is the same with merchants and craftsmen. Because which merchant has ever sailed across the seas; risking life and limb for the Common Good; bringing spices and other wares for food and better health, all the way from India, if Self-Interest or avarice did not drive him in the first place?

> Which craftsman has ever desired to work for the common good or out of love for it, if want and need for food, or insatiable greed, had driven him to it in the first place?

To explain how self-interested behaviour contributes to the common good, Smith introduces his famous metaphor of the '*invisible hand*':

> … (the merchant) … by directing that industry in such a manner as its produce may be of greatest value he intends only his own gain, and he is in this, as in many other cases, led by an *invisible hand* to promote an end which was no part of his intention. By pursuing his own interest he frequently promotes that of the society more effectually than when he really intends to promote it.[109]

There are many possible literary and philosophical sources for this metaphor.[110] Young (1996) even pointed to parallels with classical Chinese literature and philosophy that Smith may have encountered in Paris when he met Turgot. However, the reference to the '*greatest value*' might suggest that Smith understood how the system of market prices is able to direct individual interests towards a social optimum. And when he emphasises that the one´s own interest often – but not always – promotes that of society, he also seems to be very aware of the limitations of that process. He sees both social norms rooted in the individual's sympathy for others and state interventions as necessary frameworks.

We have already seen that Fronsperger draws on Stoic philosophy to explain how self-interested individuals are prevented from harming others. In *Chapter 21*, he explicitly refers to Cicero, who in '*De officiis*' quotes Chrysippus of Soli, who was for a time the leader of the classical Stoa and had compared the competition of self-interested individuals to a contest:[111]

> ... it is not our responsibility to cast aside our own self-interest for the benefit of others. The philosopher Chrysippus of Soli has a popular saying which states: He who is running a race ought to endeavour and strive to the utmost of his ability to come off as the victor; but it is utterly wrong for him to trip up his competitor or to push him aside.

The exactly same race metaphor is also used by Smith in '*The Theory of Moral Sentiments*':

> In the race for wealth, honours, and preferments, he may run as hard as he can, strain every nerve and every muscle, in order to outstrip all his competitors. But if he should jostle, or throw down any of them, the indulgence of the spectators is entirely at an end. I is a violation of fair play, which they cannot admit of. (...) They readily, therefore, sympathize with the natural resentment of the injured, and the offender becomes an object of their hatred and indignation. He is sensible that he becomes so, and feels that those sentiments are ready to burst out from all sides against him.[112]

On the one hand, this documents how strongly Smith was also influenced by Stoic philosophy.[113] On the other hand, one can also see in this quotation how Smith, under the influence of David Hume and his theory of sentiments, goes beyond the classical moral philosophy and established religious norms. By referring to the '*spectators*' who act as referees overseeing the '*fair play*', he draws attention to an additional framing of individual self-interest. As long as all individuals depend on the sympathy of others for their own well-being, they have an interest, not to say a self-interest, in not being held responsible for breaking the rules. No longer, as with Fronsperger, is accumulation of '*spiritual goods*' a necessity, but it is the goodwill of other individuals within a society, represented by the metaphor of the '*impartial spectator*', that makes self-interested behaviour compatible with the common good.

When Smith explains that self-interested action usually conforms to social moral standards not only through a love for praise but also through an innate sympathy of the individual with others, he is in a sharp contrast to Mandeville. This difference was clearly seen and expressed by Adam Smith in his discussion of *'The Fable of the Bees'* in *'The Theory of Moral Sentiments'*:

> There is, however, another system which seems to take away altogether the distinction between vice and virtue, and of which the tendency is upon that account, wholly pernicious: I mean the system of Dr. Mandeville. (…) Dr. Mandeville considers whatever is done from a sense of propriety, from a regard to what is commendable and praiseworthy, as being done from a love of praise and commendation, or as he calls it from vanity. Man, he observes, is naturally much more interested in his own happiness than in that of others, and it is impossible that in his heart he can ever really prefer their prosperity to his own.[114]

In Book 4 and Book 5 of *'The Wealth of Nations'*, Smith describes the role of governments in his economic system, which is far more than a night watchman state. The state should not only guarantee the security of society and a functioning legal system, but also restrict the self-interested activities of merchants and entrepreneurs as soon as the common good is impaired. The state should ensure that the market functions, it should fight monopolies,[115] provide for a good infrastructure[116] and invest in education, not only for young people but for people of all ages.[117]

Smith also became known as a staunch advocate of free international trade. As a critic of mercantilist economic policies who had got in contact with the leaders of French physiocracy, Francois Quesnay (1694–1774) and Anne Robert Jacques Turgot (1727–1781), during his visit to Paris, he wrote about the benefits of foreign trade in *'The Wealth of Nations'*:

> Whether the advantages which one country has over another, be natural or acquired, is in this respect of no consequence. As long as one country has those advantages, and the other wants them, it will always be more advantageous for the latter, rather to buy of the former than to make.[118] [Book IV, ch. 2, Vol. I, pp. 422-423]

But this insight that different endowments[119] make trade advantageous not only between individuals but also between countries, usually regarded as the essence of a modern theory of the benefits of international trade, was already formulated 200 years ago by Fronsperger in *Chapter 12* of the *'Praise of Self-Interest'*:

... the Lord the Creator, through His eternal wisdom directed all things in a manner that every country requires the others. No country is completely self-sufficient, and no human can live without the others' help. That is why, as you can see, no country is ever too barren; God has given every country something that another lacks so that this country can feed itself and survive [by trading with] the others. On the other hand, no country has it ever so good that it doesn't lack something that needs to be imported from somewhere else.

Finally, we can remark that Smith was well aware of the special role played by cities and their government in the emerge of a market economy in Europe since the end of the Middle Ages. In '*The Wealth of Nations*' he describes in detail how cities became drivers in economic development in Italy, Germany and the Netherlands and, following Hume, he also sees commercial activity in cities as drivers of liberty, security and good government:

... commerce and manufactures gradually introduced order and good government, and with them the liberty and security of individuals, among the inhabitants of the country, who had before lived almost in a continual state of war with their neighbours, and of servile dependency upon their superiors. This, though it has been the least observed, is by far the most important of all their effects. Mr Hume is the only writer who, so far as I know, has hitherto taken notice of it.[120]

Fronsperger and this apology of individual self-interest can be seen as part of this historical process. It not only helped to make transparent where the increase in wealth came from in a universe with multiple production processes and multiple trading activities. And it also provided the necessary new moral standards for the urban elites.

Conclusions

Fronsperger's text on self-interest, written in the form of a satirical encomium and presented to the public at the Frankfurt Autumn Fair of 1564, stands out in the German post-Reformation literature dealing with the motives of social, political and economic action. The author presents a new, realistic conception of human behaviour similar to Machiavelli´s and Guiccardini´s views in Italy, which they had applied to political science and history, and which differs markedly from the ideas of leading German reformers. Fronsperger develops the argument that self-interest is not to be condemned in everyday life, but on the contrary promotes the common good. He finds this connection realized in all social relations, but most clearly in economic actions, which he sees motivated by the fact that all actors strive for the best possible pursuit of their own benefits. He even goes one step further and outlines a world economy in which trade and the international division of labor follow the same principles as exchange between individuals. The motivation for Fronsperger's argumentation is undoubtedly his experience with the prosperity in Ulm and other Upper German cities, which coped very well with the Reformation's separation of secular and ecclesiastical life and in which economically successful merchants had become the new ruling elite.

Fronsperger's positive view on the effects of selfish behaviour on social dynamics – understood in a very broad sense – owes much to the rediscovery of Cicero's writing '*De officiis*' by German humanists in the sixteenth century. One of the leading humanist philosophers, Philipp Melanchthon, may have been in personal contact with Fronsperger and his co-author Oswald Gut, even though he is not explicitly mentioned in the '*Praise of Self-Interest*'. Fronsperger's defence of self-interested behaviour has little in common – apart from its literary genre – with the cynical analysis of self-interest presented by Bernard Mandeville some 150 years later in the '*Fable of the Bees*'.[121] It is much closer to Adam Smith's views on self-interest, developed notably in '*The Theory of Moral Sentiments*'[122] of 1759 and elaborated further in '*The Wealth of Nations*' of 1776. While Smith sees a natural, innate sympathy as the main reason for individual self-interest, Fronsperger, who is much more influenced by traditional religious considerations, suspects a self-interest in the accumulation of '*spiritual goods*'. For him, a strong motivation for good deeds to others should be the self-interest of entering paradise after a life pleasing to God. Other frameworks, also shared by Smith, derive from written laws that form the basis for any good government and sustainable social order.

In summary, Fronsperger's book on self-interest breathes the spirit of a new era in which economic activities increasingly follow their own logic based on self-interest. Since Max Weber (1904-05/2009), this spirit has been called the '*spirit of capitalism*', and thanks to Albert Hirschman (1977) and Pierre Force (2003), we know how long its normative emergence and explicit formulation took. It spread throughout the economically prosperous trading cities of the Holy Roman Empire, most of which joined the Reformation to secure – quite selfishly – the foundations of their success. With the outbreak of the Thirty Years' War at the latest, the economic dynamism in Upper Germany collapsed. When a new culture of profit-oriented economic activity then emerged in the Netherlands and in England, this was also accompanied by the emergence of a liberal economic and social theory, represented among others by the writings of Bernhard Mandeville and Adam Smith. While Mandeville became an advocate of relatively unrestricted individual self-interest, Smith sees both self-interest and sympathy for others at work in human nature. Fronsperger, who, like Smith, draws on principles of the Stoa that played no role for Mandeville, offering an alternative framework for self-interested action, should therefore be regarded as a genuinely German precursor of the Scottish founder of modern economics.

Notes

1 See Willer (1564, 17).
2 In the following we will use the English term '*self-interest*' as the best modern language translation of the early modern German '*Eigennutz*' oder '*Eigen Nutzen*'. We are aware of the linguistic specificities and traditions in both languages and discuss them at length in Part IV below.
3 See Fronsperger (1564a).
4 Different spellings can be found for the name of Leonhard Fronsperger: the first name is sometimes also rendered Leonhardt, Leonhart or Lienhart, while for the family name one finds also spellings as Frönsperger or Freundtsperger.
5 So far, 'On the Praise of Self-Interest' has only been discussed by German-speaking authors. Cilly Böhle (1940) und Alexander Rüstow (1945) refer to some selected parts of the book; see Klump/Pilz (2022). Winfried Schulze (Schulze 1986; Schulze 1988) and Bertram Schefold (Schefold 2003) mention it without giving a detailed analysis of the text. Birgit Biehler (Biehler 2011) deals intensively with the text, its form and its origins, but does not reflect on its importance for the history of economic thought.
6 See Klump/Pilz (2021).
7 Half penny, German small change coin. See translation for further comments.
8 See Kohnle (2007, 55).
9 See Schulze (1986).
10 See Biehler (2011, 182 f.).
11 See Weyermann (1829, 114 f.).
12 See Pronk (2012, 2012 f.).
13 See Fronsperger (1556).
14 See Fronsperger (1567).
15 See Fronsperger (1555), Fronsperger (1565) and Fronsperger (1578).
16 See Fronsperger (1564c).
17 See Fronsperger (1557) and Fronsperger (1564b).
18 See Fronsperger (1573a).
19 See Fronsperger (1573b).
20 See https://www.inschriften.net/pforzheim-stadt/inschriften/nr/di057-0151.html
21 See Kohnle (2007, 95 ff.).
22 See Borst (1968, 379 f.)..
23 See Stoll (2016).
24 See Machiavelli (1519-20/2003).
25 See Schmidt (1903, 240 f.).
26 See Benzing (1961).
27 See Biehler (2011, 183 f.).

28 Biehler (2011, 184) suggests that Oswald Gut and Leonhard Fronsperger might have deliberately chosen this literary form, since they were quite aware of the political (and theological) problems of their theses.

29 Brant (1494/1962). Sebastian Brant (1458-1521) was a Professor of Law at the University of Basel and later Chancellor of the Free Imperial City of Strasbourg.

30 At the end of *Chapter 4* also the conversation between Hannibal and Scipio on the three best military commanders is mentioned. This is a reference to the Roman historian Appian's book on The Syrian Wars.

31 See Hutten (1521/2014).

32 Brant (1501).

33 Erasmus (1509/1994).

34 Franck (1534/1995, 248).

35 In Franck (1541, 41) one reads: 'Wer sich selb liebt/den hassen vil.' (Who loves himself, is hated by many.).

36 See Fronsperger (1564a, 9).

37 See Schefold (2003, 110).

38 See Aristotle (1980, 1168a F.).

39 See Cicero/Schwarzenberg/Neuber (1531, 71). In the first English translation of 'De officiis' by Nicolas Grimald, printed 1556 in London, the term 'owne comodities' stands for 'sua utilitas'. Later 'self-interest' was commonly used as an English equivalent to the German term 'Eigennutz', see Bailey (1736). It did not appear in economic writings, however. Adam Smith, for example, preferred to speak of 'own interest', see Hawley (2019).

40 See Sachs (1535) and Arnold (1982, 298 ff.).

41 See Plessner (1928).

42 For an English translation of Bryon's fragments and an extended analysis of his work, in particular its influence on medival Islamic economic thinking, see Swain (2013).

43 See Frölich (1551, 427). Georg Frölich (1500-after 1552) was a legal advisor to the city governments of Nuremberg and Augsburg.

44 See Swain (2013, 6).

45 Lehmann (1630, 560): 'Eygener nutz ist ein böser putz.'

46 Lehmann (1630, 599): 'Heimlicher Neid / Eigener Nutz / junger Rath / Rom und andere Stäte zerstöret hat.'

47 See Biehler (2011, 38 f.).

48 For a detailed appraisal of Luther's economic approaches, see Rössner (2015).

49 See Eckert (1976, 10 ff.).

50 Ferrarius (1533).

51 Ferrarius (1533, 19 f.). The translations of the German text come from Klump/Pilz (2021).

52 Ferrarius (1533, 50).

53 See Weber (1904-05/2009).

54 See Freudenberg (2009, 3 ff.).

55 See Gordon (2009).

56 See Fronsperger (1564a, 13).

57 See Hirschman (1977).

58 Machiavelli (1513/2014, 86).

59 Phillips (1977, 77). Guicciardini either spoke of 'interesse suo' or 'interesse proprio'.
His Maxims did not become public during his lifetime. The first publication of the
Italian text happened in Paris in 1576, followed by a French translation one year
later that became very influential for the French moralists of the seventeenth century, see Heilbron (1998, 79 f.).

60 See Schefold (2003, 106). Peutinger translates 'commodum proprium' in the German
'aigennutzig handtierungen'; see Bauer (1954, 37). While Peutinger's views became
only known to a limited number of legal experts, Fronsperger's published booklet
addressed a significantly larger audience.

61 See Reinert (2016).

62 See Botero (1588/1606, 11 f.).

63 See Kern (2010, 107 f.).

64 See Eusterschulte (2018, 324 ff.).

65 See Eusterschulte (2018, 339).

66 See Melanchthon (1521/1997, 39): 'Videmus enim in aliis ingeniis alios regnare
affectus, sua quemque cupidine trahi.'

67 See Melanchthon (1559/2018, 470): ' ... politica officia ... faciebant Alexander, Sylla,
Marius et similes, cum contemptu Dei, propriae potentiae ac utilitatis causa.' One
should note that Fronsberger also speaks of 'Sylla'.

68 The statement was later quoted by Martin Luther, who had not been present at the
Augsburg Diet of 1530, and it was reproduced in the collection of Luther's writings;
see Sagitarius (1664, 519).

69 See Bauer (1965).

70 See Biehler (2011, 65).

71 See Biehler (2011, 111).

72 See Bauer (1965, 310).

73 See Goertz (2015, 159 ff.).

74 See Biehler (2011, 112).

75 See Pronk (2012, 2010).

76 See Tipton (1991).

77 Cicero/Schwarzenberg (1534).

78 See Tipton (1991, 98 f. and 117).

79 See Pronk (2012, 2013 f.).

80 It is interesting to note that when the paintings on the outside wall of Ulm's city hall
were renovated in 1905 the painting of 'Eigen Nutz' was replaced by a painting of
'Sträflicher Nutz' ('culpable interest') indicating that self-interest was no longer given
the earlier negative connotations; see Tipton (1991, 98 f.).

81 See Hundert (1994).

82 Mandeville was born in Rotterdam into a family of French Huguenots. He stud-
ied at Leiden University, where he obtained a doctorate in philosophy in 1689 and
a medical degree in 1691, and then began working as a neurologist in his home
town. When he became involved in a political uprising in 1693, he had to leave the
Netherlands and went to England, where he stayed for the rest of his life, working as
a doctor in London, specializing in hypochondria and hysteria. At the same time, he
became known as the author of satirical texts and pamphlets on topics such as the
education of lower-class children in poorhouses, the usefulness of prostitution or the
excessive consumption of spirits; see Jansen (2019).

83 The second edition of 1723, to which Mandeville added two new parts 'An Essay on Charity and Charity-Schools' and 'A Search into the Nature of Society', was denounced as a public nuisance and even brought before a jury, which condemned the 'diabolical attempts against religion'. In a new edition in 1729, Mandeville added a second part to the 'Fable', which contained six dialogues between the two fictive discussants Cleomenes and Horatio. Further dialogues were included in the 1732 edition as part of a new section titled 'An Inquiry into the Origins of Honours and the Usefulness of Christianity in War'; see Appeldorn et al. (2016, iv).
84 Euchner ((1968, 7).
85 Mandeville (1723, 11).
86 Mandeville (1723, 25).
87 See Luban (2015, 834).
88 Mandeville (1723, 1).
89 See Montaigne (1571/1988).
90 Mandeville (1723, 32 f.).
91 See (Luban 2015, 841).
92 (Luban 2015, 844).
93 See Dekker (1992), Bick (2008), Weststeijin (2012) and Verburg (2016).
94 Verburg (2016, 685).
95 Hobbes (1651/2010).
96 Mandeville (1723, 201).
97 Mandeville (1723, 410).
98 Mandeville (1723, 413).
99 Adam Smith was born in Kirkcaldy, Scotland. He studied moral philosophy at the University of Glasgow and later went to Oxford for postgraduate studies. On his return to Scotland in 1746, he gave public lectures on philosophy and literature in Edinburgh before being appointed professor of logic at Glasgow University in 1750. In 1752 he became professor of moral philosophy, lecturing on ethics, law, political economy and natural religion. In 1764 he left Glasgow University to work as a private tutor for the Duke of Buccleuch and to accompany him on an extended study tour to France. Returning from the continent in 1766, he settled again in Kirkcaldy; in 1778 he was appointed Scottish Commissioner of Customs and moved to Edinburgh, where he died in 1790; see Ross (2010).
100 See Paganelli (2008).
101 For Adam Smith's theory and practice of irony see the study by Cremaschi (2017).
102 See https://eleanor.lib.gla.ac.uk/record=b1778550
103 Montes (2006, 3).
104 Hume (2019), 401).
105 Smith (1759/2016,13).
106 See Smith (1759/2016, 38 ff.).
107 Smith (1776/2012, 686).
108 Smith (1776/2012, 19).
109 Smith (1776/2012, 445).
110 See the study by Kennedy (2009).
111 See Cicero (2013/2019, III, 310 f.).
112 Smith (1759/2016, 81 f.).
113 See Hawley (2019).

114 Smith (1759/2016, 268).
115 Smith (1776/2012, 442 ff.).
116 Smith (1776/2012, 721 ff.).
117 Smith (1776/2012, 758 ff.).
118 Smith (1776/2012, 448).
119 We leave it open here whether Smith when talking about '*advantages*' had absolute or comparative advantages in mind.
120 Smith (1776/2012, 402).
121 Mandeville (1723).
122 Smith (1759/2016).

References

Appeldorn, Larens van, Maas, Harro, and Olsthoorn, Johan (2016), Science, Politics, and the Economy: The Unintended Consequences of a Diabolic Paradox (Editorial), *Erasmus Journal for Philosophy and Economics*, 9, iii–vii.
Aristotle (1980), *The Nicomachean Ethics*. Oxford University Press, Oxford.
Arnold, Klaus (1982), damit der arm man vnnd gemainer nutz iren furgang haben ...: Zum deutschen ‚Bauernkrieg' als politischer Bewegung: Wendel Hiplers und Friedrich Weygandts Pläne einer ‚Reformation' des Reiches, *Zeitschrift für historische Forschung* 5, 257–313.
Bailey, Nathan (1736), *English Dictionary Shewing Both the Orthography and the Orthopedia of that Tongue*. Leipzig.
Bauer, Clemens (1954), Conrad Peutingers Gutachten zur Monopolfrage, *Archiv für Reformationsgeschichte*, 45, 1–43 and 145–196.
——— (1965), Melanchthons Wirtschaftsethik(1958), in: Bauer, Clemens (Eds.), *Gesammelte Aufsätze zur Wirtschafts- und Sozialgeschichte*. Herder, Freiburg i. Br., 305–345.
Benzing, Josef (1961), Feyerabend, Sigismund, *Neue Deutsche Biographie* 5, 119. https://www.deutsche-biographie.de/gnd118683527.html#ndbcontent.
Bick, Alexander (2008), Bernard Mandeville and the 'Economy' of the Dutch, *Erasmus Journal of Philosophy and Economics*, 1, 87–106.
Biehler, Birgit (2011), *Der Eigennutz – Feind oder wahrer Begründer des Gemeinwohls?* Wallstein, Epfendorf/Neckar.
Böhle, Cilly (1940), *Die Idee der Wirtschaftsverfassung im deutschen Merkantilismus*. G. Fischer, Jena.
Borst, Otto (1968), *Alte Städte in Württemberg*. Prestel, München.
Botero, Giovanni (1588/1606), *Delle Cause della Grandezza delle Città / A Treatise Concerning the Causes of the Magnificency and Greatness of Cities*. London.
Brant, Sebastian (1494/1962), *Das Narrenschiff/The Ship of Fools*. Dover Publication, New York.
——— (1501), *Fabelbuch des Äsop. Esopi appologi sive mythologi: cum quibusdam carminum et fabularum additionibus Sebastiani Brant*. Basel.
Cicero, Marcus Tullius (1913/2019), *De Officiis/On Duties*. III Volumes, Cambridge University Press, Cambridge, MA.
Cicero, Marcus Tullius, and Grimald, Nicholas (1556), *Marcus Tullius Ciceroes thre Bokes of Duties to Marcus his Sonne*. London.
Cicero, Marcus Tullius, and Schwarzenberg, Johann von (1534), *Der Teutsch Cicero*. Augsburg.

Cicero, Marcus Tullius, Schwarzenberg, Johann von, and Neuber, Johann (1531), *Officia M.T.C. Ein Buch so Marcus Tullius Cicero der Römer zu seynem Sune Marco Von den tugendsamen ämptern…in Lat.* Geschriben, Augsburg.

Cremaschi, Sergio (2017), Adam Smith's Irony and the Invisible Hand, *Iberian Journal of the History of Economic Thought*, 4, 43–62.

Dekker, R. (1992), Private Vices, Public Virtues revisited: The Dutch background of Bernard Mandeville, *History of European Ideas*, 14, 481–98.

Eckert, Brita (1976), *Der Gedanke des Gemeinen Nutzens in der Lutherischen Staatslehre des 16. Und 17. Jahrhunderts.* Goethe University, Frankfurt am Main.

Erasmus of Rotterdam (1509/1994), *Moriae Encomium/In Praise of Folly.* Penguin Classics, New York.

Erasmus of Rotterdam (1517), *Sileni Alcibiades.* Basel.

Euchner, Walter (1968), Versuch über Mandevilles Bienenfabel, in: Mandeville, Bernard (Ed.), *Die Bienenfabel.* Suhrkamp, Frankfurt am Main, 7–56.

Eusterschulte, Anne (2018), Zur Rezeption von ‚De officiis' bei Philipp Melanchthon und im Kreis seiner Schüler, in: Eusterschulte, Anne and Frank, Günther (Eds.), *Cicero in der Frühen Neuzeit.* Frommann-Holzboog, Stuttgart, 323–361.

Ferrarius, Johannes (1533), *Von dem Gemeinen Nutze.* Marburg.

Force, Pierre (2003), *Self-interest before Adam Smith: A Genealogy of Economic Science.* Cambridge University Press, Cambridge.

Franck, Sebastian (1534), *Paradoxa Ducenta Octoginto.* Ulm.

——— (1541), *Sprichwörter. Schöne, Weise und Herrliche Clugreden, und Hoffsprüch.* Frankfurt am Main.

Freudenberg, Matthias (2009), Economic and Social Ethics in the Work of John Calvin, *HTS Theological Studies*, 65, 1–7.

Frölich, Georg (1551), *Stobaios, Ioannes: Scharpffsinnige Sprüche.* Basel.

Fronsperger, Leonhard (1555), *Fünff Bücher von Kriegß Regiment vnd Ordnung.* Frankfurt am Main.

——— (1556), *Einn fast nützlich Weinkauffbüchlin.* Frankfurt am Main.

——— (1557), *Von Geschütz und Feuerwerck, wie dasselb zu werffen und schiessen.* Frankfurt am Main.

——— (1564a), *Von dem Lob deß Eigen Nutzen.* Frankfurt am Main.

——— (1564b), *Kriegs Ordnung Vnd Regiment sampt derselbigen Befehl statt vnd Ampter zu Roß vnd Fuß auch an Geschuetz vnd Munition in Zuegen … zu gebrauchen mit schoenen Figuren auffs neuw zugericht gemehret.* Frankfurt am Main.

——— (1564c), *Besatzung.* Frankfurt am Main.

——— (1565), *Geistliche Kriegßordnung.* Frankfurt am Main.

——— (1567), *Von Burger vnd nachbarlichem Bauhen in Staetten Marcken vnd Dorffern.* Frankfurt am Main.

——— (1573a), *Von Wagenburg und Feldtleger.* Frankfurt am Main.

——— (1573b), *Kriegsbuch.* Frankfurt am Main.

——— (1578), *Von kaiserlichen Kriegsrechten, Malefiz und Schuldhändeln Ordnung und Regiment.* Frankfurt am Main.

Goertz, Hans-Jürgen (2015), *Thomas Müntzer: Revolutionär am Ende der Zeiten. Eine Biographie.* Herder, München.

Gordon, Bruce (2009), *Calvin.* Yale University Press, New Haven.

Hawley, Michael C. (2019), Cicero's Duties and Adam Smith's Sentiments: How Smith Adapts Cicero's Account of Self-interest, Virtue, and Justice, *History of European Ideas*, 45, 705–720.

Heilbron, Johan (1998), French Moralists and the Anthropology of the Modern Era: On the Genesis of the Notion of 'Interest' and 'Commercial Society', in: Heilbron, Johan, Magnusson, Lars, and Wittrock, Björn (Eds.), *The Rise of the Social Sciences and the Formation of Modernity. Conceptual Change in Context, 1750–1850.* Kluwer, Dordrecht/ Boston/London, 77–106.

Hengstmengel, Joost W. (2016), Augustinian Motifs in Mandeville's Theory of Society, *Journal of Markets & Morality*, 19 (2), 317–338.

Hirschman, Albert O. (1977), *The Passions and the Interests.* Princeton University Press, Princeton.

Hobbes, Thomas (1651 /2010), *Leviathan. Or The Matter, Forme, & Power of a Common-Wealth Ecclesiasticall and Civill.* Yale University Press, New Haven.

Hume, David (2019), *A Treatise of Human Nature*, retrieved from https://ebookcentral. proquest.com

Hundert, E.G. (1994). *The Enlightenment's Fable: Bernard Mandeville and the Discovery of Society.* Cambridge University Press, Cambridge.

Hutten, Ulrich von (1521/2014), *Gesprächsbüchlein.* Holzinger, Berlin.

Jansen, Arne C. (2019), *Bernard Mandeville M.D. de eerste moderne psychiater. Biografie en genealogie*, retrieved from http://www.bernard-mandeville.nl/category/view/biografie -en-genealogie, 15.06.2019

Kennedy, Gavin (2009), Adam Smith and the Invisible Hand: From Metaphor to Myth, *Econ Journal Watch*, 6, 239–263.

Kern, Margit (2010), "Omnia mea mecum porto". Soziale Interaktion und Autonomie – die Rolle des Gelehrten in bildlichen Darstellungen des 16. Jahrhunderts, in: Schorn-Schütte, Luise (Ed.), *Intellektuelle in der Frühen Neuzeit.* Akademie-Verlag, Berlin, 105–134.

Klump, Rainer, and Pilz, Lars (2021), The Formation of a "Spirit of Captialism" in Upper Germany: Leonhard Fronsperger's "On the Praise of Self-Interest", *Journal of the History of Economic Thought*, 43, 401–419.

——— (2022), *"Den Fronsperger finde ich geistesgeschichtlich aufregend interessant". Zum Briefwechsel von Alexander Rüstow und Walter Eucken über das Buch "Vom Lob deß Eigen Nutzen" von 1564.* Draft, Goethe University, Frankfurt am Main.

Kohnle, Armin (2007), *Kleine Geschichte der Markgrafschaft Baden.* Lauinger, Karlsruhe.

Lehmann, Christoph (1630), *Florilegium Politicum. Politischer Blumengarten.* Wittenberg.

Luban, David (2015), Bernard Mandeville as Moralist and Materialist, *History of European Ideas*, 41 (7), 831–857.

Luther, Martin (1532/1962), Von weltlicher Obrigkeit, wie weit man ihr Gehorsam schuldig, ist / Secular Authority: To What Extent It Should Be Obeyed, in: Luther, Martin (Eds.), *Selections from his Writings.* Quadrangle Books, Chicago, 363–402.

Machiavelli, Niccolò (1513/2014), *Il Principe/The Prince.* New York. http://ebookcentral .proquest.com/lib/senc/detail.action?docID=1807411.

——— (1519–20/2003), *Dell'Arte della Guerra/The Art of War.* The University of Chicago Press, Chicago.

Mandeville, Bernard (1723), *The Fable of the Bees or, Private Vices, Publick Benefits*, II Volumes. Oxford.

Melanchthon, Philipp (1521/1997), *Loci Communes*, ed. and transl. by Hans Georg Pöhlmann, 2nd ed. Bertelsmann, Gütersloh.

——— (1559/2018), *Loci Praecipui Theologici*, ed. and transl. by Peter Litwan and Sven Grosse, Vol. I. Evangelische Verlagsanstalt, Leipzig.

Montes, Leonidas (2006): Adam Smith: real Newtonian; in: Dow, Alexander, and Dow, Sheila (Eds.), *A History of Scottish Economic Thought*. London, 102–122.

Oncken, August (1897), The Consistency of Adam Smith, *Economic Journal*, 7, 443–450.

Paganelli, Maria Pia (2008): The Adam Smith Problem in Reverse: Self-Interest in *The Wealth of Nations* and *The Theory of Moral Sentiments*, *History of Political Economy*, 40, 365–382.

Phillips, Mark (1977), *Francesco Guicciardini: The Historian's Craft*. The University of Toronto Press, Toronto/Buffalo.

Plessner, Martin (1928), *Der OIKONOMIKOC des Neupythagoreers 'Bryson' und sein Einfluß auf die islamische Wissenschaft*. Winter, Heidelberg.

Pronk, Theo (2012), Ulm, in: Adam, Wolfgang, and Westphal, Siegrid (Eds.), *Handbuch kultureller Zentren der frühen Neuzeit. Städte und Residenzen im alten deutschen* Sprachraum, *Band 3: Nürnberg-Würzburg*. De Gruyter, Berlin/Boston, 2005–2059.

Reinert, Erik S (2016), Giovanni Botero (1588) and Antonio Serra (1613): Italy and the Birth of Development Economics, in: Reinert, Erik S., Ghosh, Jayati, and Kattel, Rainer (Eds.), *Handbook of Alternative Theories of Economic Development*. Edgar Elgar Publishing, Cheltenham/Northampton, 3–41.

Ross, Ian Simpson (2010), *The Life of Adam Smith*, 2nd ed. Oxford University Press, Oxford.

Rössner, Philipp Robinson (2015), *Martin Luther on Commerce and Usury*. Anthem Press, London/New York.

Rüstow, Alexander (1945), *Das Versagen des Wirtschaftsliberalismus als religionsgeschichtliches Problem*. Europa Verlag, Istanbul/Zürich.

Sachs, Hans (1535), *Das schedlich Thier des Eygen nutz, mit sein verderblichen zwölff Eygenschafften*. Nürnberg.

Sagitarius, Johann Christfried (1664), *Hauptregister über Herrn D. Mart. Lutheri Seel. Gesampte Teutsche Schriften*. Altenburg.

Schefold, Bertram (2003), Wirtschaft und Geld im Zeitalter der Reformation, in: Schefold, Bertram, *Beiträge zur ökonomischen Dogmengeschichte*. Schäffer-Poeschel, Stuttgart, 101–126.

Schmidt, Rudolf (1903), *Deutsche Buchhändler. Deutsche Buchdrucker*, Vol. II. Weber, Berlin/Eberswalde.

Schulze, Winfried (1986), Vom Gemeinnutz zum Eigennutz – Über den Normenwandel in der ständischen Gesellschaft der frühen Neuzeit, *Historische Zeitschrift*, 243, 591–626.

——— (1988), Das Wagnis der Individualisierung, in: Cramer, Thomas (Ed.), *Wege in die Neuzeit*. Fink, München, 270–286.

Smith, Adam (1776/2012), *The Wealth of Nations*. Wordsworth, Ware.

——— (1759/2016), *The Theory of Moral Sentiments*. Enhanced Media, Los Angeles.

Stoll, Christian (2016), Stirrup, Composite Bow and Traction Trebuchet: Some Remarks on the Interdependence of War and Technology in the Early Middle Ages, in: Dworok, Gerrit, and Jacob, Frank (Eds.), *The Means to Kill – Essays on the Interdependence of War and Technology from Ancient Rome to the Age of Drones*. McFarland&Co., Jefferson, NC, 30–45.

Swain, Simon (2013), *Economy, Family, and Society from Rome to Islam: A Critical Edition, English Translation, and Study of Bryson's Management of the Estate*. Cambridge University Press, Cambridge.

Tipton, Susan (1991), Tugendspiegel einer christlichen Obrigkeit: Die Fassadendekorationen des Ulmer Rathauses, *Ulm und Oberschwaben. Zeitschrift für Geschichte und Kunst*, 47/48, 72–118.

—————— (2015), Bernard Mandeville's Vision of the Social Utility of Pride and Greed, *European Journal for the History of Economic Thought*, 22, 662–691.

—————— (2016), The Dutch Background of Bernard Mandeville's Thought: Escaping the Procrustean Bed of Neo-Augustianism, *Erasmus Journal for Philosophy and Economics*, 9 (1), 32–61

Weber, Max (1904-05/2009), *Die protestantische Ethik und der Geist des Kapitalismus / The Protestant Ethic and the Spirit of Capitalism*. Routledge, New York/London.

Weststeijin, Arthur (2012), *Commercial Republicanism in the Dutch Golden Age. The Political Thought of Johan and Pieter de la Court*. Brill, Leiden.

Weyermann, Albrecht (1829), *Neue historisch-biographisch-artistische Nachrichten von Gelehrten und Künstlern, auch alten und neuen adelichen und bürgerlichen Familien aus der vormaligen Reichsstadt Ulm*. Stettin, Ulm.

Willer, Georg (1564), *Novorum librorum, quos nundinae autumnales, Francoforti anno 1564. Celebratae, venales exhibuerunt, Catalogus*. Frankfurt am Main.

Young, Leslie (1996), The Tao of Markets: Sima Qian and the Invisible Hand, *Pacific Economic Review*, 1, 137–145.

Chapter 4

LEONHARD FRONSPERGER
'ON THE PRAISE OF SELF-INTEREST' (1564)

Translated from the original Early New High German
by Philipp Robinson Rössner with Julia McLachlan

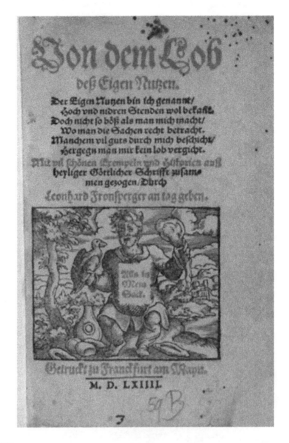

TITLE PAGE
On the praise of Self-Interest

I am known as Self-Interest,
well known to all ranks of society high and low.
But not as bad as I am made out to be
when the matter is considered clearly.
Much good is brought by me to some,
But people do not generally grant me praise.

With many illustrative examples and histories gathered
from Holy Scripture, delivered by Leonhard Fronsperger

Image: Everything in my sack

Printed in Frankfurt-am-Main
1564 AD

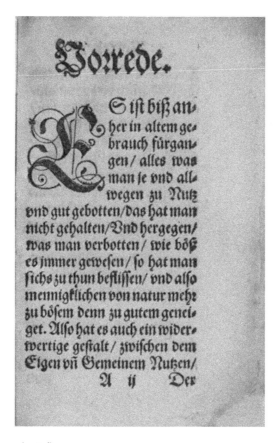

PREFACE (unpaginated)

Since the earliest of times, whatever needed to create
usefulness and good would be neglected;
however, anything that was forbidden, no matter how bad
or evil, would be eagerly attempted. From this it follows
that humanity is naturally more inclined to bad[1] than
good. Therefore, there exists a despicable rift between
Self-Interest and the Common Good.

PREFACE (unpaginated)

Self-Interest has had to let itself be disgraced and reviled
by everybody, but most commonly by those who have
received great riches, honour and goods from and through
it. In turn, the Common Good is exalted and praised, as if
no one had ever lost a *heller*[2], or had incurred any damage
or shortcomings because of it.

About this world view, custom and tradition I once
spoke to

PREFACE (unpaginated)

a gentleman and friend of mine known by the name
of Doctor Oswald Gut (may God rest his soul), then
chancellor to the Margrave [*of Baden-Durlach*] and still
alive. He had a thirst for history and old tales;
among other things we dwelled and spent much time
on the topic of Common Good, and we considered
and concluded that the matter had almost never been
examined closely; but that instead always and throughout
the history of the world, it was Self-Interest alone which
stood behind everything.

Vorrede.

allein zu thun gewesen/ vnnd
noch also darmit geschaffen ist/
solcher gestalt/ Hette oder bekeme ich nur vil/ Gott geb was
mein nechster Nachbawer hat
oder bekeme.

Dergleichen vrsachen/ Ge-
dachter mein günstiger Herr
Cantzler/ vor der selbigen zeit
im Werck ein vnterscheyd/ zwi-
schen dem Eigen vnnd gemeinen Nutzen zu beschreiben/ für-
habens gewesen/ vnd mich darzu gebetten/ als ich denn selbiger zeit mein vorhabed Kriegs-
ordnung wider auffs neuw inn
Truck auß zugehen lassen/ wil-
lens

PREFACE (unpaginated)

It is generally assumed that Self-Interest takes the following form: If only I owned or earned as much as possible; pray God give me what my neighbour has or owns.

Based on this line of thought my good chancellor set out to write about the difference between Self-Interest and the Common Good. Whilst intending to do so he asked me – as I was about to put my military manual[3] into print again – whether I was willing

Vorrede.

lens gewesen / ich wolte / oder
solte doch sein angefange werck
sein helffen auß führen / darmit es getruckt möcht werden/
zu welchem ich mich gutwillig
gegen jm erbotten / Jn dem a-
berermelter Herr Cantzler ge-
leich darauff von Gott durch
schwacheit ersucht / auch mit
Tod abgangen/vnd in Christo
dem HERRN entschlaffen / so
haben mich aber nun selbiger
zeit her / meinem bewilligeten
versprechen nach zu kommen/
hierinn vil guter Hertzen vnnd
Freunde ermahnet/welches ich
mich denn schuldig zu vollen-
den erkennt.

A   iiij   Wie-

PREFACE (unpaginated)

to help complete the little volume which he had started,
so that it could be put in print. I willingly offered him
my services; yet shortly afterwards the aforementioned
chancellor was struck by God with weakness, died and
passed away in Christ. Since this time many gentlemen
and friends have reminded me of my willing promise; and
I thus declare myself responsible for having to fulfil it.

PREFACE (unpaginated)

Even though this purpose – in this case to commence with
printing – was difficult to fulfil in this transient[4] world, I
nevertheless did not dare neglect it. I wanted to preserve
the blessed good name of the chancellor and provide an
immortal and praiseworthy memory. Therefore, I took
up the task; to carry it out in good order. I ventured
to achieve this as well as I could given my humbly
intellectual capacities, especially given the scope and
purpose of the work, and the space afforded to elaborate
on this important matter.

PREFACE (unpaginated)

Everyone should strive and provide a good example to
others and work to earn one's idleness; striving for the best
rather than spending one's life akin to the wild and foolish
beasts who only eat and drink but whose work and joyful
lives are covered by the grave and forgotten.

Lest those acting in the common interest and others
interpret what I write as shameful (I don't want to be
treading upon someone else's toes), I plan in the future to
produce a similar analysis of the Common Good

Vorrede.

ßen wolfart inn seinem werd/
nicht mit minderem lob vnnd
preyß inn sonders theil zu erörff-
nen vnd erheben/ Demnach es
aber mit der warheit zu bezeu-
gen/ wie das nichts allhie auff
Erden für recht/ gut/ oder wol
angefangen worden/ welches
nicht mit gnaden vñ gunst deß
Eignen Nutzen fürgenommen
wirdt/ derwegen es auch in al-
tem langwirigen gebrauch für
gangen/ daß man nichts/ wie
schlecht oder gering es immer
welches von hertzen vnd getreu
wer wol meynung/ darzu men-
nigklich one nachtheil vnd scha
den in eignem nutzen her fleußt
ver-

PREFACE (unpaginated)

with similar scrutiny and care; containing no less praise
and glory. Nevertheless, I hereby testify truthfully
that nothing here on earth that is right, good or well-
conceived is undertaken without the grace and favour
of Self-Interest. That is why traditionally one has not
condemned anything, no matter how bad and lowly it was
in the estimation of the heart and goodwill, if it causes no
disadvantage or harm and serves Self-Interest;

Vorrede.

verachten / sonder geneigtem
willen es auff vnd annemmen/
Vnd was aber hierin̄ von mir
dem Buchstaben nach / oder
sonst nicht wol / mit form oder
zierlichen worten auß gefůhrt
vnd gesetzt wer worden/ solches
mehr meinem wolmeinen
denn dem verstand
oder schreiben
nach zumes-
sen.

Register.

PREFACE (unpaginated)

instead it has been accepted and willingly received. And
anything below that has not been elaborated well with
letters, or nicely stated in good form and graceful words,
should be attributed to my good intentions and not the
quality of my intellect and writing.

Index

Index for this little book

On Self-Interest / chapter 1 folio 1.
On wine / and how it is the noblest creation among all /
chapter 2 folio 3.
Why flattery is better than truth / chapter 3 folio 4.
How the Goddess Folly has endeavoured to praise Self-
Interest /chapter 4 folio 8.
On the praise and good deeds of Self-Interest /
chapter 5 folio 10.

Index

Register.
der allwegen ein Eigner Nu
tzen gewesen/Cap.11. Fol. 22.
Wie der Eigen Nutzen bey den
Gelehrten bißher sein woh-
nung gehabt hat/ Cap.12.
Fol.   25.
Wie auch die Höchsten der Ni-
drigsten hilff bedörffen/
Cap. 13.   Fol.26.
Von der Welt Güter / wie die
gemein seyen / Cap. 14.
Fol.   28.
Von verwaltung eines grossen
Herren Hof. Cap. 15. Fol.29.
Was rechter Gemeiner Nu-
tzen sey/ belangt vnd inhalt/
Cap. 16.   Fol. 30.
Wie Gott kein müssiggang ge-
felt/

Index

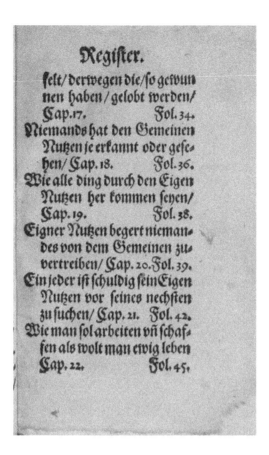

Index

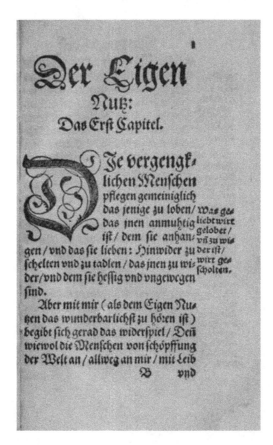

Folio 1 recto
Self-Interest: The first chapter

Mortals generally tend to praise that which they cherish;
which they are attached to and love:
On the other hand, they scold and criticise what
they dislike and towards which they feel spiteful and
unyielding.

But with me (Self-Interest, which is strange to hear)
it is the opposite way. Humans have been attracted to me
since the creation of the earth; with their bodies

What is loved is praised;
and what is abhorrent, is
scolded.

Von dem lob deß

vnd Blut / Haut vnd Har gehangen /
mich auch zum höchsten geliebt vñ geehrt / nichts one meinen Raht vnd zu-
thun angefangē / geendet oder gethan.
Also gar / daß auch der erst von Gott
selbs gemachter Mensch / durch Raht
der Schlangen / von der sie das wissen
Guts vnd Böß / begert / vnd daß der
erst Bruder / seinen Bruder vnd neben
Menschen / tod geschlagen / nichts anders denn jren eigen nutz / Glorj vnd
Ehr gesucht haben.

So hab ich doch nit allein nie kein
lob von jnen erlangen mögen / sonder
bißher leyden vnd gedulden müssen /
daß sie sich mein beschemt vnd verläug
net / mich auch zum höchsten vnd ergs
sten gelästert / geschennt / geschmecht /
vnd gescholten haben / als ob ich sey ein
Landtwerderber / ein zerstörer aller guter Pollicey / Erbarkeit / Sitten / Ei-
nigkeit / Fridens / gemach vnd ruwen /
von dem auch nichts guts je bekommen

Marginalia: Aigē nutzen wirt geehret vñnichts one sein Raht gethan. — Bruder / sein Bruder tod geschlagen vmb aigēs nutzen wegen. — Jr viel sich deß aigen nutzē beschemet / vnd verleugsnet. — Als ob er ein Lādtverderber vnd zerstörer were.

Folio 1 verso

and blood, skin and hair; and have loved and cherished me to the highest level and done, started or ended nothing without my advice and support. Even the first human created by God, when he took the advice of the snake from which he desired knowledge about good and evil, and the first who beat his brother and neighbour to death, sought nothing else than Self-Interest, glory and honour.[5]

Self-Interest is widely adhered to and nothing done without its advice.

Brother beat his brother to death due to Self-Interest.

However, I have never been praised; instead I have had to bear and suffer. People have been ashamed of me and have denied me my praise; have slandered, shunned, reviled and scolded me, as if I were a destroyer of the land, a destroyer of all good order[6], honour, customs, unanimity, peace, tranquillity and calm; as if nothing good has ever come

One has often been ashamed and denied Self-Interest its praise.

As if Self-Interest was a destroyer and corrupter of land.

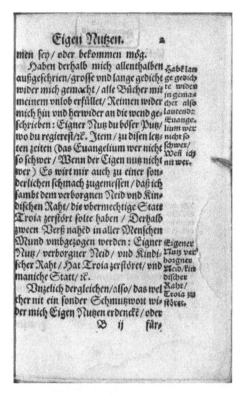

Source: MDZ Digitale Sammlungen: https://www.digitale-sammlungen.de/en/details/bsb00020768
Reprographic of the original text held by Bayerische Staatsbibliothek Munich

Folio 2 recto

or will ever come from me. Everywhere people have criticised me loudly; written big and long poems against me; filled all their books with criticisms of me; created rhymes against me and written on the walls: Self-Interest, you are bad dress[7], wherever you reign, etc. Just as in recent times (the saying goes 'The Lord's Gospel would not be so hard to follow if there was no Self-Interest'[8]). I am particularly humiliated by the belief that I together with hidden envy and childish [*immature*] advice am to be held responsible for the destruction of the powerful city of Troy. That is why two verses have been put in nearly all people's mouths: 'Self-Interest, concealed envy, and childish advice destroyed Troy and many other big city.'[9] Equally countless are those who do not condemn and insult me, Self-Interest

They wrote long poems against me, such as: The gospel would not be so hard to follow if it wasn't for me.

Self-Interest, hidden envy, childish advice destroyed the city of Troy.

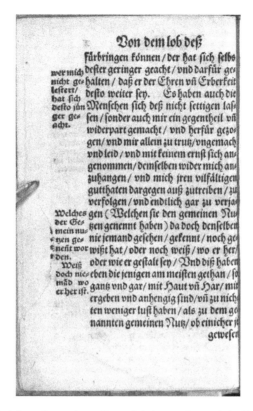

Source: MDZ Digitale Sammlungen: https://www.digitale-sammlungen.de/en/details/bsb00020768
Reprographic of the original text held by Bayerische Staatsbibliothek Munich

Folio 2 verso

and who therefore think they have to think badly of themselves, and believe they are not honourable or respectable. People have not been satisfied by this, and have made an adversary and opponent of me; have opposed and defied me, to my detriment and suffering, and have not considered me seriously. Instead they have shut me out and denied my influence on their many good deeds (which they attributed instead to the Common Good), even though no one has ever seen, recognised, or known the Common Good, or knows where it has come from, or which shape it takes. And this was done mostly by those who are wholly, with skin and hair, devoted and attached to me, and who want to do nothing less than contribute to said Common Good, regardless of whether the latter ever had existed (or still exists).

Those who do not gossip about me, have to think badly of themselves.

This was called Common Good.
But nobody knows where it comes from.

Eigen Nutzen.   3

gewesen oder noch wer / welches nicht
ein kleine vndanckbarkeit gegen mir/
so doch dargegen die warheit ist / vnd
hernach mit bedeutlichen vnd begriff-
lichen Argumenten / sol bewisen vnd
dargethan werden/ daß ich nicht allein *Eigē nu-*
nit so böß bin / als mir meine vndanck- *ze ist nit*
bare Kinder zulegen / sonder auch daß *so böß/*
sondern
die gantze Welt / durch mich in guter *die gantz*
Ordnung vnd Policei friden / bestand *welt wirt*
vnd wesen erhalten würd/ vnd von an- *erhaltē.*
fang erhalten worden ist/ one mich auch
nicht bestehen köndt oder möchte.

    Die wort lauten wol hart/ vnd sind
schwer vnd seltzam zu hören/ Das ma-
chet / daß ich so gar allenthalben ver-
schrien/ vnd in meiner verantwortung *Eigē nu-*
nie gehört bin/ sich deren auch nie nie- *ze ist nie*
mand vnterzogen hat.   Aber wenn jr *zuuerant*
wortung
die sach in jr selbs mit gleichem vrtheil *komen.*
bedencken/ so werdet jrs befinden/ daß
ich recht vnd war sag vnd hab/rc.

    Denn vil ding sind bey den Men-
            B iij   schen

Folio 3 recto

This is not only doing me quite a disservice, but a
disservice to the truth. And in the following I shall prove
with meaningful and illustrative arguments that not only
am I not as evil as my ungrateful children think, but
also that through me the whole world is maintained and
preserved in good public order, shape and peace; and
was maintained from the beginning; and could not be
maintained without me.

Self-Interest is not that
bad or evil; instead the
whole world is maintained
through it

These words sound harsh and might be difficult and
strange to digest. That's because I have such a bad
reputation, and my responsibility is never acknowledged;
and no one has ever devoted themselves to this proposition
seriously. But if you regard the matter in itself with
objective judgement, you will find that I am right and
speak the truth.

Self-Interest's responsibility
has never been
acknowledged.

Because many things are regarded by people

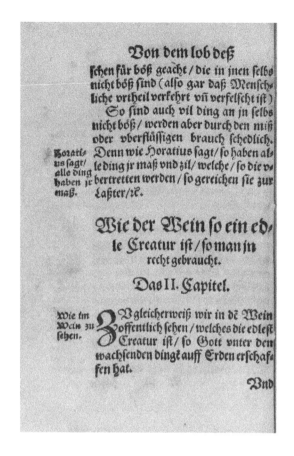

Folio 3 verso

as evil, that are not evil in themselves (this means that
human judgement is likely wrong and distorted).

And there are many things that are not evil in themselves,
but become harmful through misuse or excessive use.
Because as Horace said, all things have a certain measure,   Horace says there is a
and when this measure is overstepped, they become a   middle ground in (all)
vice.   things

**How wine is a noble creation / as long as it is
used correctly
Chapter II**

This is how the public sees wine, which is the noblest   As we can see in wine
thing that God has created on earth.

Folio 4 recto

And who wants to speak about its great and exuberant
virtues and uses? It gives to people health, long lives,
refreshment, happiness of mind and heart; all books are   Wine brings good health
full of it. Even the Psalmist has not been able to restrain   and sorrow alike
himself from praising wine, and he says: The wine makes
people's hearts happy.

But if wine, the noble creation, is used too heavily and
excessively, who wants to tell every now and then of the   Wine brings not as much
great disadvantages, misfortunes and unfortunate damage   usefulness as damage to
it causes people and their bodies, souls, honour and   expect when abused.
wealth? There is not so much usefulness in wine as there is
great damage and spoil when abused. However, this must
not be attributed to wine, or its nature in itself (which is
good), but rather its

Folio 4 verso

excessive use. And so it is with all things in this whole wide world: nothing is ever so good that it couldn't also cause damage and detriment in numerous ways through abuse or excessive use. On the other hand, nothing is so bad that it couldn't principally serve a useful and good purpose when used skilfully and right. And this I want to bring to light clearer as shall be heard in the following chapter.

This is the same for all things in the world

About flattery and how it is sometimes better than the truth
Chapter III

Flattery should be considered highly.

Who could not hold that flattery is the best, whereas usually the truth, contrary to flattery (we

Folio 5 recto

want to talk about the truth here) is regarded and thought
of as the highest, best and most exquisite thing in the
world, so that all books of the wise and the learned are
full of truth's praise? However, if you look at the matter at
its core, flattery may, when used correctly and well, bring
good; whereas the truth can lead to bad things. Yes, this
may sound highly surprising, but flattery and truth do not
stand in each other's way.

Flattery can cause good,
while the truth can cause
bad.

Therefore, watch out for it: if everyone freely told the
other one the truth about what he carried in his heart and
how he truthfully felt about the other, may God help us!
what a life, what slaughter, envy, hate, war, strife, uproar,
unpleasantness and infinite evil would grow out of it! How
could or would anyone possibly want

Should everyone tell each
other the truth, what would
be the result?

Folio 5 verso

to stay or live with one another.

Some people wish others a good evening or morning and thank them for their service, and [say] much good about them, following common habit; whereas in fact they would rather that all the misfortunes befell the other. Some tell the others sweet words, but in reality would rather be at the other's neck instead.

One tells the other kind words, but would rather hit him in the neck

Now decide for yourselves: Would flattery not be better here than the truth? It is through flattery that friendship between people is upheld; discord and enmity are avoided. Flattery creates much good. The youth are educated by it. The father flatters the child; the child flatters the father; the lord his vassal; the vassal his lord; one friend and neighbour flatters the other, and through such flattery

That is why flattery is better than the truth.

Folio 6 recto

all things are preserved in order, peace, chastity, and their natural character. However, the truth (which we are speaking about here, which I often have to repeat lest my words be twisted) often causes offensiveness, discord, quarrel, disorder, destruction and huge disadvantages.

Through flattery all things are preserved in order but the truth causes discord.

For flattery has such wondrous powers, that even though the recipient recognises it and knows it is flattery, he prefers this to the blunt truth.

Through flattery better things are created than through truth

Because he thinks it is an honour that the person who flatters him thus holds him in such high esteem, and is afraid to tell him the truth outrightly and bluntly without the cover of flattery. This is why Terence said: Friends are won through flattery, truth gives birth to hate.[10]

Terence says Friends are won through flattery; truth gives birth to hate.

Folio 6 verso

From all this we have to and want to conclude that flattery is inherent to all beings and was given to them by nature, as one can also see clearly in the example of animals who are not blessed with reason. Therefore, when flattery is scolded and reprimanded by wise men and scholars, this shouldn't apply to flattery in general, but rather the bad and mischievous kind of flattery, where one wants to cause another person damage and disadvantage; but not the good flattery, which preserves and sows peace, love and unanimity. On the other hand, the sort of truth that creates quarrel and discord builds nothing and brings no good; it should not be praised. But the truth which serves good and is necessary should be. Mariamne the most beautiful and beloved

Bad flattery is not good; it causes harm to the world

Truth is praised if it doesn't create quarrel and discord.

Eigen Nutzen.   7

liebgehabteſt / Königliche Gemahel /
deß groſſen Herodis / ſagt nicht vnwar
daran / da ſie jrem Herrn dem König
auffhub vnd verwiß / das er vnedel vnd
von Beuriſchem herkommen war /
Warzu war aber ſolche Warheit jr o=
der andern nutz / ja auch von nöten / da=
durch ſie den mechtigen vnd gewalti=
gen König Herodem dermaſſen zu zo=
ren bewegt / das er ſie vmb ſolche jr fre=
fel reden tödten ließ / darauß nachmals
vil vbels entſtunde.

(margin: Königes Gemahel jrē Herrn auff hub / ſein Beu= riſch her= kommen / Warzu war ſolch Warheit nutz / ſie war dar= umb ge= tödt.)

Jr vnd andern / ja auch dem gan=
tzen Land / wer vil nützer vnd darzu löb=
licher geweſen / das ſie jm geſchmeich=
let vnd liebkoſet / vnd diſe warheit ver=
ſchwigen / vnd bey jr behalten hett / die
zu keinem guten / aber wol zu groſſem
argem dienen mocht.

(margin: Hette ſie dafür / o= der die= weil ge= ſchmeich= let / were jr Beſſer geweſen)

Wer könnt oder möcht nicht zum
höchſten dargegen loben die vbertref=
fenliche dapffer vnd redlichkeit / deß al=
lerheyligiſten von Frawen leib geborn
Johan=

Folio 7 recto

royal wife of Herod the Great, did not lie when she opened her heart to the king and disclosed to him that he was not of noble blood but had descended from farmers. But what necessity or use was this truth to her or others, since it moved the mighty and powerful King Herod to such anger that he had her killed for her act of sacrilege, and great evil came from it.

Royal wife opening her heart and telling the truth about his peasant roots; what use was that? She was killed because of it

For her and others, in fact for the whole country, it would have been much more useful and commendable if she had flattered and caressed him instead and kept this truth a secret and kept the secret with her. It did not serve her any good, but great evil.

If she had flattered him instead, she would have been better off.

On the other hand, who would and could not want to praise the unsurpassable bravery and integrity of the most holy Saint John the Baptist

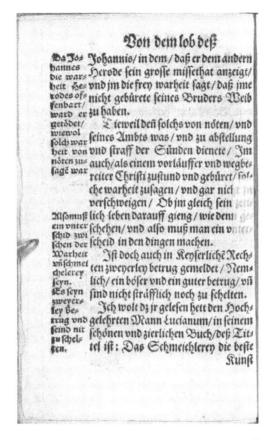

Source: MDZ Digitale Sammlungen: https://www.digitale-sammlungen.de/en/details/bsb00020768
Reprographic of the original text held by Bayerische Staatsbibliothek Munich

Folio 7 verso

as he advised the other Herod[11] of his wrongdoing and freely told him the truth, which was that he did not deserve to have his brother's wife.

Because Saint John told Herod the truth, he was killed; although it was necessary to tell this truth

While this was necessary and was his duty, to punish and prevent further sin, he was also ordained and entitled to tell this truth and not keep silent, because he was a predecessor and later on companion of Christ; even though he paid with his worldly life as it were. Thus one has to carefully distinguish between these matters.

Therefore there must be a difference between the truth and flattery

There are two types of fraud in imperial law, namely an evil and a good fraud, the latter of which should not be deemed criminal.

Two types of betrayal, they shouldn't both be scolded

I wish you had read the erudite Lucian's[12] beautiful and delicate book on how flattery is the highest art

Folio 8 recto

on earth, and he speaks about the subject with this understanding of flattery. I know you will not be able to contradict me in this, there are two sides to all things in the world; just as was the case with the *Sileni Alcibiadis*.[13] And everything can bring forth good or evil, depending on whether used for evil or for good, as has been stated above.

Of the Goddess Folly[14]/ how she undertook the praise of Self-Interest
Chapter IV

I will now return to my initial undertaking. I know forthright that I, Self-Interest, bring good things and need little defense; especially not against those who turn against me only in words

All things have two sides to them

Von dem lob deß

Die dem mir zu wider/ vnd der that gantz anhen-
gen zu wi- tzen zu wi- gig sind/ sonst wo das nicht wer/ würd
der seyen ich mich vnselig schetzen / in dem/ das
vnd doch mir nicht auch ein solcher trefflicher
götz an- hangen. fürsprech zugestanden.

Als die Göttin Narrheit/ob sie an-
derst ein Göttin zu vernemmen ist/ einen bekommen / der sich meins lobs vnterzogen hat/ welche/ wiewol sie vor-
mal gar veracht vnd verspottet gewe-
sen/ Jedoch durch den Hochgelehrten
Eraß. võ vbertrefflichen beredten Mann/Eraß-
Roterdã meldet. mus von Roterdam/ also gelobt vnd
herfür gestrichen ist / das man jetzt darfür halt/vnd glaubt/das sie Menschlichem Geschlecht nicht geringen verstand vnd nutz schaffe/ vnd derhalb nit
wenig geehrt wirt/ wiewol dasselb E-
Göttin narrheit rasmus in solchem andern meinen vn-
lobnit jr/ danckbarn Kindern nit vngleich sich
sonder dé Eigē Nu- gehalten / in dem/ das er der gemelten
tzen entzo- gen. Göttin Narrheit fast alles das lob (so
mir eigentlichen zugehört/ zugezogen/
vnd

Folio 8 verso

but are very attracted to me in their actions. If this wasn't so, I would consider myself unfortunate, because I would not deserve such splendid endorsement.

Even the Goddess Folly – if she can indeed be understood to be a goddess – found someone who would undertake her praise, although she was once despised and mocked. However, she was praised and affirmed by the erudite and unsurpassably eloquent Erasmus of Rotterdam, so that now one is of the opinion and believes, that she is of great use to mankind and its wit and therefore is not so sparsely praised. However, at the same time Erasmus did not treat me fairly, since he – not unlike some of my other ungrateful children – bestowed upon the aforementioned Goddess of Folly almost all the praise (which should have been mine and had been

Those who oppose Self-Interest, but are actually attached to it

According to Erasmus

Praise for the goddess of folly should not be given to her but to Self-Interest.

Folio 9 recto

unjustly taken from me). At the same time, I have been
more than a little bewildered at what could be the reason
that nothing on earth is so disdainful that it hasn't found
someone who has bestowed praise upon it: Erasmus and
his folly; Ulrich von Hutten and the fever; even baldness –
such a disdainful thing! And the drunkenness during our
times, praised through fables of the virtuous poet Aesopus.

I alone am poor Greten's [Greta/Gretchen] son; someone
through which the existence and essence of the whole
world is preserved. But not only am I not praised by
anyone; I am also also reviled, despised and scorned by
all humanity, even by those who are attracted to me and
who love me. However, I console myself with the thought
that the learned and virtuous men tend to take to the most
disdainful things and praise them,

Self-Interest is poor Greta's
son; not praised by anyone;
but scolded instead

Von dem lob deß

damit sie jren scharpffen verstand vnd
Kunst / daß sie auß nichts etwas ma=
chen / vnd ein ding das bey jedermann
veracht / hoch erheben / desto mehr er=
zeigen vnd beweisen mögen / darauß
denn mir / als dem Eigen Nutzen ein

Ein still= stillschweigend lob zuwechst / wie Ha=
schwei= nibal geacht / vnd Scipian in dem ge=
geb lob/
wie Han= sprech / zu erst zugemessen haben / in de
bal vnnd daß er jn auß der zal der dreyen fürtreff
Scipion
zu ehr ge lichsten Haubtleut außschloß / vñ sich
messen. selbs für den dritten der ganzen Welt
Höfflich setzt / aber darneben gar höfflich schmei
schmeich
ler vnnd chelt / vnnd sagt: Wenn er obgelegen
sagt. wer / er sich nicht für den dritten / son
der für den ersten gesetzt haben wolt/
Also wil vnd muß ich auch darfür ach
Die Ge= ten / das die Gelehrten für ein geringe
lehrten Kunst geacht haben / mich zuloben/
für ringe vnd sich der vrsachen dessen nicht vn=
Kunst ach
ten. terzogen / dieweil sie darmit kleinen
ruhm getrauwet zu erlangen / Wel=
ches nicht ein klein stillschweigend be=
kannt=

Folio 9 verso

creating something out of nothing; elevating a thing which
everyone despises, so that they can demonstrate and
prove their sharp intellect and abilities even more. But
implicit praise is bestowed on me from this, similar to the
case of Hannibal who, in his conversation with Scipio[15],
excluded him [Scipio] from his list of the three greatest
military commanders and named himself [Hannibal] as
the third greatest in the whole world. But at the same time
he politely flattered Scipio by saying that if he [Hannibal]
had suffered defeat by [Scipio], he would not have named
himself as the third greatest, but as the greatest military
commander in the world. So I propose that learned men
consider it too lowly a skill to write my praises, without
fully considering the reasons for it. Through this omission
they hoped to gain some small honour; which all in all is a
not unsubstantial yet tacit

An implicit praise as
Hannibal bestowed on
Scipio politely flattered
and said.

The learned men consider
it a lowly skill.

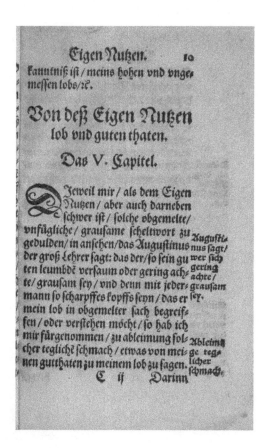

Folio 10 recto

acknowledgement of my high and immeasurable praise.
(Summary of argument: Learned men praise things which are
considered despicable to prove their rhetorical and intellectual
abilities; Self-Interest has not been praised as it is not that
despicable; therefore, this implicitly praises Self-Interest)

On the praise of Self-Interest, and its good deeds
Chapter V

However it is difficult for me as Self-Interest to tolerate
these unreasonable and cruel insults mentioned above;
considering how Saint Augustine the great teacher
said that he who doesn't think highly of himself is cruel
[upon himself]. Therefore, to ensure that everyone is of
keen mind and can understand my praise, I intend to
compensate for this daily humiliation, by praising myself
and saying something about my good deeds as stated
above.

Saint Augustine said he
who thinks little of himself
is cruel.

Compensation for daily
humiliation.

Folio 10 verso

A common and traditional saying goes that he who praises himself approvingly and righteously will not be praised by anyone else and has bad neighbours.[16] But this might be interpreted less to the disadvantage of my reputation than it would for others; for I am Self-Interest itself. Therefore writing my own praise does not befit me so badly.

For I am Self-Interest itself

I am aware that it is not necessary at the start of my speech to ask for your goodwill and your willing attention; because I have always known that you are all favourably inclined and attracted towards me, opposing me only in words; but you are not particularly serious about this opposition.

For this reason, I don't doubt that my speech will appear simplistic to you. I only ask one thing: that you do not force yourselves, after you've heard me, to pass judgement against me when this is against what your hearts and thoughts are telling you.

Many of you will pass judgement against me, which goes against what your heart is telling you.

Eigen Nutzen.   11

hertzen sey / so zweiffelt mir nicht / ich
wölle mit meiner / wiewol schlechten
red/ vnd guten greifflichen Argumen=
ten/ euch dahin bringen / daß jr beken=
nen werdet/ vnd müßt/ daß jr mich biß
her/ wiewol allein mit worten / vnbil= *Eigener
lich geleſtert vnd geſchmecht habt/ vnd Nutze iſt
das alles daß gut/ ſo auff Erden iſt/ biſher
nach dem waren allmechtigen ewigen mit vn=
Gott/ von dem vrſprüngklich alles her worte ge
kombt/ mir fürnemlich ſol vnd muß zu leſtert
gemeſſen werden/ vñ auff das ich euch worden.
durch lang Vorred nit auffhalt / vnd
mein ſach in zweiffel ſtell / ſo wil ich es
kürtzlich angreiffen.

Wie die Welt bißher
durch den Ehſtand
vnd Eigen Nutzen
erhalten ſey.

Das VI. Capitel.
C iij   Vnd

Folio 11 recto

Do not doubt me, despite my badly articulated speech, using good and illustrative arguments I will bring you to the point at which you will have to admit that until now, although only with words, you have gossiped and reviled me unreasonably; and that everything on earth which is good, after the true almighty and eternal God created everything in the beginning, has to and must be attributed first and foremost to me. This is why I won't bother you with a long opening speech with which to cast doubt upon my issue, but will address the matter now presently and swiftly.

Self-Interest has been the subject of unjustified gossip so far.

How the world has so-far been preserved through marriage and Self-Interest
Chapter VI

Folio 11 verso

If we begin by asking through what the world, from its very
first beginnings and creation, has so far been preserved
and expanded; and how it will expand and be preserved
in times to come, until the end of the world, there could
and would be no other answer than that this happens
through marriage. If you were to give a different answer,
you would be disproven not only by Holy Scripture but by
natural reason also. Holy Scripture clearly shows that the
true Almighty and Eternal Lord, after He created heaven
and earth and everything contained in it, and created
Man, too; created nothing more valuable and precious
than marriage. Through His eternal divine word, He
ordered Man to be fruitful and expand the world[17], as He
recognised in his divine wisdom and council that the world
without matrimony and marriage

No other answer could be
given than marriage.

The Lord created heaven
and earth; marriage was
created within.

Eigen Nuꜩen.   12

Eheſtand nicht könnt oder möchte be- *Die Welt*
ſtehn/ oder erhalten werden.   *one den*
      Ehſtand
    Denn warzu were es gut oder für- *nit könne*
treglich / wenn gleichwol Kinder auß *beſtehn.*
anreizung der Natur geboren / wenn *Von Kin-*
nicht auch dieſelben ernehrt / erzogen/ *derziehe.*
vnd vnterhalten würden.

    Nun kan aber ein jeder auch auß
Menſchlicher vernunfft außrechnen/
daß die erziehung der Kinder one den
Eheſtand nicht ſeyn könnte / ſo alle ge-
burten gemein/ vnd vermiſcht ſeyn ſol-
ten / Alſo / daß man bekennen müſſe/
nicht allein auß zwang der heyligen
Schrifft / ſonder auch auß Menſchli- *Der Eha-*
cher vernunfft / daß der Eheſtand ſey *ſtand ein*
ein einziger erhalter vnd erweiter deß *erweite-*
Menſchlichen Geſchlechts.   *rung vñ*
      erhaltũg
    Nun wöllen aber wir den befelh vñ *Menſch-*
ewigen willen Gottes hindan ſeꜩen/ *lichs Ge-*
welchem alle Geſchöpff vnd Creatu- *ſchlechts.*
ren billich ſollen vnd müſſen gehorſam
leiſten / dem auch billich alle ehr zu for-
            C iiij   derſt

Folio 12 recto

could and would not exist, nor be preserved.

Because what good or advantage would it be if children
were born only because of natural allure[18], without
a perspective of being fed, educated and properly
maintained?

Now everyone endowed with human reasoning skills
can work out that raising children would be impossible
outside matrimony, since all offspring would be mixed and
raised by all in common. Therefore, one has to recognise
that marriage alone preserves and expands the human
race, not just following the commandments of the Holy
Scripture but also due to human reasoning.

But for now, we will set aside the commandments and the
eternal will of God by which all creatures and beasts must
abide, to which respect shall be paid above all else

The world could not exist
without marriage.

On raising children
marriage expands and
preserves humanity.

Von dem lob deß

derst zugelegt sol werden / von alle Creaturen / vnd allein betrachten vnd für
vns nemmen / auff was vrsachen vnd
bewegungen die menschē jrem menschlichem affection nach / in den Ehestand
kommen / vnd was sie darinn suchen /
als vil sie antrifft / werdet jr fürwar be
finden / daß ich Eigner Nutz / deß Ehestands bey den Menschen die gröst vñ
erst vrsach bin.

Denn auß was vrsachen vnd bewegungen kommen die Menschen zusammen in die Ehe / geschicht dz allein auß
vrsach / daß sie fürsatz vnd willen haben / nach dem Göttlichen ewigen befelch die Welt zu mehren / jme zu lob
vnd zu ehren Kinder zu ziehen / oder
Heuraten die Leut vmb gemeines nutz
willen / vnd demselben zu gut zu acht nit /
das jemand so vnbesind sey / der solches
sagen werd / oder auch mit warheit könne / wiewol es also gemainglich in die
Heuratsbrieff / mehr auß einer gewonheit

Folio 12 verso

by all creatures. Instead we shall only consider people's reasons and motivations to follow their feelings and seek marriage. And you will surely find that I, Self-Interest, am the greatest and first reason for matrimony.

Because for which reasons and motivations do people come together in marriage? It happens for the sole reason that they are planning and willing to follow God's eternal commandment to populate the world; to raise children in His praise and honour. Or do people marry for the sake of the Common Good? You would not think that someone would be so unwise as to seriously claim such a thing, just because the marriage certificate is commonly written according to the customs

Self-Interest is the main reason for marriage.

People do not marry for the Common Good but for Self-Interest.

> ### Eigen Nußen.   13
>
> heit vnd form der Schreiber/denn daß
> also inn warheit vnd ernst sey/gesetzt
> wirt/sonder geschicht solches mehrers
> theils/durchauß/auß sonderlichem af=
> fect/gesuch/ annmuhtig vnd eigen nutz=
> barkeit der gemeinen befelhen Raht/
> auß Natürlicher begirligkeit/die von
> der Natur eingepflantzt ist/folgt nach
> seinem gelust vñ willen/demselben ein
> genügen zu thun/ Vnd so demselben
> durch ander weg/denn den Eheftand
> ein genügen zu thun/zügelassen/würd
> er die Ehe nicht begeren/ Vnd weil es
> gleichgute vrsachen bey jm hat/so be=
> gert er der Ehe darumb/daß er one den   Jm Ehe
> Eheftand nicht füglich kan haußhal=   stand su=
> ten/vnd also sucht er doch dariñ nichts   chet jeder
> anderfts denn sein eigen nutzen.   sein eige
>   nutzen.
>   Die so höhers stands seyn/habē ein
> jeder auch sein sonder bedencken/vnd je
> einer anderß denn der ander/nach dem
> eins jeden gelegenheit vñ gemüt sichet/
> vnd gemeinigklich durchauß ist/ daß
>   C v   bey

Folio 13 recto

and conventions of the scribes who certify the marriage that way
[i.e. *implying that marriage takes place for a higher goal such as Common
Good*]. Truth is instead that marriage occurs because of affection,
wooing, grace and the fact that its pursuit serves Self-Interest and
natural desires implanted by Nature. If people had alternative
options to satisfy such lust and desires, they would not seek
marriage. And even if they had other good reasons, their main
motivation to seek marriage is because they could not manage[19]
without it. Therefore pursuing matrimony, they do only seek their
own Self-Interest.

In marriage
everyone seeks to
fulfil Self-Interest.

Those of upper rank and status have their own concerns, one
different than the other, depending on opportunity and disposition.
And in fact it often is the case that

Von dem lob deß

Doch bey allen/hochs vnd niders stands köñe
standtkön oder möcht man künlich one Ehe ge=
nen nicht seyn/also dz der natürlich eigennützig
affect/oder natürlich eingepflantzte be=
girlichkeit nicht dahin drünge vnd rei=
gete/so were zu besorgen/dz von Gott
oder deß gemeinen nutz wegé niemand
oder wenig Heuraten würden/ich wil
hie geschweigen/wenn man also auß
eigennützigen vrsachen entschlossen ist
zu Heuraten/was demnach weiter am
forderisten gesucht vnd angesehen wirt.
O wie wer das so für gut an zunem
men/daß man doch alßdenn nach der
lieb Heurate/daß doch der Heydnisch
Poet nicht hat wöllen lassen gut seyn/
da er scheltender weiß spricht: Die ge=
stalt/nicht die Haußfrauwen wirt lieb
gehabt/als wolt er sagen: Man Heu=
rat nicht vmb der vrsachen willen/dar=
umb man Heuraten sol/sondern auß
Fleischlicher begirligkeit vnd anmuth/
denn eben dasselb auch frömbkeit vnd
Ehr/

Folio 13 verso

everyone, upper or lower rank of people couldn't and wouldn't want to be married unless Self-Interest or natural desire urged and appealed them to. Nobody or only very few would marry for the Lord's sake, or for the Common Good. I do not want to elaborate further about marrying out of Self-Interest and what other drives and motivations stand behind it.

Upper and lower ranks cannot be without marriage and me, Self-Interest.

Few marriages take place for the Common Good.

Oh, how good it would be if we could assume that instead one married for love. But the heathen poet did not accept this and said scoldingly: The body is loved, not the housewife; as if to say: One doesn't marry for the reasons for which one should marry, but for bodily desire. For the same reason even piety and honour

The heathen poet affirms that marriage doesn't usually take place for the reason that it ultimately should (love) but rather for utility and pleasure.

Folio 14 recto

are cast aside. Instead most marry for property, power, land and people. Just consider how many wars you have seen and experienced, that resulted from marriages; because one ruler used force and cunning and other things to push the other ruler away and steal their promised spouse, just for the sake of kingdoms, land and people; while the other ruler thus robbed had sought marriage first and foremost for exactly the same reasons, but without using unfair practices. These examples are spiteful, but I could just as easily demonstrate how in your times this has occurred even amongst those of lower rank. Property and money clearly are preferred, so here, too, nothing else is sought and considered. Honour, piety and beauty are hardly important; this is why a woman old and wrinkly

Most people marry for property; nothing good comes from this.

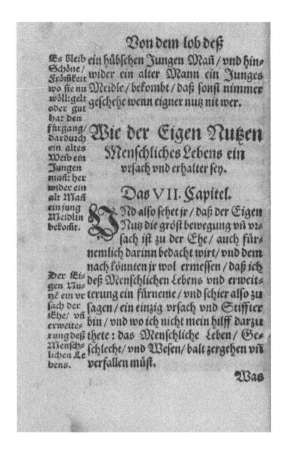

Folio 14 verso

can get a handsome young man; and on the other hand, an old man can marry a young girl. This would not happen if Self-Interest didn't exist.

How Self-Interest is the origin and preserver of human life
Chapter VII

And so you can see how Self-Interest is the greatest motivator and reason for marriage, and is considered above all else. Therefore, you will surely acknowledge that I am a key if not the only reason for the preservation and expansion of human life. And if it were not for my aid: human life, lineages and character would soon dissolve and decay.

Beauty and piety don't matter: money and property have priority; this is why an old woman can get a young man: on the other hand, an old man can marry a young girl

Self-Interest is a reason for marriage and expansion of human life.

Folio 15 recto

What greater thing can be said or stated in my favour than
that I cause, initiate, spread and preserve all human life and
character?

I also wanted to show that I not only cause and initiate
matrimonial friendship, but all friendships in general. I am
aware that this is no small factor in my praises; as Cicero
said (and all others agree with him): if someone were to take
friendship from the people, it would be the same as if they
pulled the sun away from the earth. Thereby he clearly
wanted to show that human life could not exist, and would
be nothing, without friendship.

Self-Interest is not only
the cause of marriage
but also all other actions;
Cicero said this; all others
agree with him.

As I have proved many times, matrimonial friendship,
which is the highest of all,

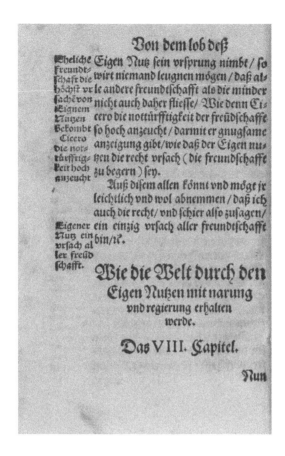

Folio 15 verso

has its cause and roots in Self-Interest. Therefore no one will be able to deny that all other friendship stems from Self-Interest, as well. When Cicero demonstrated the necessity of friendship, he gave plenty of evidence that Self-Interest is the true origin (of seeking friendships).

Matrimonial friendship is the highest kind of friendship.

Cicero demonstrated how necessary it is.

From all this you surely can and will want to deduce, that I am the true, nay even to say, the only cause of all friendships.

Self-Interest is the cause of all friendship.

How the world is nourished, governed and preserved through Self-Interest
Chapter VIII

[N.B. *Nahrung* – literally "nourishment", "food" or "sufficiency" is an idiosyncratic term from early modern German economic language: it covered, on top of its literal meaning ("food on the table"), also "professions"; the way the necessary income is earned, and also that income itself]

Folio 16 recto

However, all of this is not yet sufficient proof, if I don't also testify and demonstrate that food and *Nahrung*, clothes, government, and all goods necessary to preserve us humans, after we are born and raised, come first from God; but then from my graces. Therefore I want to show clearly that if it wasn't for me, Self-Interest, humans would not only never be born; but if they were, they would be wanting of all things.

Clothes and *Nahrung* come, first from God, but then from me, Self-Interest

This I want to demonstrate with blunt and tangible evidence. It is well-known that all human life and public order (*Policey*) are preserved chiefly through two things: firstly, food and *Nahrung*; secondly, temporal [secular] authority.

Nahrung and government [*Regierung*]

Nahrung covers not only food and drink, but also clothing, housing, medicine and what[ever else] people require

Maintaining the body.

Folio 16 verso

and need to maintain their bodies.

The world is divided into spiritual and temporal [secular] government [Ger. *Regierung*], that is the perception of God and observance of prayer, and the protection of the secular order [as princes, Kings and rulers do]. That's why in ancient times the human governance and social structures (Ger. *menschliche Policey*) were skilfully divided into three.

Spiritual and secular order.

Namely, into the Emperor, Pope and Farmers [as a collective third estate], as can be seen in all those paintings with the title *Tu supplex ora; tu protegeme; tu labora*, meaning that the Pope [the Church] shall pray; the Emperor [the State] shall protect, and the farmer shall work.

Pope / Emperor / farmer.

To pray means the proclamation and teaching of the word of God and His commandments; praying to God for everything that the human race deserves in the face of the Lord.

Teaching God's will.

To protect means guarding everything that is necessary to support and preserve human life

Eigen Nutzen. 17

schen erfordert wirt/vnd fürwar/wo
es bey solcher theilung blieben wer/vñ
noch blieb/vnd ein jeder seins Ambts *Einjeder*
vnd beruffs warnemme/vnd auff sich *seines*
selbs/vnd seinen stand/darein er gese- *Ambts*
tzet vnd verordnet/acht hette/so wür- *warten.*
de gewißlich alle ding in der Welt bey
den Menschen inn guter ordnung stehen.

   Weñ aber der Babst/als der Geist *Weñ der*
lich stand/das Gebett vnd Gottes- *Babst be*
dienst verlest/vnd sich deß schirms der *tē verlest*
Regierung vnterziehen wil. Deßglei- *vnnd sich*
chen der Keyser den schirm/das ist/das *deß welt-*
Weltliche Regiment versaumbt/vnd *lichen an*
sich der Geistlichkeit beladen. Vnd *nimbt.*
der Pauer sich der beyder annemmen *Der Key*
wil/so müssen von not wegen alle ding *ser den*
vermischt werden/vnd in vnordnung *schirm*
vnd zertrennung kommen/wie sich zu *versau-*
vnsern zeiten offenbarlich an den tag *met.*
vnd zuerkennen gibt/vnd noch vil er- *Der pau*
ger vnd böser wer/wo ich Eigener Nu *er sich sol*
         O   tzen *der an- nimt wie denn ge sehen,*

Folio 17 recto

and surely, if this division had remained, and continued
to remain in place, and everyone stuck to their office and
profession and stayed within their own status [social order]
into which they had been born, then surely all things would
be in good order.

> Everyone should stick to their ordained office and profession.

But if the Pope, representing the spiritual order, left his
prayer and worship and instead wanted to appropriate
the guardianship of the government [i.e. usurp powers
of temporal authority], or if the Emperor neglected his
guardianship that is the worldly order [temporal or secular
authority] seeking spiritual authority instead; or if the
farmer wanted to assume either of the other two, then all
things would inevitably become confused. The public order
would be in disarray and divided, as so often happens these
days. And the state of things would turn out even worse, if it
wasn't for me, Self-Interest

> When the Pope leaves prayer and turns to worldy matters instead.

> When the Emperor neglects his guardianship.

> When the Farmer usurps both, as happens to be the case in our days.

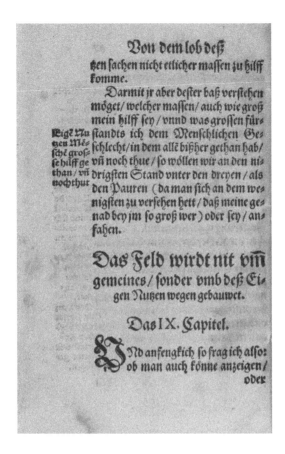

Folio 17 verso

coming to aid.

But just so you understand what exactly and how great my help is really, and what great assistance I have delivered to the people in everything so far, and still do, let's look at the lowest order [status] of the three, that is the farmers (so you can see with those who have least how great my mercy is).

Self-Interest was and is a great aid to humans.

The field is not tilled for the Common Good / but for Self-Interest
Chapter IX

To start off I shall therefore ask: Is it possible to determine or say that

Eigen Nußett. 18

oder sagen / daß je ein Pawers Mann
erfunden sey worden / oder noch zu
erfunden sey / der vmb gemeins Nuß
willen / fürnemlich / vnd inn betrach-
tung desselben die Ecker gebawt / oder
welcher einen Pflug in das Feld gefü-
ret würd haben / wenn jn nicht Eigner
Nuß darzu gedrungen oder verrsacht
hette.

Die Pauren bawen nit vmb gemeinen / sondern vmb deß Eigen Nußen wille die Ecker

Fürwar / jr müsset alle Hungers
sterben / wenn jr kein Brot essen solt /
welches also nur von gemeines Nuß
wegen erbawet würd / weñ man aber
wolt sagen / es würdẽ alle Stend durch
deß Pauren arbeit vnterhaltẽ / so kñe
man aber dennoch nit sagen / daß er nit
auch gemeinem Nuß zu gut bauwete.
Ich bekenn solchs selb waar seyn / aber
ich sag / daß solchs nicht freywillig geschicht / sonder auß einem drang. Deñ
wenn man einem Pauren zuließ / daß
er allein für sich selbs bawet / oder sonst
solchs nit ander seiner notturfft halb /

Alle stend de werdẽ nit durch der paurẽ arbeit erhaltẽ.

D ij   die er

Folio 18 recto

you could or would find a single farmer who cultivated
and drove the plough into his field purely for the Common
Good, if Self-Interest had not caused and driven him to it in
the first place?

The farmers do not
cultivate the fields
for the sake of the
Common Good, but for
Self-Interest.

In fact, you would starve to death if you were only to eat
bread, whose grain had been cultivated for the sake of the
Common Good alone. However, if you wanted to say that
the farmers' work provides nourishment for everyone and
all ranks in society, one could not deny that the farmer
cultivates the field for the Common Good also. I will admit
that this is true; but I will also say that all this doesn't
happen voluntarily, but due to some sort of urge. Because if
you let the farmer cultivate crops only for himself and only
to fulfil his own material needs

All classes are provided
for by the farmers.

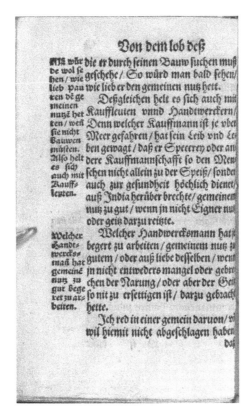

Folio 18 verso

you would soon see how fond he really is of the Common Good.

It is the same with merchants and craftsmen. Because which merchant has ever sailed across the seas; risking life and limb for the Common Good; bringing spices and other wares for food and better health, all the way from India, if Self-Interest or avarice did not drive him in the first place?

Which craftsman has ever desired to work for the Common Good or out of love for it, if want and need for food, or insatiable greed, had driven him to it in the first place?

I am generally speaking about the fact and don't want to deny that

One would see how fond the farmers are of the Common Good if they did not have to farm. It is the same with merchants.

Which craftsman desires to work for the Common Good?

Folio 19 recto

one could find many who are of a different opinion; at the
same time I find it difficult to believe that one could find
somebody who did something or worked for the Common
Good alone, if Self-Interest had not caused him in great
measure to do it. A single swallow does not make a summer,
as the proverb says. So now you can see that it is not only
your life, but everything great and good that comes within
it: Food, drink, clothing, houses, and everything else
making up the necessities for human life: all this you receive
through my grace; because if Self-Interest did not exist, you
would have to want for all of this. How deeply would you
want for it, because you couldn't live without it.

You may find some who
do; but it is generally
speaking difficult to believe
that someone would work
for the Common Good
exclusively.

Therefore, I want and shall legitimately conclude with
just one sentence, that is: you could not and would not
want

If Self-Interest did not
exist, there would be lack
and dearth of everything.

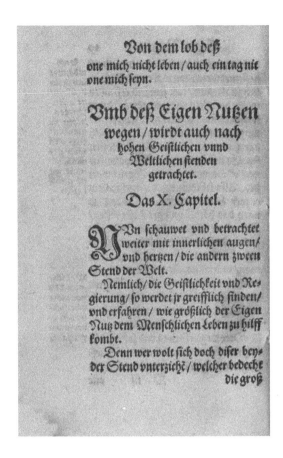

Folio 19 verso

to live without me; or be without me for even just one day.

**People strive for rank and file in the clergy and
nobility out of Self-Interest
Chapter X**

Now go on and consider with your inner eye and heart the
other two orders in the world.

That is, the clergy and temporal [secular] authority
[*Regierung*, i.e. the state]; and you will experience and find
how greatly Self-Interest aids human life.

Because who would want to be in either of these two orders,
considering the huge responsibility

Folio 20 recto

and burden that goes with them, a burden which they bear
against God; and what is demanded of these orders, not just
from God, but in terms of worldly matters also.[20]

If I, Self-Interest did not exist, one would have to search to
the end of the world (in order to recruit a pope, bishop, or
someone else of this order; or emperor, king, prince or other
peer) and one would have to force him with the sword or
threaten him with incarceration.

However, in these present times (for this you should be
grateful) no great pressure is required; instead so much is
achieved through my help and assistance. Therefore these
offices and honours are not only accepted gladly, but also
being strived for with life and limb, with great diligence and

If Self-Interest did not
exist, even the highest
orders would have to
be forced to take their
posts. But this pressure
isn't necessary; they
automatically strive for it
out of Self-Interest.

Von dem lob deß
allerley Practicken getracht vnd geſtel
let/ vnd zu erlangung derſelben / alle
Brüderliche lieb vnd freundtſchafft/
Recht vnd billichkeit neben ſich geſetzt/
vnd vberſchritten / auch ring geacht
wirt/ ob man auch deßhalb Krieg vnd
Auffruhr gemacht/ auch Land vñ Leut
verderbt/ Witwen vñ Waiſen gema=
chet/ Menſchen blut vergoſſen/ vnd al
les vbel vnd vnglück dardurch ange=
richt/ wie man denn das alles in tegli=

Krieg vñ cher erfahrung hat/ daß alle Krieg vnd
Auffrur Auffruhr vnter den Menſchen mehrer
vmb Ei= theils von der Herrſchung vnd Regie=
ges Nu= rung gewalt vnd Oberkeit wegen ſich
nē wegē erheben/ꝛc.
erhaben.

Eraſ. võ Vnd wiewol der vber hochtreffen=
Roterdã lich Mann/ Eraſmus von Roterdam
der Narr inn ſeinem zierlichen vnnd künſtlichen
heit lob Büchlein / von dem lob der Narrheit/
ſolchs. ſolchs mehrer theils alles der Narrheit
zuſchreibt / als ob dieſelb ein vrſach ſolt
ſeyn diſer gutthat/ daß niemand be=
dacht

Folio 20 verso

all sorts of practices and tricks; and to attain these positions, all brotherly love and friendship; all righteousness and fairness are cast aside and overstepped and held in low regard. Whether this causes war and turmoil, devastates land and people, turns wives into widows and offspring into orphans; whether human blood is spilled, and evil and misfortune caused, one can experience every day how wars and turmoil among people stem from the governance and powers of their rulers.

War and turmoil result from Self-Interest.

And although the distinguished man Erasmus of Rotterdam has stated in his delicate and artful book on the *Praise of Folly* that folly was a reason for good deed, nobody considered

Erasmus of Rotterdam praised folly.

Eigen Nutzen.   21

dacht/was solche hohe stend der Regie=
rung für beschwerd vnd laast mit jnen
brechten/vnd darumb desto minder ge=
scheucht würden / auch wol sein möcht
daß solches auch etwan zum theil von
der Narrheit her fliesse/ so hab ich doch
eigentlich darfür/ daß ich Eigner Nu=
tzen die nechst vrsach sey / vnnd mir diß
lob zu forderst sol zugemessen werden.

*Dem Ei=
gen Nu=
tzē zuge=
messe sol
werden.*

Denn ob wol etwan die Menschen
verstehen/ was grosse gefehrligkeit hie=
rinn sey (wie es denn nicht mag seyn/
daß sie es/vorab der mehrer theil nicht
verstehen) vnangesehen / daß gantze
Bücher vol daruon geschrieben sind/
vnd die Prelaten / auch grossen Herrn
selbs/ vnd sonderlich/ so es jnen zu nutz
reicht/ gantz sicherlich daruon reden/
vnd die beschwerden so darauff stehen/
nach aller leng erzelen könten/ so schaff
ich doch/ daß sie diser gefahr vnd alle
beschwerligkeit nicht allein nicht ach=
ten/ sonder auch darüber mit darstre=

*Ws gros=
sen Her=
ren zu nu=
tz reicht.*

D v   ckung

Folio 21 recto

the high burden and weight that these high posts of ruling bring with them, and thus would be much eschewed. It is possible that this is partly due to folly; but I, Self-Interest, am the proximate reason, and therefore this praise should first and foremost go to me.

It should be attributed to Self-Interest.

Even though most humans generally understand how dangerous these offices and responsibilities can be (it seems unlikely that they don't understand anything of it, at least some bits); even though whole books have been written on that matter, and the prelates [high ecclesiastical dignitaries] and powerful counts and dukes themselves surely speak about it, when useful for them, and elaborate on the difficulties; I nevertheless not only manage to make them forget the dangers and difficulties, but also make them desire and strive for

What benefits the great lords.

> ### Von dem lob deß
>
> ckung Leibs / Lebens / Ehren/ Bluts/
> vnd Guts/ nach allem jrem höchsten
> vermögen/ nach solchen Stenden stel=
> len vnd trachten / Gott vnd die Welt
> zu zeiten vnd viel malen deßhalb vber=
> geben/ damit sie die vberkommen/ wie
> hie oben erzelt ist/ vnd in einer Sum=
> ma dauon zu reden / so hat jener nicht
> vnbillich außgeschrien / Wer hat baß
> die Tugend an jr selbs/ wenn die be=
> lohnung auffgehebt wirt?
>
> Der Hirt hütt der Schaf nit von
> der Schafen/ sonder sein selbs Eigens
> Nutzens wegen / nichts dester minder
> haben die Schaf den Nutz von mir/
> daß sie mitler weil auff der Weyd ge=
> führt/ vnd für den Wolffen/ vnd an=
> dern wilden Thieren zu zerreissen vber
> geben werden.
>
> Darumb/wenn man wolt warten/
> biß einer kem / so der Schafe vmb jres
> nutz willen vergebenlich hüttet/ kan
> ich nicht wissen/ ob jemand denn allein
> Christus

Folio 21 verso

these posts, ranks and orders; risking their bodies, lives, honour, blood and earthly possessions with their highest capabilities, disregarding God and the world many times, so that they may receive these high posts; just as I have argued above. To sum up: you may just as well ask: who would want to be virtuous, if there was no reward for it?

People strive with all their might for the highest positions

The shepherd does not tend the sheep for the good of the sheep, but out of Self-Interest; thus the sheep profit from me as well, since they are in the meantime led to the meadow, and not left unprotected to be devoured by wolves and other wild animals.

Self-Interest makes the shepherd tends his sheep

Therefore, if one were to wait for someone who tended to the sheep only for their good, I could not think of anyone but Christ

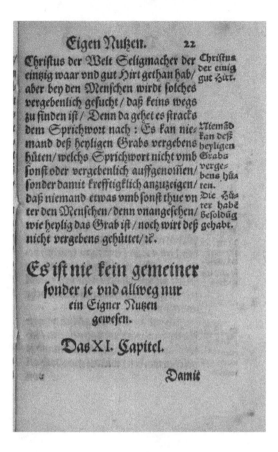

Folio 22 recto

who blessed the world and was the only good shepherd. But among us mortals you would search for this in vain; it cannot be found, and the old saying is true: no one tends the Holy Sepulchre for free. This saying is not without its reason; it illustrates that no human does anything for free; no matter how holy the grave is, no one tends it for free.

There has never been Common Good, but only Self-Interest
Chapter XI

The only good shepherd is Christ.

No one tends the Holy Grave for free.

Shepherds were paid.

Folio 22 verso

Now I want to return to my initial argument that the world should be thankful to me, Self-Interest, above all else; for spiritual and worldly power to prevail; without which the world could and would not exist. My favours are so abundant that no one cares much about how much effort it is to reign over a diocese, a kingdom or country; even if one was denied such a post, they would still strive for it with highest diligence and effort. That is how sweet and light I can make even heavy burdens. If you were to regard it in the light (as the German proverb goes [*on the face of it*]), it has never been different from the very beginnings of the world, and we can be certain that this will never change.

Self-Interest makes heavy burdens light.

I have not said in vain: There is no Common Good, and I am certain that no one has ever seen it, no matter how much one

There has never been a Common Good.

Folio 23 recto

has blabbered or written about it, or still does.

In fact, I go as far as saying that you won't find a spark of Common Good on this earth; amongst any social rank, status and orders, no matter where you turn to look for it.

You won't find a spark of Common Good.

To explore this point I do not want to go too far astray and use only one example, even though there are many. Just take the Romans who are thought to be a mirror and example for the entire world of what they, the Romans, Cicero, and all others have called the Common Good. But this label was unwarranted; because if one were to truly and rightfully consider the Common Good, one would find that Rome was nothing but a single state[21] that overpowered and oppressed all its neighbours through Self-Interest, arrogance and greed.

The Romans have been called an example and mirror of the Common Good.

Rome, a single state made it far due to Self-Interest.

Von dem lob deß

vnd vnter getruckt / ja die gantz Welt beraubt / vnd beleſtigt / deren ſie auch ein herꝛſcherin zu werden / vnterſtanden hat / vnd zu groſſem theil worden iſt / Denn was der Statt Rom vnnd dem gantzen Römiſchen ſtand vnd weſen zugangen / das iſt allein jren Nachbaurn vnd der gantzen welt abgangen / wie jr ſelbſt auch bekennen müſt / vnd was jr nutz vnd auffgang / das iſt der andern / vnd in der gantzen welt ſchad / abgang / vnd verderben geweſen / Vnd weñ man jetzt recht daruon reden wil / ſo kan vñ mag man wol frey öffentlich ſagen / daß Rom nichts anderſt ſey geweſen / denn ein lauter Eigner Nutz / auch ſo man jre Nachbaurn vnnd die gantze Welt betrachten / vnd erwegen wil / ſo wirt man ſehen / daß Rom kein gemeiner Nutz / ſondern ein Eigner Nutz genennt werden mag vnd ſol.

Was ich nun von Rom red / dz wil ich von allen Stetten vñ Stenden der gantzen Welt verſtanden haben.

Rom durch Eigen Nutzen auffgangen / hergegē jre Nachbauwrn verderbet.

Vñ Rom iſt nichts deñ lauter Eigē Nutze geweſen.

Folio 23 verso

Yes, it robbed and harassed all those parts of the world, over which it was Rome's intention to rule, and succeeded by and large. Because what the city and empire of Rome and the Romans gained was only taken from its neighbours and the rest of the world. You will have to admit that everything that benefitted Rome's ascent was to the damage, detriment and decline of others and the entire world. And if one wanted to speak the truth about it one could and would publicly say that Rome was shaped by nothing else than pure Self-Interest: considering her neighbours and the rest of the world, one would see that Rome cannot be said to have constituted a Common Good, but represented Self-Interest in its clearest form instead.

What I have said about Rome, one can say about all cities and estates in the whole world.

> Rome rose to greatness out of Self-Interest; however its neighbours declined in consequence.

> Rome acted out of nothing but pure Self-Interest.

Folio 24 recto

Because should that be called a Common Good where only
a minority from a single city can claim power over land
and people, authority and posessions to their neighbours
and everybody else's detriment and damage, by usurping
and overpowering them; then it follows that any *Hausvater*[22]
[i.e. head of the household, *oeconomus, pater familias*] with
his children and all his servants would be excused on
the same grounds for profiteering, robbing, stealing and
overcharging his neighbours using violence, cunning and
fraud, following this line of argument and perhaps with
much better reasons than laid out thus far, that this was
done for the benefit of the Common Good. There is no
difference between a household and an entire city or state;
the difference between them is just the same as between
Alexander the Great and Diomedes the Pirate, who
justifiably complained that he should be called a pirate, just
because he robbed ships

Should Common Good
mean usurping foreign
land?

Alexander and Diomedes
the Pirate.

Folio 24 verso

but Alexander the Great who had robbed from the whole world with the strength of an army, was proclaimed a king. And therefore, one wants to say here if one were to carefully consider it, one would find that Mucius Scaevola, Decimus Brutus or patrician dynasties such as the Scipiones, the Cachones, the Metelli, the Fabius family and all other exceptional Romans were seen to act out of this presently-discussed misinterpretation of the Common Good. However in truth they were motivated by their own honour, glory and Self-Interest. This became particularly evident in the last days of Rome, especially in Sulla, Emperor Marius and Pompeius, when they showed their true face: for no other reason than that they had been brought up that way, and that they had nothing and nobody to fear.

Alexander the Great brought the whold world under his control.

The Romans wrongly called it the Common Good, where in truth they acted out of Self-Interest, honour and glory.

Folio 25 recto

It was either shame or fear, or Self-Interest itself that made
them pause and think, and cover their Self-Interest with the
cloak of acting for the Common Good.

**Self-Interest has affected scholars, too; many are
quite attached to it still
Chapter XII**

If one truly wanted to discuss the Common Good properly,
one would have to contemplate it even more deeply and
broadly. But I am unsure if it is appropriate for me, Self-
Interest, to discuss the Common Good.

It is not appropriate for
Self-Interest to argue with
the Common Good.

Folio 25 verso

However, I have been in scholars' minds since the beginning of the world, and I have had a steady place within their studies. From their discourses and disputations and writings, which they produce on a daily basis, I have realised and learned a lot.

Self-Interest has always had a habitat with scholars

I can be quite relaxed that no one will turn their back on me and turn to the Common Good instead, which would be to my disadvantage. Thus, I won't shy away from detailing my argument (which was formed by closely examining the work of other scholars).

No one turns away from Self-Interest to the Common Good.

The wise Lord Almighty, Creator of all things, made the world in such a way, that everything within its realm should be subjected to the same common public order (*Policey*); everything should be like one big city or state, just as Cicero confirmed (using his natural gift of reason) in his

Eigen Nutzen.   26

seinem ersten Buch / von den Gesa- *Cicero in*
tzen / Darumb Socrates / der allein bey *seinem er-*
  ste Buch
den Heyden den Tittel der Weißheit *meldet.*
von dem Gott Apolline erlangt / als *Socra-*
er gefragt ward / woher er wer / von *tes.*
der Welt / gleichsam wolt er darmit
anzeigen / daß die gantze Welt ein ein-
tzige Policey / Heurat / vnnd Wesen
wer.

   Vnd darmit der Göttelich will vnd
wolgefallen / in solchem dester klerli-
cher vnnd deutlicher verstanden vnnd
gemerckt würd / so hat Gott der Schö-
pffer als durch sein ewige Weißheit al- *Ein Lad*
le Ding dahin gericht / daß je ein Land o- *ander*
deß andern nottürfftig ist / vnd so gar *nehret.*
nottürfftig / daß man nichts kan oder
mag entrahten oder emberen / vnd kein
Mensch one deß anderen hilff vnd zu
stand leben kan.

   Derowegen so sehet jhr / daß keine
Lands art so rohe ist / Gott jr etwas
geben / daß eines anderen Lands art
     F ij   man-

Folio 26 recto

first book of *De Legibus* [On the Laws] that Socrates who was recognised by the heathens as having obtained his wisdom from the god Apollo, when asked where he was from answered "from the entire world." With this he wanted to illustrate that the whole world was connected by the same public order, like marriage, and everything made of the same essence.

Cicero speaks of Socrates in his first book.

Divine will and pleasure are nowhere more clearly and explicitly recognised and shown than by the fact that the Lord the Creator, through His eternal wisdom directed all things in a manner that every country requires the others. No country is completely self-sufficient, and no human can live without the others' help.

One country feeds the other.

That is why, as you can see, no country is ever too barren; God has given every country something that another lacks

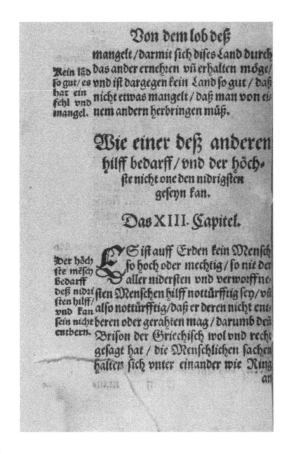

Folio 26 verso

so that this country can feed itself and survive [by trading with] the others. On the other hand, no country has it ever so good that it doesn't lack something that needs to be imported from somewhere else.

No country is so good that it has no lack and need [of goods].

How one needs the help of others, and even the highest [ranks] can't live without the lowest
Chapter XIII

No one on earth would ever be so high or mighty that they would not occasionally need the help of the lowest and depraved. In fact, the need is so great that one cannot do without them. Therefore [the Greek philosopher] Bryson rightly said that human interactions are like links in a chain

The mightiest requires the help of the poorest and cannot exist without it.

Eigen Nutzen.   27

an einer Ketten/ die in einander ver- *Ketten.*
schrenckt sind/ vnd einer dem anderen
nachfolgt/ also/ ob du einen darunter/
es sey welcher es wöl/ zu dir zeuchst/ so
folgt die gantze Kettë hernach mit jrem
anhang/ also auch/ was du inn den
Menschlichë geschefften für dich nim-
mest/ so würdestu befinden/daß die andern von nöten/ vnd mit starcker ordnung nachfolgen/ rc.
    Als Exempels weiß: So sich je-
mand auff den Ackerbauw gibt/ muß
nicht zuuor da seyn die Kunst der Zim
merleut vnd Schmid/ vor derë schmel
ter/ deren denn widerumb die Kunst *Ertzgra-*
deß Ertzgrabens von nöten/ vorgehet/ *ben von*
Nun denen die Ertzgraben/ darmit sie *nöten.*
auff dem Feld bleiben mögen/ist von
nöten/ daß sie bedeckt seyen/ zu welchem Weber/ vnd die Heuser machen
können/ erfordert werden/ also für vñ
für/ je eins das ander erheischt/ vnd so
du das ersuchst vnd erforschest/so wür-
                    E iij   dest

Folio 27 recto

which are entangled; therefore one person is directly   Links in a chain.
connected to another, just as though you had someone
beneath you and pulled him towards you, then the whole
chain would follow with all its links. So that whatever
business you have with others you will find that other
activities inevitably follow suit, all according to a greater
order.

Take this as an example: If someone cultivates a field, does   Mining is necessary.
he not first need the craft and product of the carpenters
and blacksmiths? And before them the art of the smelters,
who in turn need the miners? Now for the miners, in order
for them to stay at work, they need to cover themselves and
have shelter, which is why they need the weavers and the
builders. It's one thing for another; one craft requires the
other. And so if you sought out the truth and researched it
properly you would find

Von dem lob deß

deß du befinden / daß alle ding an einander geknüpfft seyen.

Nun hat Gott die ewig Weißheit diß alles also geordnet / damit die menschen vrsach hetten / vnd gleich also zu reden / gezwungen würden / an einander zu lieben / so sie sehen / daß keiner on den andern nichts vermöcht.

Gott (dieweil er die Lieb selbs ist) erfordert er von den Menschen nichts denn die Liebe / vñ wil / das sie jm gleich seyen / wie er sie denn zu seiner gleichnuß erschaffen hat.

Der Allmechtig Gott hat alle ding vmb sein selbs willen / vñ zu seinem lob vnd Preyß gemacht / dieweil er dz höchste vnd einig Gut ist / Deßhalb er auch nichts anders / denn die Lieb den Menschen gebotten hat.

Dieweil denn nun keiner ohne deß andern hilff leben oder seyn kan / so fordert auch die Lieb vnuermeidenlich / vnd one alle außred / daß je ein mensch dem

Folio 27 verso

that all things are connected.

The Lord in His eternal wisdom has arranged everything just so that people would have a reason to talk to each other, and to love each other, because they would see that nobody can achieve anything without the others.

God (who is pure love) requires nothing of the people but love, and wants them to be just as He created them in His own image.

The Almighty God created all things for His own sake; for His own praise and glory, which is the highest good of man. That is why he gave nothing to the people but love.

Because no one can live or be without the help of others, love inevitably demands without excuses that one person shall

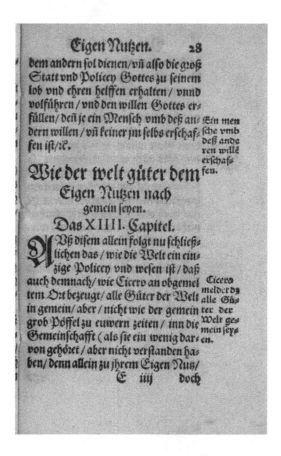

Folio 28 recto

serve the other and thus preserve God's magnificent [political and economic] order (*Policey*) of the world[23], to His praise and glory, and perform and fulfil God's will, because every person is created for the benefit of others, and no one is created just for themselves.

Each person is created to help others.

On worldly goods, and how they are common due to Self-Interest
Chapter XIV

From this follows that just as the whole world shares one grand scheme of [political and economic] order (*Policey*) and nature, as Cicero demonstrated (see above) that all goods in the world are held in common, but not like the common mob has done in your times, by making them communal (they had some knowledge about this, but did not truly understand the concept and instead acted out of Self-Interest[24]

Cicero said that all goods are common.

Von dem lob deß

doch vnsicherlich vnnd vnfüglich ge=
blaßt/ vnd vermeint haben/ die Güter
mit gewalt/ gewicht vnd maß zu thei=
len/ vnd es alles gleich zu machen / bey
welcher gleicheit / ob die gleichwol er=
langet wer/daß doch nicht müglich ist/
Got wils denn Gott wils nicht alls gemein ha=
nit habe ben/ hats auch nicht also geordnet) so
also. würd die Welt auch nicht können be=
stehen oder erhalten werden / einen au=
genplick/denn es wirt weder in dem Hi
mel noch auff Erden einiche gleicheit
nicht erfunden werden / sondern / wer=
den alle geschöpff in vngleicheit gespü=
ret / vnd seyn gegen einander inn streit
gesetzt/ aber durch die vngleicheit vnnd
streitende gegensatzung erscheint die al=
ler gröst gleichheit / vnd aller lieblichest
Hermoney vnd einigkeit/die kein zung
genug außsprechen oder voll lob/noch
kein hertz sich gnugsam verwundern
kan/ gleichsam als in einer Orgel vil
vnd mancherley Pfeiffen sind / kurtz
                                          vnd

Folio 28

and pounced on the goods and wrongly attempted to
introduce communal ownership of goods by force and
make everything equal; even if equality of some sorts could
somehow have been achieved, it would not have been
allowed, because God does not want things to be owned
in common property and did not arrange things this way),
because that way the world could not continue to exist nor
be preserved, not even for a moment. Because true equality
will never be found either in Heaven nor on earth. Instead
all creatures will experience inequality and will be pitted
against each other in competition and opposition. But
through this inequality and opposing forces the greatest
equality will emerge in turn, and sweetest harmony and
unity, which no tongue can speak of or praise highly
enough; so wondrously in fact, just like an organ which has
many sorts of pipes, long and short

God doesn't want things
to be like that.

Folio 29 recto

big and small; none of which are sounding equal and alike.
But from all these uneven voices rises the sweetest musical
harmony. Writ large this allegory means just as Audius said:
There should be such an equality and communality among
people that everyone knows that nothing he owns, in fact
everything he has, be this his title of nobility, power, wealth,
reason, wisdom, strength, craft and talent and other worldly
goods, has been given him by God so that he can serve and
help his neighbours and thus play his part in establishing
and keeping God's chosen order (*Policey*) as mentioned
above. One should manage one's worldly goods not like one
owned them, but rather as a steward[25] held accountable by
God[26]

Audius speaks about equality.

Nobility / power / riches.

God gave this so one would help the poor.

We are all *oeconomists* (stewards).

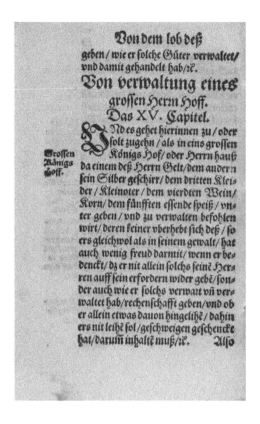

Folio 29 verso

for how he has managed and transacted with them.

On the management of a large estate (*demesne*)
Chapter XV

Here matters are or should be the same as in (managing) a large royal court or noble estate, where one is responsible for handling the lord's money [i.e. income and expenses]; another for his silver ware; a third one for his clothes and jewels; the fourth for his wine and grain; the fifth for food; no one must embezzle or misappropriate any of these goods but manage with them properly. Even though they have the goods within their power, they get little joy from them; because they know that not only will they have to return them to their lord when asked to do so, but they also have to produce accounts for how they have kept, maintained and managed them. They are held to account and have to testify whether they lent some of them out even though they should not, let alone giving any of them away as presents.

Example of a large royal estate.

Eigen Nutzen. 30

Also wirt es auch vnter allē menschē
seyn/ weñ sie dise ding bedechten vñ be-
trachtetē/dz es in obgemelter gstalt alls
gmein ist/ vñ keiner jm selbs allein wed
ehr/adel/reichthumñ/gwalt/sterck/oder
lüst/od weißheit zuziehē mag/sond solches alles dē nechsten zu dienst seyn sol.
Was kan sich deñ der reich seins guts
vberhebē/weñ er weiß dz es nit sein/son
der schuldig ist/ seinē nebē Menschē/ d
mind oder nichts hat dauon zu helffen
d gewaltig od edel ist/ dz solcher gewalt
ehr vñ adel/ d gantzē gemein zugehört/
vñ er dagegē schuldig ist/ dz Regiment
zu führē od helffen führē/ fridē vñ recht
zu schaffen vñ hand zu habē/ witwē vñ
waisen zu schützē vñ schirmē/ den armē
für gwalt zu erhaltē/wid vnrechtē glau
bē zuuerhütē/ vñ daran sein leib vñ lebē
zustreckē / vñ dz jn zu solchē nit enthebē
mag/ ob er gleichwol fürwenden wolt/
er het von seinem eigen Zinß vnd gül-
ten/ oder andern seinen Gütern zu le-
ben/ bedörfft keins Herrn oder dienst/

Marginal notes: Was wir haben dē nechsten zu dienē sten seye sol. — Witwen vnd waisen zu beschützen.

Folio 30 recto

It is the same with all people as can easily be considered
and contemplated, that everything is common and
connected as outlined above, and no one can claim for
himself exclusively glory, nobility, riches, power, strength,
artistic talent – everything must be used so as to one's
neighbour. How could a rich person waste or spend all
his goods, knowing they aren't his, but that instead he is
obliged to use them to help his neighbour who has less or
nothing? And he who has power or the status of nobility
must know that he holds and must use this honour and
noble status on behalf of the community; therefore he is
responsible to partake in or assist in upholding government
and temporal [secular] order; establish and keep the peace,
law and order; to protect widows and orphans and the poor;
fight and prevent false faith; sacrificing for this cause his
body and his life. And he cannot be freed from this duty,
even if he were to claim that he needed the proceeds from
his estates, his rents and annuities to live on and needed
neither lord nor vassal

Marginal glosses: What we have shall serve our neighbours. — Protect widows and orphans.

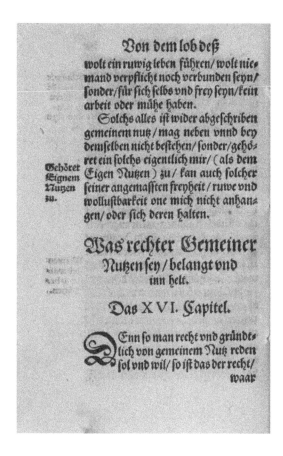

Folio 30 verso

wanting to live a quiet life without being bound, obliged or someone else's liege; but himself wanting to be free without work or toil.

All this goes against Common Good as it has been described here and cannot co-exist with it; instead it actually pertains to me (Self-Interest). No one can pursue their common and accustomed·freedom, peace and lust without me.

Belongs to Self-Interest.

Concerning true Common Good
Chapter XVI

It is quite appropriate to engage in a full and thorough discussion of the Common Good.

> **Eigen Nutzen.**   **31**
>
> waar gemein Nut/ daß obgeschriebe
> ner massen alle ding in der welt/ es sey
> Gewalt/ Kunst/ oder Gut/ gemein
> seyn sollen vnnd müssen/ vñ je eins dem
> andern/ darmit Gott dem Schöpffer
> zu lob vnd Preyß/ dienen/ zu hilff kom
> men/ die hand biegen vnd stewer thun/
> welchs Christus der Son Gottes vnd
> Seligmacher der Welt/ vnnd rechte
> Lehrer vnd Stiffter deß gemeinen Nu
> tzen/ wiewol allenthalben/ aber jr doch
> sonderlichen an zweyen Orten/ seinen
> Göttlichen vnd Euangelischen lebend
> machenden Lehrer/ gar klar vnd auß
> trücklich angezeigt hat.
>
>   Nemlich für das ein/ an dem Ort/
> da der jenig fragt/ was er solt vnd müst
> thun/ daß er möcht Selig werden? vñ
> Christus jn auff das Gesätz gewisen
> hat/ vnd gesagt: Er solt Gott lieben/
> vnd den Nechsten als sich selbs/ vñ der
> Jung antwort/ vnd sprach: solchs het
> te er von seinen jungen tagen angefan
>   gen/
>
> *Margin:* Gemeiner Nutz/ d₃ einer dem anderen zu hilff komme. — Gott vil hernach den Nehesten lie ben.

Folio 31 recto

True Common Good as outlined above means that all things in the world, whether power, artistic talent or material possessions should be and are received to be held in common and on behalf of others[27]; and one should help out the other, offering his hand to praise and serve God the Creator, work and toil and pay his dues; just as Jesus Christ the son of God and redeemer of the world, and true teacher and founder of the Common Good, clearly and explicitly demonstrated everywhere in his divine teachings, but on two occasions in particular.

Margin: Common Good means helping others.

In one occasion someone asked him what he ought to do to become blessed? And Jesus Christ reminded him of the commandments and said [Matthew 22:36-40; Mark 12:30-1]: Love the Lord and love thy neighbour as thyself, and the lad replied and said: He had done this from an early age on.

Margin: Firstly, love God and then your neighbour.

Von dem lob deß

gen/wolt jm Chriſtus anzeigen/ das er
diß Gebett wie tieff es gründet / vnd
vmb ſich griff noch nie erfahren het/
vnnd thete jm ſein red bas bedeutten/
wie er meint/ daß er liebhaben ſolt/ vnd
Verkauff ſagt / eins manget dir / gehe hin / vnd
was du v:rkauff was du haſt/ vnd gibs den ar=
haſt/ vnd men / vnd folge mir nach / darab aber
gibs den der Jüngling erſchrocken vnd traw=
Armen. rig hin gegangen / Denn er war ſehr
reich/ꝛc. Darauff Chriſtus den ſchwe=
ren Sententz gefellt hat/ daß es leichter
ſey/ daß ein Kamelthier eingieng durch
ein Nadel Or / deñ daß ein Reicher in
den Himmel koñie/ denn diſer war ſehr
Reich / wie das der Text mit bringt.
    Nun laſſe ich ſeyn / daß ein groſſer
theil der Leut / diſen Text auff die vol=
kommenheit deuten/ alſo/ daß welcher
volkoñien ſeyn wil / daß ſein verkauf=
fen/ vnd Chriſto nachfolgen ſol / jeder
daß ſein verkauffen vnnd verlaſſen
muß/ ſo er anderß wil Selig werden/
                                    Chriſto

Folio 31 verso

[Mark 10:17-31] Now, Jesus wanted to show him how deep and far-reaching this commandment was and that he had never properly understood it. He explained clearly what he really meant by this saying about loving one's neighbour and spoke: you lack one thing; go, sell what you possess and give to the poor; and come, follow me. When the young man heard this, he went away sorrowful, for he had great possessions. Thereafter Jesus passed the grave sentence that it is easier for a camel to go through the eye of a needle than for a rich person to enter the kingdom of God; because this man was very rich, as Scripture says.

Now, I will acknowledge that many people interpret this text *verbatim*, meaning that those who want to be perfect, have to sell all that is theirs and follow Jesus Christ. Everyone should sell and abandon all their possessions, so they become blessed;

Sell what you have and give it to the poor.

Folio 32 recto

follow Christ and thus become a member of the body of
which Christ is the head. Therein lies all eternal bliss and
nothing else; therefore [as this common interpretation
goes] this passage of the Bible ought to be interpreted as
"physically selling your posessions."

Follow Christ.

However, in my opinion the meaning is more spiritual
than physical; referring to the act of spiritually loving God
and thy neighbour, rather than doing everything for your
neighbour and suffer in consequence; or having no own
posessions. [The purpose is] to unite all things and efforts
in a common cause, for the praise of God and the love of
one's neighbour.

The passage about
selling your possessions
is more about spiritual
than temporal [secular]
matters.

What would it mean to sell everything that one has; to shed
and deny everything that one possesses; to own nothing,
just as the apostle St. Paul showed even more clearly when
he said in 1 Corinthians 7:29–31: those that have wives be
as though they had none,

Von dem lob deß

vnd die weineten / als weineten sie nie /
vnd die sich freuweten / als freuweten
sie sich nicht / vnd die diser Welt braucheten / als braucheten sie sich jr nicht /
denn das wesen auff diser Welt zer-
gehet.

Jnn Summa / Christus Lehre ist
Geistlich / darumb wirdt one zweiffel
Christus hie Christus mehr von dem Geistli-
von dem chen / denn von dem leiblichen verkauf-
Geistli- fen geredt haben.
chen ver-
kauffen Wie er auch gleich an einē anderen
deutet. Ort von dem Geistlichē Handabhau-
wen / Augen außstechē geredt hat / deñ
es sol vnd muß alles in Geist gezogen /
vnd Geistlich gedeut vnnd außgelegt
werden / Deñ was wer darmit außge-
richt / daß gleichwol einer das sein euf-
serlich vñ leiblich verkauffte / wie etwa
Die Phi- die Philosophi gethan haben / die jr gut
losophi
haben jr in das Meer geworffen / darumb / das
Güter in sie der Philosophi frey vnd vnuerhin-
dz Meer
geworffē dert anhangen / vnd obligen möchten /
vnd

Folio 32 verso

and they that weep, as though they wept not; and they that rejoice, as though they rejoiced not; and they that use this world, as not abusing it: for the fashion of this world passeth away.

In sum, Christ's teachings are spiritual. Therefore, Christ will without a doubt have spoken about giving away one's spiritual rather than material posessions.

Christ spoke about the spiritual selling.

Just as another time he spoke about the spiritual [metaphorical] cutting off of hands and gauging of eyes. Everything has to be interpreted in a spiritual context, because what trouble would be caused if one sold all one's material posessions, just as the philosophers did so that they could freely and eagerly pursue philosophy[28] –

The pilosophers threw their posessions into the sea.

Folio 33 recto

possessions to which he was wholly devoted with heart and mind? God on the other hand wants the heart and not the physical body; the Bible tells of this everywhere.

Where would one find enough merchants, if everyone sold their worldly possessions, seeking to become perfected and blessed, as everyone was created in that purpose? If one gave everything to the poor, the poor would become rich, and the givers would become poor and in turn would seek assistance. So that the same poor to which they had given would also have to sell their goods and give them to the poor, who had before been rich.

If one understood this commandment as having to sell one's worldly possessions, this would be an incorrect and foolish interpretation, which can't be attributed to the Lord in his eternal wisdom. Because the Lord doesn't want for us material poverty, but the poverty of the spirit.

If everyone sold their possessions, where would be enough merchants.

If one gave everything to the poor, many would become rich.

God wants poverty.

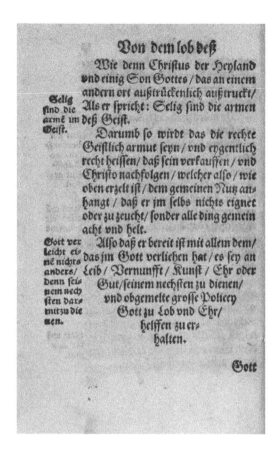

Folio 33 verso

Just as Christ our Saviour and the Son of God explicitly
stated somewhere else, when he said: blessed are the poor
in spirit.[29]

Blessed are the Poor in
Spirit.

Therefore, true spiritual poverty means selling everything
and following Christ, which would as outlined above
serve the Common Good, owning and acquiring nothing;
considering all things common.

But what this actually means is the state of being prepared;
to help preserve the Lord's great order (*Policey*) to His
praise and glory, with everything given to us by the Lord,
be it body, reason, arts and crafts, honour and material
possessions.

God gives only so one can
serve one's neighbour.

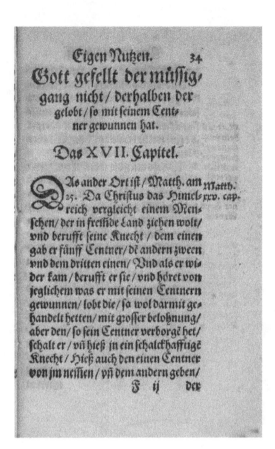

Folio 34 recto

God dislikes idleness; this is why those were praised that earned more with their bag of gold Chapter XVII

Another example is Matthew, Chapter 25[30] where Christ compares heaven with a man about to travel to a distant land. He called his servants to him; to one he gave five bags (*talents*[31]) of gold; another two bags (*talents*), and to another one bag (talent). When the master returned and heard how much the servants had earned with their gold he praised those who traded well with it and gave them great rewards. But he scolded the servant who hid his gold, and called him a wicked fool and lazy servant. So he took his bag (*talent*) away from him and gave it to the other

Matthew, Chapter 25

Von dem lob deß
der fünff Centner empfangen hett.
Auß diser gleichnuß ist nichts anders zu verstehen / denn daß Gott mit
seinen gaben wol gewircket / kein müß-
Gott wil siggang / sonder dem nechsten darmit
kein müs- gedient wil haben / das ist der Wucher
siggang/ daruon diser Text redt.
sonder dē
nechsten Welchs auch der from theur Heyd
gedient Seneca für der ankunfft Christi deß
haben. Heylands der Welt / allein auß natür-
Der fro-
me Heyd lichem liecht / also sich halten / gefület
Seneca. hat / Als er fast auff dise meynung in
seinem Buch von den wolthaten also
redet: Was schoneft du deß als wer es
dein / darüber du doch nur allein ein
Schaffner bist ꝛc.
Alle ding die vns auffgeladen / vnd
vber Menschliche gelegenheit erheben/
dahin reitzen / zwingen / vñ wöllen / daß
ir vergessen sollen / euwer gebrechlig-
keit / die ding / so ir mit gewaptneter
hand / in eisen Schlössern / bewaren/
die ir auß frembdem Blut geraubt/ mit
euwrem

Folio 34 verso

who had originally received five bags (*talents*). From this
parable it is clear that God wants us to do good with His
offerings. He dislikes idleness, but wants us to serve our
neighbour. That is the essence[32] of the text.

God does not like
idleness, but wants us to
serve our neighbours'
needs.

Just as the pious heathen Seneca said before the arrival of
Jesus Christ the Saviour, using natural reason, reflecting
almost exactly this opinion in his book 'On Benefits' [*De
Beneficiis*]: why do you keep hold of your posessions as
though they were yours when ultimately you are only the
steward[33]?

The devout heathen
Seneca.

All those things bestowed on us allowing us to carry on
with our lives; those that tempt and force and try to make
us forget our mortality; all the things that you protect
with your steeled hand, behind iron gates; which you have
robbed spilling the blood of others

Eigen Nußen.   35

euwrem Blut beschirmen/vmb wel=
cher willen jr die Schiff in das Meer   Die schiff
sencket/daffelb mit Blut zu retten/vñ   inn das
welcher willē jr die Stett erschnitten/   Meer
vngeacht/wieuil der Pfeil/in die wi=   sencken.
derwertigen das Glück zuricht/vmb
welcher willen so offt mit verbrechung
der Bündtniß vnd Freundtschafft ge=
setzt/durch zween mit einander streiten
de/der vmbkreiß der Erden bequesche
wirt/ist alles nicht euwer/sonder allein
behaltens weiß euch gegeben/vnd wirt
gar bald einem andern Herrn zugehö=
rig werden/es werden entweder solche
ding angriffen der Feind(oder der Er=
ben feindtlich gemüt.

    Fragstu wie du es dein mögest ma=
chen/gibs hin/oder schencks hinweg/
vñ thu darmit deinen sachen raht/rich=
te dir selbs diser dingē ein vnvberwind=
liche besitzung zu/darmit würdest du
dieselben nicht allein ehrlicher/sonder
auch sicherer machen.

                    F iij   Denn

Folio 35 recto

that you protect with your own blood; things for which you
sink ships into the sea; things that you save with your own
blood; which make you destroy cities, however many evil
fools will be destroyed by the arrows in the process; things
that cause alliances to break and friendships to crumble;
which give rise to animosity and fight amongst people with
whom the earth is crammed and squeezed – none of these
[material possessions] are yours. They were only given to
you to keep until you return them; they will sooner than
later have another steward; either your adversaries will try
and take them (or those inheriting your property and their
unfavourable disposition).

If you ask me how you should make them yours: give them
away; bestow them upon others; thus creating yourself
eternal property in them and make them inalienable to you.
Thereby you will not only make these things more honest,
but also safer.

Sink the ships into the
sea.

Folio 35 verso

Because what you presently value so much, making you
feel rich and mighty on a whim – what concerns your
posessions, it all comes down only to a disdainful name
or title; be it houses, or servants, or money. But if you give
whatever you have away or bestow it upon others it is a
blessing and good deed.

It all comes down to a
disdainful name or title

Thus speaks Seneca: You should live your life, as if you
owned nothing, but only were a manager and steward of
the things given to you by God. This is fully in line with
Christian teaching.

Seneca says.

Therefore: If you have two garments and someone else has
none, you should share; also, whatever food and drink one
has on top of one's needs one should give away to those in
need of it. And therefore, let all things be in common; serve
and be industrious all day and night; one shouldn't rest or
be idle. Even if God bestowed great riches upon some

Folio 36 recto

that person should regard himself as nothing more than a
donor and vendor of those riches; and hold authority for no
other reason than out of love for God and his neighbours.
Therefore think carefully about the happiness and pleasure
you have, or desire to have on this earth, and whether this
would also be a life worth pursuing.

**No one has ever truly recognised or seen the
Common Good
Chapter XVIII**

Now consider, whether the Common Good has ever been
recognised or cherished on this earth, and how many
there were who were attached to the Common Good and
followed its promise. How long would fields lay fallow

Where has the Common
Good ever been
recognised?

Folio 36 verso

before someone began to till them for the sake of the
Common Good?

In summary I say: how long would the world be without
spiritual and worldly government, if no one wanted to rule
over it and be its overseer, because the Common Good was
the sole and only reason to accept this responsibility?

In sum I say

For now I do not want to speak about the love of God, just
as you have seen when I spoke about the people mentioned
above – clergy, monks, parsons, preachers of the words of
God. Just assume that in another city they will get paid ten
or twenty florins more as yearly pay, and many preachers
of the gospel would leave their flock at once; and take on a
new one instead, who gave them more money.

About the clergy:
whoever - bishop, parson,
priest - wherever they get
paid 10 florins more they
will quit their job and
move to that place

Thus pastors would no longer come to church and preach if
you did not pay them for it. Countries would have no rulers

Folio 37 recto

and rulers would be without council, court-masters and chancellors; officials and other administrators and subservients. And the world would forever be without ministers, pastors, and preachers, if it were not for me, Self-Interest.

Members of the clergy would no longer come to work unless they are paid.

Not to mention the less prestigious posts and professions: Who would want to be a knacker, an armourer, executioner[34]; a gravedigger, a chimney sweep, and accept work that is not only unpleasant, but in fact abominable and contemptuous – if it wasn't for me, Self-Interest? And how long would you have to wait for someone to accept these tasks for the Common Good; tasks which no one wants to do, but which no one can do without, roles that are just as important as the more pleasurable prestigious posts?

Who would want to be a hangman, gravedigger, armourer or chimney sweep if it wasn't for me, Self-Interest.

It is me alone who not only ensures that there is no lack of these professions, but that instead there is strife and competition,

Von dem lob deß

vnd danck darumb ist / wenn ein solch
Ambt ledig wirt. Darumb hab ich hie
oben gesagt / welchs ich offt repetieren
muß. Man redt von einem gemeinem
Nutz / vnnd kennet jhn doch niemand /
hat jhn auch niemand gesehen / oder er
kennt / Aber dennoch schilt mich jeder
mann dargegen / vnd doch jedermann
an mir / wirt auch die gantz welt durch
mich erhalten / vnd regiert / noch hab
ich deß weder danck / lohn / ob ich gleich
wol alles guts bey den Menschen
wirck / vnd thu / vnd ob ein gemeiner
Nutz auff Erden ist / oder seyn kan /
so hat er doch von mir seinen vrhab
oder vrsprung / also / daß ich wol
sein Vatter mit recht ge
nennt werden
möchte /
ec.

Man redt viel von gemeine nutzen/a ber es kennet jn niemand/ mich Eigen nutz aber kennet jeder wol. Die gantze Welt wirdt durch eigen Nutz erhalten.

Alles

Folio 37 verso

when these positions are to be filled. That is why I said above, and have to repeat often: People speak about the Common Good, but yet no one knows it; no one has ever seen or recognised it. Still everyone scolds me, even though the whole world is preserved and governed by me. I have not received much gratitude or praise, even though I cause and do much good for the people. And if there is, or if there ever were, a Common Good on this earth, then it has originated from me; therefore, I can be rightly called its father.

One speaks a lot about the Common Good, but no one knows it; however, everyone knows me, Self-Interest.

The whole world is preserved by Self-Interest.

Folio 38 recto

Everything originates out of Self-Interest
Chapter XIX

It has been rightly said that things happen according to the
principle: *Primum mihi, secundum tibi* [Firstly I, Second you].

I truly influence everything: through me the field is tilled
for the nourishment of the people. Towns and castles have
been built by Self-Interest. For the shelter and protection
of the common people, for the maintenance of public
order and control – through Self-Interest worldly and
spiritual authority is instated. Nothing is created without
Self-Interest; it is through Self-Interest that merchants travel
foreign countries; activities from which all people benefit.
Self-Interest has incentivised craftsmen and artisans

The whole world is built
due to Self-Interest.

Self-Interest supplies
worldly and spiritual
authority.

Folio 38 verso

to invent, improve and manufacture those things in life that people need and which let them thrive; and nothing that people require is too small or insignificant for Self-Interest to create. Self-Interest creates everything and makes sure that this earth lacks nothing.

Self-Interest creates arts and crafts (manufacturing).

Just so I can close this chapter and go even further I propose something that may sound horrible to some ears; but when you consider it carefully, it is true: in my opinion even the Lord is praised through Self-Interest.

This is my conclusion on Self-Interest; but I will pick this up again further down.

Because how many good works do you think would be done by people, if Self-Interest did not exist, hoping to go to Heaven and gain eternal life? Just as David says in the Psalms: I have given my heart to the Lord's righteousness

If Self-Interest did not exist; no good deeds would be done.

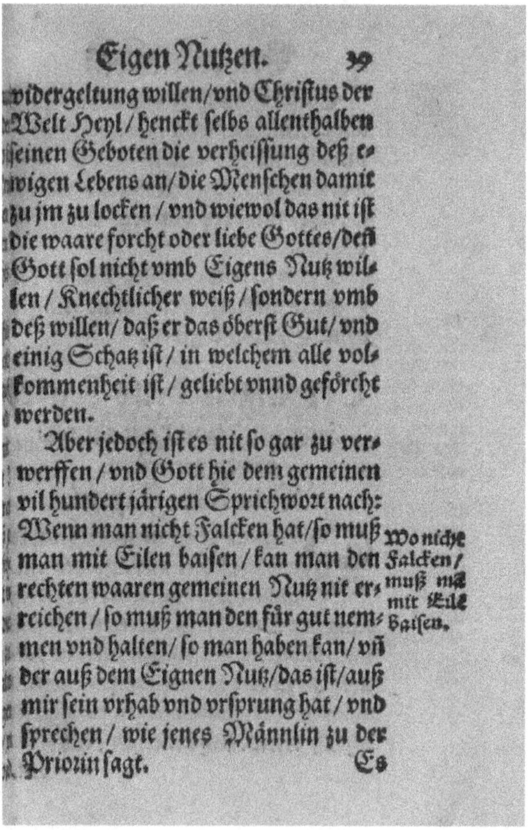

Eigen Nutzen. 39
widergeltung willen/vnd Christus der
Welt Heyl/ henckt selbs allenthalben
seinen Geboten die verheissung deß e-
wigen Lebens an/die Menschen damit
zu jm zu locken/vnd wiewol das nit ist
die waare forcht oder liebe Gottes/dann
Gott sol nicht vmb Eigens Nutz wil-
len/Knechtlicher weiß/sondern vmb
deß willen/daß er das öberst Gut/vnd
einig Schatz ist/in welchem alle vol-
kommenheit ist/geliebt vnnd geförcht
werden.
Aber jedoch ist es nit so gar zu ver-
werffen/vnd Gott hie dem gemeinen
vil hundert järigen Sprichwort nach:
Wenn man nicht Falcken hat/so muß
man mit Eilen baisen/kan man den
rechten waaren gemeinen Nutz nit er-
reichen/so muß man den für gut nemmen vnd halten/so man haben kan/vñ
der auß dem Eignen Nutz/das ist/auß
mir sein vrhab vnd vrsprung hat/vnd
sprechen/wie jenes Männlin zu der
Priorin sagt. Es

Wo nicht Falcken/ muß man mit Eile baisen.

Folio 39 recto

to be rewarded, and Christ the Saviour of the world has added to his commandments the promise of eternal life; to attract people to his teachings. And surely this is not the true fear or love of God, because God should not be loved and feared out of Self-Interest or compulsion, but because He is the most valuable and greatest treasure in which perfection can be found.

Yet the following common saying which is many hundreds of years old is still valid here: If you have no hawk you have to hunt with owls [i.e. you have to be content with what you got] and if one cannot achieve the true and just Common Good, then one has to accept the motivation which has its root and origin in me, Self-Interest and speak just as the man said to the prioress.

If you have no hawk, you have to hunt with owls.

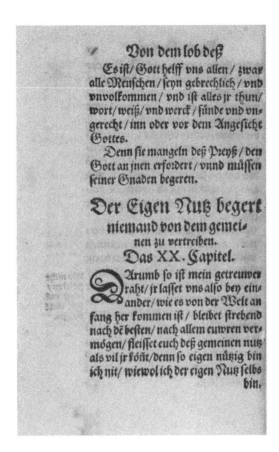

Folio 39 verso

God help us, people are fragile and flawed; and all their deeds, words, wisdom and work are sinful or injust before the eyes of God.

Because humans are imperfect[35], they are dependent upon His grace and mercy.

Self-Interest does not desire to drive anyone away from the Common Good
Chapter XX

That's why it is my sincere advice: leave the two of us [Self-Interest and the Common Good] together, just as it has been since the beginning of the world. Keep striving for the best, using all your ability and might; diligently work towards the Common Good as much as you can, because I am not that egoistic, actually – even though I am Self-Interest itself.

Eigen Nußen.   40

bin. Daß ich euch daruon beger ab zu-
weisen / sonder ich bekenn selbs / daß allein Gott darinn ein wolgefallen hat /
daß er auch von den Menschen zum
höchsten erfordert / vnd haben wil / vnd
darumb seind die Menschen auff Erden erschaffen / daß sie Gott / vñ Gottes willen an einander lieben sollen.

    Aber darneben lasset mich als den ei-
gen nuß auch bleiben / vnnd vnterstehet
mich nicht so gar zu verjagen / denn ich
mich nit also vertreiben laß / ich hab zu
lang vnd vil eingewurßelt / bin von an-
fang der welt gewesen / also / daß so vil
den Adel betrifft / welcher auch nit ein
gering ansehe bey der welt hat / mir niemand gleichen mag / dieweil Adel zum
grossen theil auff dem alter vnd lenge
der zeit besteht / so bin ich auch an mir
selbs nit böß / als man mich außschreit
thut / sonder wie obgehört ist / wirdt die
Welt durch mich in bestand vñ wesen
erhalten / Vnd ob wol etwa zu zeiten
                        etwas

Marginal notes: Eigē nuß bē Bekennet / daß Gott an jm einen wolgefallen hab. — Eigener Nuß ist von an-fang der welt gewesē / welcher auch nicht ein geringes ansehen.

Folio 40 recto

Not that I would desire to try and make you reject the
Common Good; for I have to admit that God takes
pleasure in it. He therefore wants and demands that people
continuously strive for the Common Good. And that's why
He created Men, so that they would love the Lord and each
other according to the Lord's will.

> Self-Interest admits that the Lord takes pleasure in him.

But at the same time you should also let me, Self-Interest,
be; and should refrain from trying to drive me away. I am
not easily driven away; I am too deeply rooted and have
been for a long time; from the beginning of the world. Not
even the state of nobility, so highly regarded in this world,
can compete with me; and the system of aristocracy too is
based on tradition and the great length of time for which
it has existed. I, myself, am not so bad. There is no need
to curse at me, because as you have heard above, through
me the world is preserved in essence and nature. And even
though sometimes

> Self-Interest has existed since the beginning of the world and was not regarded badly.

Von dem lob deß

etwas durch mich schadens vnd nach-
theils begegnet / als ich den meins lobs
so gar frey oder begirig nicht bin / daß
ich deß inn abreden seyn wolt/ vnd geschicht doch selbs allein durch die böse
bräuch/ wie in andern dingen sich auch
begibt/ ꝛc.

Ich wil nicht von denen Herren/
noch die in meiner Gesellschafft haben
oder erledigen/ die von meinet wegen
böß würcken / ihre nechsten betriegen/
mörden/ rauben / vnd stelen / Ich hab
hie oben im anfang gesagt/ daß durch
den mißbrauch alle ding mögen zu argem gerahten/ so mögen an jm selbs böse ding auch zu gutem dienen / als der
guts ge-zoren sonst an jhm selbs ein lastersam
schentlich ding / wenn der auß Göttli-
chem Eiffer / vnd vmb der Gerechtig-
keit willen geübt wirt.

Ist in al-
len dinge
ein miß-
brauch/
guts kan
böß/ vnd
böß für
guts ge-
achtwer-
den.

Ist doch auch nit alle Melancolia/
wie die Philosophi lehren / vnlöblich/
sonder eine/ wie sie den Helden zuschrei-
ben/

Folio 40 verso

damage or disadvantage is caused by me – and I am not
so desperate for praise to deny this – the harm is caused by
bad improper use, as it is the case with many other things
as well.

I don't want those souls in my company, who do bad things
because of me; who defraud their neighbours, kill, rob
and steal; As I said in the beginning, all things can be evil
if they are misused. But even bad things can serve good
causes, such as fury in itself is a bad and vicious thing, but
can result in good outcomes when practiced due to religious
fervour with the aim of achieving justice.

All things can be
misused; good can serve
evil, and evil can serve
good.

At the same time the philosophers teach us that not all
Melancholia [wistfulness] is disgraceful; there is a certain
type of it ascribed to heroes

Eigen Nutzen. 41

ben/ löblich vnd gut / vnd befindt sich
auch (daß einer zu vil vñ schedlich kan   *zu vil*
witzig seyn) wie gesagt ist / daß die vn=   *einer wi-*
zeitige weißheit Catonis das Römisch   *tzig seyn*
wesen mehr zerstört vnd vmbkehrt hat/
deñ der freuel Julij deß Keysers / habt
ir nicht gesehen/wie auch sonderlich zu
vnsern zeiten dz heylig Seligmachend
wort Gottes/vnd Euangelium/miß=
bräuch/ vñd vnter desselben schein/
Krieg/vnd Blutvergiessen angericht/
Land vnd Leut beraubt/zerstört/ vnd
verderbt seyn worden/vnd je einer dem
andern daß sein abgezogen/ vnnd ge=
noũen hat / alles in krafft deß Euan=
geliums/so doch dasselb nichts anders
denn Lieb/gedult/vnd leyden lehret.
    Darumb/ wie hie oben gemeldet/
es alles vñterschied/ vnd ein zwifaches
ansehen vnd gestalt hat/ Aber vber das
alles gebürt sich nicht/vnd stehet vbel/
daß ir die jenen/so mir mit Haut vnnd
Har ergeben sind/ Tag vmd Nacht
           G   mit

Folio 41 recto

that is praiseworthy and good, while at other times people may be harmfully intelligent: for example, it has been said that the exceptional wisdom of Cato[36] contributed to the transformation and eventual destruction of (the late republic of) Rome more than the sins of the emperor Julius Caesar. And have you not seen how, especially in our times, the Holy and Blessed Scripture is abused, and how under the pretext of the Gospel wars and bloodshed have occurred; people and whole countries have been robbed, destroyed, and spoiled; and one has taken away the other's posessions, all under the guise of the Gospel, even though it teaches nothing but love, patience and endurance.

It is possible for someone to be too intelligent.

That is why, as I have said above, there is a [qualitative] difference [in everything], and everything has two sides to it. Despite all this it is still not fair or just that those who are completely devoted to me, who seek my company day and night

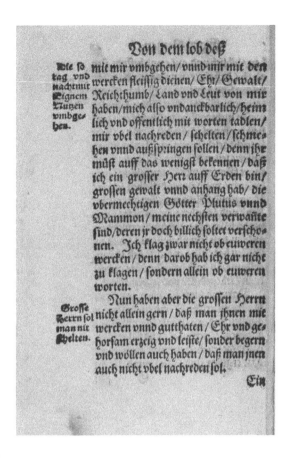

Folio 41 verso

and serve me diligently with their work; those who have received honour, power, riches, land and people from me, scold me publicly and secretly, speak about me badly, chide and revile me. Because you must admit that I am a great lord in this world and have great power and many followers. The mighty gods Pluto[37] and Mammon are my closest relatives, which you should justifiably spare as well.[38] I don't complain about your actions, for there I have nothing to complain about; but only about your words and how you speak about the matter.

Not only do great princes and lords desire that people obey and pay respect to them through deeds and useful actions, but also ask that one does not speak ill about them.

Those who are surrounded by Self-Interest day and night.

One should not scold great lords.

Folio 42 recto

Everyone is responsible to seek their Self-Interest
before their neighbour's, without impeding others
Chapter XXI

Cicero has written: It is justifiable that a person strives
for its own Self-Interest more fervently than for their
neighbour's good. On the other hand, nature prevents
that one person's wealth and capabilities are increased by
harming or robbing others. This is not only a principle of
natural law, that all people adhere to justice and honour
with everything they own and do. It is also codified in the
written laws of all peoples and is a common principle of
governance

Folio 42 verso

that no one should harm another person for their own
Self-Interest.

Further he writes, that it is not our responsibility to cast
aside our own Self-Interest for the benefit of others. The
philosopher Chrysippus of Soli has a popular saying which
states: He who is running a race ought to endeavour and
strive to the utmost of his ability to come off as the victor;
but it is utterly wrong for him to trip up his competitor or to
push him aside.

> The person running
> a race should strive to
> win, but not trip his
> competitor.

Therefore in life it is righteous for one to seek for himself
what may benefit him; but it is not right to take it from
another.

That's why usefulness or need drive spending and earning.
And this rule is the best, as the wise man says:

> The usefulness of income
> and expenses.

Folio 43 recto

Whatever you buy for a *heller*[39] without really needing it is too expensive.

All rulers should – for common ["public"] Self-Interest – strive to have a supply of all necessary things. There can be little debate about how one should accumulate these supplies: these necessary things should be earned through hard work and then multiplied. But this has to be done according to God's commandments, as shall be discussed briefly now.

Because the Almighty and eternally gracious God created Man in His own image and love, He gave them orders and laws according to which they should strive, especially for these temporal goods (which change a person more

Folio 43 verso

than other gifts from the Lord do by His providence and grace). These gifts we have been given by the Lord, we are only servants and guardians of. They should serve only our needs and we ought to use them with great gratitude, but not in excess or wasted. When a person has received from God an abundance of earthly goods covering more than his needs, he should reach out and give to his poor brother in Christ, and generally manage his possessions well and carefully.

We are guardians and servants [i.e. *stewards*] to all goods and material possessions.

In Luke 16 we find the rich man (whose name was not written into the Book of Life) who did not think to share his great wealth with poor beggar Lazarus; and doubtlessly he didn't share with other poor people either. He did not consider

Give alms to the poor.

Folio 44 recto

that when he died he would have to suffer the agony of
Hell; while the poor Lazarus was carried to Abraham's
Bosom [*i.e. went to Heaven*[40]]. This rich man was not cursed
because of his wealth, but because of his selfishness[41] and
mercilessness. He rather wasted his wealth in a superfluous
and useless manner, not sharing it with the poor (where it
would have been well and justly invested). If he had used his
wealth according to God's commandments, and had given
away what he did not need, he undoubtedly would not have
been cursed but would have become blessed. Unfortunately,
in our times there are a lot of people who have received
much wealth from God; but they waste and use it to no
good, forgetting about the poor. And they think that what
they got they have earned by themselves and not from God.
But this is not true; because everything we have, has been
given to us by God alone,

The rich man has wasted
his wealth.

In our times many people
can be found who forget
about the poor. What
we have is given to us by
God.

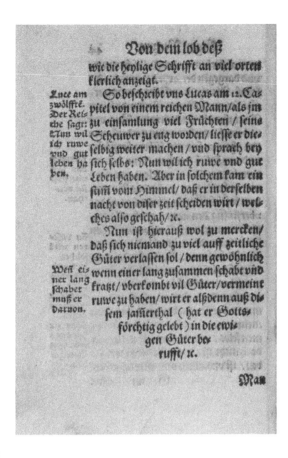

Folio 44 verso

as Holy Scripture indicates so clearly passim.

As Luke [12:13-21⁴²] describes there was a rich man, and when he harvested his crops, did not have enough space in his barn, so he had it built bigger, saying to himself: Now I can rest easy and have a good life. But in that moment a voice came from Heaven, telling him that he would die that night; which is what happened.

Luke 12. The rich man says: Now I can live in peace.

From this we have to learn that no one should rely too heavily on worldly goods. Because usually when someone scrapes and scrabbles [i.e. *accumulates, saves*] for material goods all the time, purely for accumulation's sake, thinking he will live in peace, he will soon be called from this valley of tears (into Heaven, if he has lived piously).

If someone accumulates too much he will die eventually.

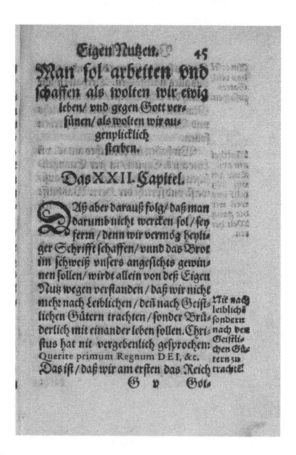

Folio 45 recto

One should work and toil as if one lived forever, and atone as if one were to die immediately
Chapter XXII

But to conclude from this that one should not work nor toil could not be further from the truth. Because Scripture commands that we ought to work; our daily bread we should earn by the sweat of our brow. And this can only be understood through Self-Interest, because rather than for worldly we should strive for spiritual goods, and should live together brotherly and neighbourly. Christ did not say without reason: *Querite primum Regnum Dei* [seek ye first the Kingdom of God]. This means that we should first seek God's Kingdom,

One should not seek temporal but spiritual goods.

Folio 45 verso

and everything else will follow [i.e. *fall into place*]. That is why we should justly strive to follow the Gospel of Christ, and not Mammon, the idol of the body and of earthly lust.

First we ought to see the Kingdom of God.

In the Gospels of Matthew 16 and Luke 8 God says: "What good will it be for someone to gain the whole world, yet forfeit their soul?"[43] Furthermore, this is what the Lord says, according to Matthew 6 and Luke 12[44]: Do not strive for treasures here on earth that will be eaten by rust or moths, or stolen by thieves. Instead collect your treasures in Heaven, so that your heart will be where your treasure is; this is much more useful. From all this one can conclude, that Christ did not utter this prohibition for nothing, but with good reason,

Matthew 16.

Luke 8.

Folio 46 recto

because if he had not done so, people would have only
thought about their own Self-Interest and not about the
praise of God and their salvation.

In Matthew 9, Mark 2 and John 1 it is also described how
Jesus Christ came to Simon Peter and his brother Andrew,
both fishermen, and spoke to them and told them to
follow him. Soon thereafter they left behind their nets and
everything they owned, and followed Christ; just like the
Apostles Philip and Matthew the tax collector did, and many
others who followed Christ. Without a doubt they would
have continued seeking their own Self-Interest and worldly,
rather than the spiritual and eternal goods, if they hadn't
followed Christ our Lord. In Acts 5 Ananias committed
fraud when he sold his field [*handing over only part of the proceeds
to the apostles*], and he immediately departed from this life;
both he and his wife were punished with death.

Matthew 9, Mark 2,
John 1 / one should
follow Christ.

In Act of the Apostles 5,
Anania sells his field.

Von dem lob deß

Darauß haben wir leichtlich vnnd wol zu verstehen / daß wir Gott / vnnd nicht dem Mammon nachfolgen sollen / Doch so der Reich seine von Gott zugeordnete Güter (als ein Schaffner derselben) recht braucht / nemlich / daß Reich sei er seinem mit Bruder darvon gebüren nem mit de handreichung thut / ist jm solch sein Reichthumb zum ewigen leben keine verhinderung / sonder ein fürdernuß / denn Gott will / daß wir seine verlihene Gnaden vnd gutthaten / wie billich danckbarlich erkennen / vnd nicht vnnützlich vmbbringen / oder verzehren sollen / darff gleichwol sonst vnserer armen werck nit / aber wir seind schuldig / seinen Göttlichen gebotten / so vil vns müglich / nach zu setzen / vnnd jm vmb alle seine Gnaden / Gutthaten / vñ grosse Barmhertzigkeit alzeit danckbar zu seyn/rc.

Wir lesen Marci am 12. vnd Luce 21. von einer armen Wittwe / welche nicht

Weß der Reich sei er seinem mit Bruder hilff zu Kombt ge bürende handreichung thut. Gott wil daß wir jm dancken sollen.

Folio 46 recto

From [all] this we can easily conclude, that we should follow God and not Mammon. But if the rich man uses the goods he has been given by God (as a steward would) rightly, helping out his neighbours with his wealth, then his wealth is not an obstacle but advantage to gain eternal life. God wants us to recognise the favours and blessings He has bestowed upon us. We shouldn't waste or use them up in our arms' work. Instead we are responsible to obey His divine commandments as best we can and be grateful for all His graces, blessings and His abundant mercy.

When the rich man helps the poor man his brother.

God wants us to be grateful.

In Mark 12[45] and Luke 21 we are told about a poor widow, who only

Eigen Nußen. 47

b nicht mehr denn ein Heller hett / lege
d den selbigen inn Gotts Kasten / Auch
l spricht Luce am dritte / der Herr spricht
t wer zween Röck hat / der geb dem ein
r so kein hat. Johannis am 4. Einer
f Sáet der ander Schneid. Item / wir
n lesen in der Apostel Geschicht / am 4.
in Die darumb Christi willen verkauffen
t was sie hetten / dieselben haben in diser
i/ zeit nie mangel gehabt / sonder nach e=
s wiger Glori / alda sie jetzund sind / ge=
h tracht.
w   So haben wir auch in Paulo / der
m da gesprochen wenn wir haben zimlich
r essen / trincken / vnd kleidung zu vnse=
l rer notturfft sollen wir solchs mit grof
il sem lob vnd danck von Gott annem=
m men / vnnd vns wol genûgen lassen.
n/ Es spricht auch der Heylig Apostel
d Sanct Mattheus am dritten Capitel.
Das Himelreich ist nahe herbey kom=
t men / vñ die Axt ist schon an den Bau=
h me geleint / rc.
ft   Darumb

Folio 47

had a mite (*heller*)[46] left, but she put it in the temple treasury
[i.e. *collection or donation box*]. In Luke 3 we learn that the
Lord says that anyone who has two shirts should share with
the one who has none.[47] In John 4[48] we are told that 'One
sows and another reaps'. Just as in Acts [of the Apostles]
4 the apostles sold everything they had for Jesus Christ, but
none of them ever suffered from deprivation; instead they
sought eternal glory which they ultimately found.

Paul too said that if we have all the food, drink and clothing
that we require, we should gratefully accept it from God
and enjoy it.

The holy apostle Matthew says in the third chapter: The
kingdom of heaven is at hand, and the axe is laid unto the
root of the trees.

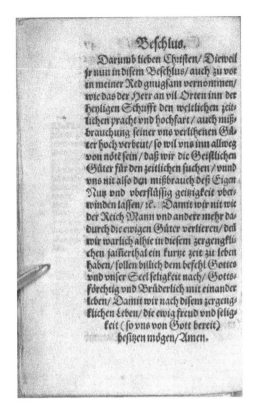

Source: MDZ Digitale Sammlungen: https://www.digitale-sammlungen.de/en/details/bsb00020768
Reprographic of the original text held by Bayerische Staatsbibliothek Munich

Conclusion

That is why, my dear Christians, in this conclusion as in
my speech before, you will have learnt how the Lord in the
Holy Scripture commands us to refrain from temporal and
worldly strife for riches, forbidding the misuse of the goods
He has given us. And therefore, we have to seek spiritual
over worldly goods, and we should not succumb to misusing
the force of Self-Interest and be excessively avaricious and
greedy, lest we miss out on the eternal goods, like the rich
man and many others did. Because we really only live
in this earthly valley of tears for a short and transitory
time, we should righteously follow God's commands and
live piously and neighbourly with others, to ensure the
blessedness of our souls; so that we may, following this
transient life, gain eternal salvation (hopefully given to us
by God). Amen.

Notes

1 In the early modern German usage, the term *bös(e)* – which is used throughout in Fronsperger's text and today may translate depending upon context as 'bad', 'evil' or, in the case of children, 'naughty' – may also refer to capital depreciation when used in business, as in 'to be written off' (i.e. debts, capital depreciation), and so on. See Philipp Robinson Rössner, *Deflation – Devaluation – Rebellion. Geld im Zeitalter der Reformation* (Stuttgart: Franz Steiner, 2012), introduction and chs. III, IV. In the present context Fronsperger most likely refers to an ontological dialectic between 'good' and 'bad', in the sense of 'good' vs. 'evil'.

2 Half penny, German small change coin. Original term stems from the city of Hall in Tyrol, an important Austrian mining town and mint. For money in the German speaking lands, Michael North, *Kleine Geschichte des Geldes. Vom Mittelalter bis heute* (Munich: Beck, 2009); Bernd Sprenger, *Das Geld der Deutschen. Geldgeschichte Deutschlands von den Anfängen bis zur Gegenwart* 3rd ed. (Paderborn / Munich / Vienna / Zurich: Schöningh, 2002); Herbert Rittmann, *Deutsche Geldgeschichte 1484–1914* (Munich: Battenberg, 1975), Arthur Suhle, *Deutsche Münz- und Geldgeschichte von den Anfängen bis zum 15. Jahrhundert* 8th ed. (Berlin: VEB Deutscher Verlag der Wissenschaften, 1975); Ferdinand Friedensburg, *Münzkunde und Geldgeschichte der Einzelstaaten des Mittelalters und der Neueren Zeit* (Munich / Berlin: Oldenbourg, 1926); A. Luschin v. Ebengreuth, *Allgemeine Münzkunde und Geldgeschichte des Mittelalters und der Neueren Zeit*, 2nd ed. (Munich / Berlin: Oldenbourg, 1926); Wolfgang Trapp, *Kleines Handbuch der Münzkunde und des Geldwesens in Deutschland* (Cologne: Anaconda, 2005).

3 Leonhard Fronsperger, *Kriegs Ordnung und Regiment sampt derselbigen befehl statt vnd Ampter zu Roß und fuß* … (Frankfurt-am-Main: Feyerabend, 1564).

4 Ger. original: *geschwinden*. A modern translation for *geschwind* would be 'fast' or 'fast changing'.

5 Reference is being made to Adam and Eve (Genesis 2:4-3:24), and Cain and Abel (Genesis 4).

6 Fronsperger uses the idiosyncratic term *Policey*, a polyvalent term which underwent considerable conceptual changes throughout the early modern period. It roughly translates as 'good order', but later on – in the Cameralist age – also came to include practical policies of market regulation, social order, economic policy and general economic development. See Philipp Robinson Rössner, *Managing the Wealth of Nations. Political Economies of Change in Pre-Industrial Europe* (Bristol: Bristol University Press, 2023).

7 An idiosyncratic expression based on a German proverb, parts of which are missing or lost in the present text (denoted by the 'etc'. in the original German). 'Butz' or 'putz' in this case refers to 'cover', 'cloak', clothing, following an older German proverb, see Karl Friedrich Wander (ed.), *Deutsches Sprichwörter-Lexikon* Vol. 1 (Leipzig, 1867), col. 774.

8 This refers to a poem by George Frederick, Margrave of Ansbach and Bayreuth, as well as Regent of Prussia (1539–1603) at the Imperial Diet of Augsburg in 1530. See: Martin Luther / Johann Christfried Sagittarius, *Alle Deutschen Bücher und Schrifften: Aus denen Wittenbergischen, Jehnisch- und Eißlebischen Tomis zusammen getragen. HauptRegister über Herrn D. Mart. Lutheri Seel. Gesampte Teutsche Schrifften, Wie sie aus denen Witteb. Jenisch- und Eißlebischen Tomis in Neun Theile zusammen getragen, Volume 10* (Altenburg in Meissen, 1664), p. 519.

9 Common proverb, which rhymes in the German original, see: Samuel Singer, *Lexikon der Sprichwörter des romanisch-germanischen Mittelalters* (Berlin, 1996), p. 403.

10 Terentius: Roman Dramatist (195BC–159 BC).

11 Herodes Antipas, son of Herod the Great.

12 Lucian, Greek Lukianos, Latin Lucianus (born AD 120, Samosata, Commagene, Syria [died after 180, Athens [Greece]), ancient Greek rhetorician, pamphleteer, and satirist, see: https://www.britannica.com/biography/Lucian.

13 Erasmus's *Sileni Alcibiadis* is one of his most direct assessments of the need for Church reform. Desiderius Erasmus / Johann Froben., *Sileni Alcibiadis* (Paris, 1527).

14 Refers to: *In Praise of Folly*, an essay written in Latin in 1509 by Desiderius Erasmus of Rotterdam and first printed in June 1511, a satirical attack on superstitions and other traditions of European society as well as on the western Church. See introduction by Rainer Klump & Lars Pilz for further context.

15 For conversation between Hannibal and Scipio, see: Appian, *The Syrian Wars*, 11.2.9–10.

16 Meaning 'will have bad company'.

17 *Erwitterung der Welt* is probably a reference to Genesis 1:28: 'And God blessed them. And God said to them, Be fruitful and multiply and fill the earth and subdue it, and have dominion over the fish of the sea and over the birds of the heavens and over every living thing that moves on the earth'.

18 Sexual urges, pleasures.

19 In a sense of householding, managing a household. This is the ancient notion of oeconomics. See note 22.

20 No concept existed as yet for 'society' (with a definite article) in our modern sense in the German speaking countries, or – in the words of Thatcher – there was no such thing as society. 'Welt' here refers to roughly 'all worldly matters', as in politics, administration and economy.

21 Ambiguous term. German original *Statt*, which translates as either 'state' or 'city', depending upon context and time; this double translation possibility is cognate to the double use of the Latin term *civitas*, which usually refers to either the physical city, or the political community embodied in it, i.e. state form. In the present case Fronsperger refers to Rome which was a city and state (empire) at the same time.

22 An idiosyncratic term and concept in early modern economics, with borrowings from Classical Antiquity. In early modern political economy, the *pater familias* or *Hausvater* usually was the manager of a large agrarian estate and father of an extended household (to which belonged, on top of the nuclear family, wider groups such as domestic servants, labourers and serfs). There was an entire literary genre devoted to successfully managing such large estates, see Johannes Burkhardt & Birger P. Priddat, (eds.), *Geschichte der Ökonomie* (Frankfurt: Deutscher Klassiker Verlag, 2009); Dotan Leshem, 'The Ancient Art of Economics,' *The European Journal of the History of Economic Thought* 21:2 (2014), 201-229; Johannes Burkhardt, 'Artikel 'Wirtschaft'' in: *Geschichtliche Grundbegriffe. Historisches Wörterbuch zur politisch-sozialen Sprache in Deutschland*, Vol. 7, eds. Otto Brunner, Werner Conze & Reinhart Koselleck (Stuttgart: Cotta, 1992), pp. 511-513 (*Einleitung*); 550-594 (*Neuzeitteil* (16. - 20. Jh.); Keith Tribe, *The Economy of the Word. Language, History, and Economics* (Oxford: Oxford University Press, 2015), ch. 1.

23 In the German original, Fronsperger uses *Statt und Policey*, the latter a standard term in early modern political economy.

24 Fronsperger is obviously alluding to the German Peasant War (1524-5) and other social revolutionary movements of his time, where calls were often heard to transform private into common ownership (as some revolutionary movements like the Anabaptists would). The standard work still is Peter Blickle, *Die Revolution von 1525* 4ᵗʰ ed. (Berlin: Oldenbourg, 2014).

25 The common sixteenth century German translation of the Biblical word and Greek expression *οἰκονόμος*, Latinized as *oeconomus*, i.e. literally 'economist' or 'household manager', 'farm or estate manager', 'steward', German *Hausvater*. See previous notes on the wider conceptual notions of stewardship and management since biblical times.

26 Literally: 'will have to produce his accounts (of incomes and expenses) to God'.

27 In the sense of the previous notion of stewardship.

28 This probably refers to Diogenes and cynicism, see for example: Louisa Shea, *The Cynic Enlightenment: Diogenes in the Salon* (Baltimore, 2010), p. 86-88.

29 Matthew 5:3: 'Blessed are the poor in spirit, for theirs is the kingdom of heaven'.

30 Matthew, 25:15-25:30.

31 Luther translated this as 'Zentner' (cwt, hundredweight) of *silver* not gold, because in Luther's time the monetary systems of Saxony and central Germany were based on the silver thaler, a substitute for the medieval high value gold currency known as *Gulden* (florin). A common English-language usage has this story as the Parable of the Bags (or Talents) of Gold. On Saxon and central German currency and monetary policy in the sixteenth century, see Rössner, *Deflation – Devaluation – Rebellion*, ch. III.

32 Interestingly Fronsperger uses the word 'Wucher' here, which could also translate – apart from 'essence', 'bottom line' – as 'interest', or 'usury'.

33 See note above on the meaning of the Latinised Greek word for 'oeconomus'. On double economic and spiritual meaning of 'steward' in classical Antiquity, see Dotan Leshem, *The Origins of Neoliberalism. Modeling the Economy from Jesus to Foucault* (Columbia University Press, 2017).

34 *Nachrichter* being an antiquated expression for *Scharfrichter*, i.e. executioner.

35 Ambiguous, as the original German *Preyß* could translate as either 'price', 'prize', or 'praise'. Meaning humans are by definition sinners. This could be a hint at Luther's *Sola Fide* doctrine. An alternative translation: they do not match the value (=price) considered worthy enough for God.

36 Presumably referring to Cato the Younger (95-46 BCE), an influential Roman senator who opposed monarchical tendencies in the late Roman Republic under Julius Caesar. Another possible reference here is the *Distichs of Cato*, a fourth or fifth century AD collection of wisdom and proverbs by an obscure author known as Dionysius Cato or Catunculus, a text commented on by Erasmus.

37 Formerly known as Hades; ruler of the Underworld in Greek mythology. Fronsperger obviously juxtaposes the strife for money or avarice (Mammon) with humans' propensity to wage war and destruction upon one another (Pluto) as the two closest allies of self interest.

38 An alternative translation possibility is: 'from whose operations (i.e. war and avarice) you should refrain, as well.'

39 German halfpenny, or 504ᵗʰ part of a silver florin (Thaler) or less at Fronsperger's time. The smallest denomination coin circulating in the German speaking lands at the time of the Reformation.

40 In some early Christian and eastern/orthodox traditions the Bosom of Abraham is a place different from Heaven, but in sixteenth-century Germany, and particularly a Lutheran context, the use of 'Abraham's Bosom' was likely allegorical, i.e. referring to Heaven.
41 Literally: Self-Interest.
42 The Parable of the Rich Fool.
43 Matthew 16:26.
44 Matthew 6:19-23: 'Do not store up for yourselves treasures on earth, where moths and vermin destroy, and where thieves break in and steal. But store up for yourselves treasures in heaven, where moths and vermin do not destroy, and where thieves do not break in and steal. For where your treasure is, there your heart will be also.' Cf. Luke 12;33-34: 'Sell your possessions and give to the poor. Provide purses for yourselves that will not wear out, a treasure in heaven that will never fail, where no thief comes near and no moth destroys.'
45 Mark 12:41-44; Luke 21:1-4.
46 See above. The Old King James Version uses the term 'mite', a common late medieval and early modern coin of the smallest denomination. The New International Version translates these passages as 'two copper coins'; Luther (1534) used 'Scherflein', referring to a regional half-penny coin (*Scherf*; diminutive: *Scherflein*) that circulated in and around the city of Erfurt and the central German lands during Luther's days. In southern and central Germany, the term 'heller' would have been more common, and that is the one used in Fronsperger's text.
47 Luke 3:11.
48 John 4:37.

CPSIA information can be obtained
at www.ICGtesting.com
Printed in the USA
JSHW022033020523
40868JS00003B/3